KINGDOM HEARTS

4

Adapted by
Shiro Amano

TOKYOPOP®

HAMBURG // LONDON // LOS ANGELES // TOKYO

Kingdom Hearts Vol. 4
Adapted by
Shiro Amano

Associate Editor - Peter Ahlstrom
Retouch and Lettering - Fawn Lau
Cover Layout - Gary Shum

Editor - Elizabeth Hurchalla
Digital Imaging Manager - Chris Buford
Production Manager - Elizabeth Brizzi
Managing Editor - Lindsey Johnston
Editor-in-Chief - Rob Tokar
VP of Production - Ron Klamert
Publisher - Mike Kiley
President and C.O.O. - John Parker
Chief Creative Officer and C.E.O. - Stuart Levy

A  Manga

TOKYOPOP Inc.
5900 Wilshire Blvd. Suite 2000
Los Angeles, CA 90036

E-mail: info@TOKYOPOP.com
Come visit us online at www.TOKYOPOP.com

ISBN: 1-59816-220-9

First TOKYOPOP printing: July 2006
10 9 8 7 6 5
Printed in the USA

DISNEY • SQUARESOFT

Our Story So Far...

After being swept away from his island home and his friends Kairi and Riku, Sora finds himself lost in a mysterious new land. Soon, he meets Court Wizard Donald and Captain Goofy, who are desperately trying to find their missing King. Now the trio must travel from world to world, find the keyhole to each planet's Heart and lock it with the magical Keyblade. Only this will stop the Heartless from consuming every world in Darkness. Having defeated Ursula and Captain Hook, the companions learn that the "wise" scientist Ansem built a machine that creates Heartless! Now Riku has gained the power to control Heartless and has taken Kairi to Maleficent, who is collecting all the princesses with pure hearts. But it seems Kairi's heart may already be lost...

KINGDOM HEARTS: VOLUME 4
TABLE OF CONTENTS

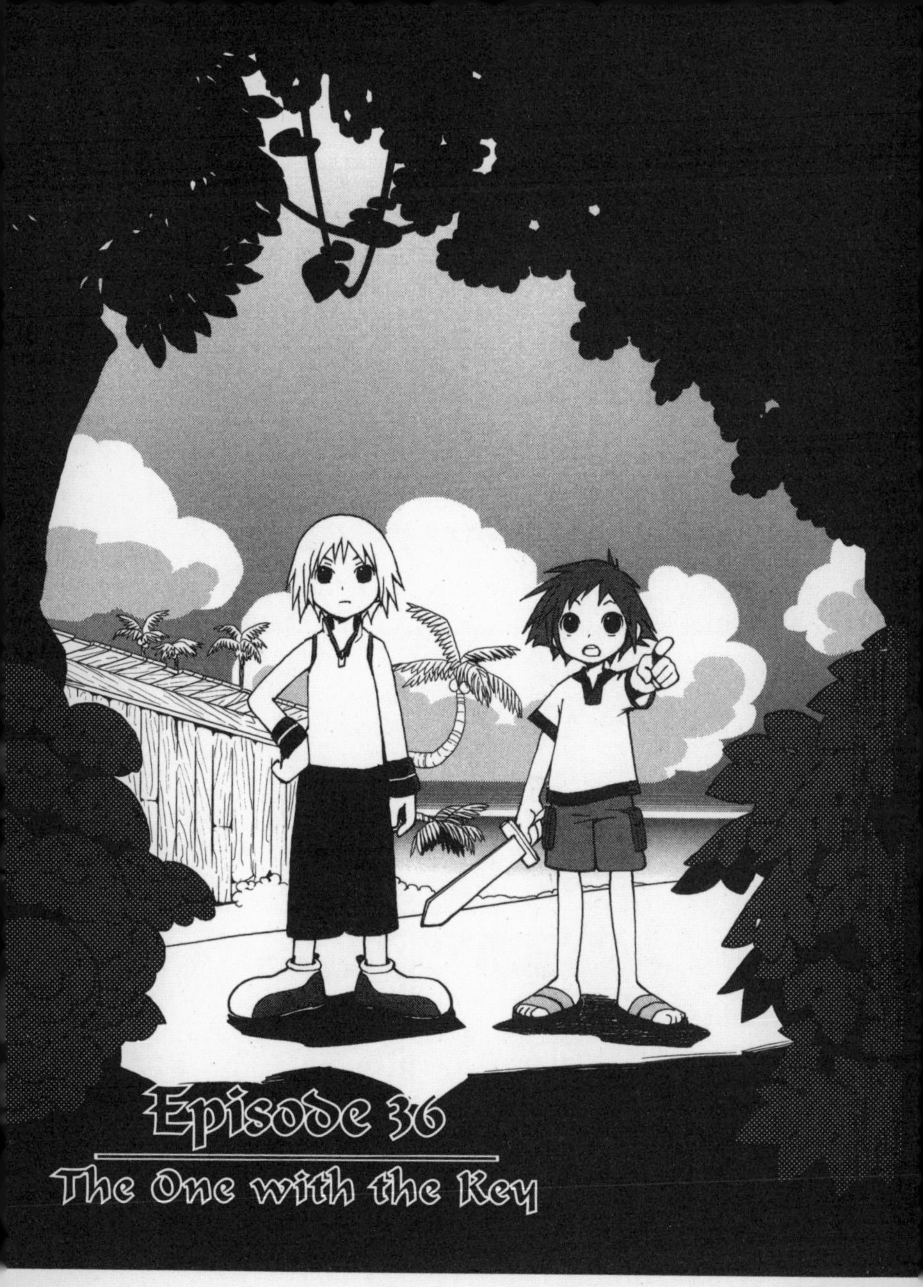

Episode 36

The One with the Key

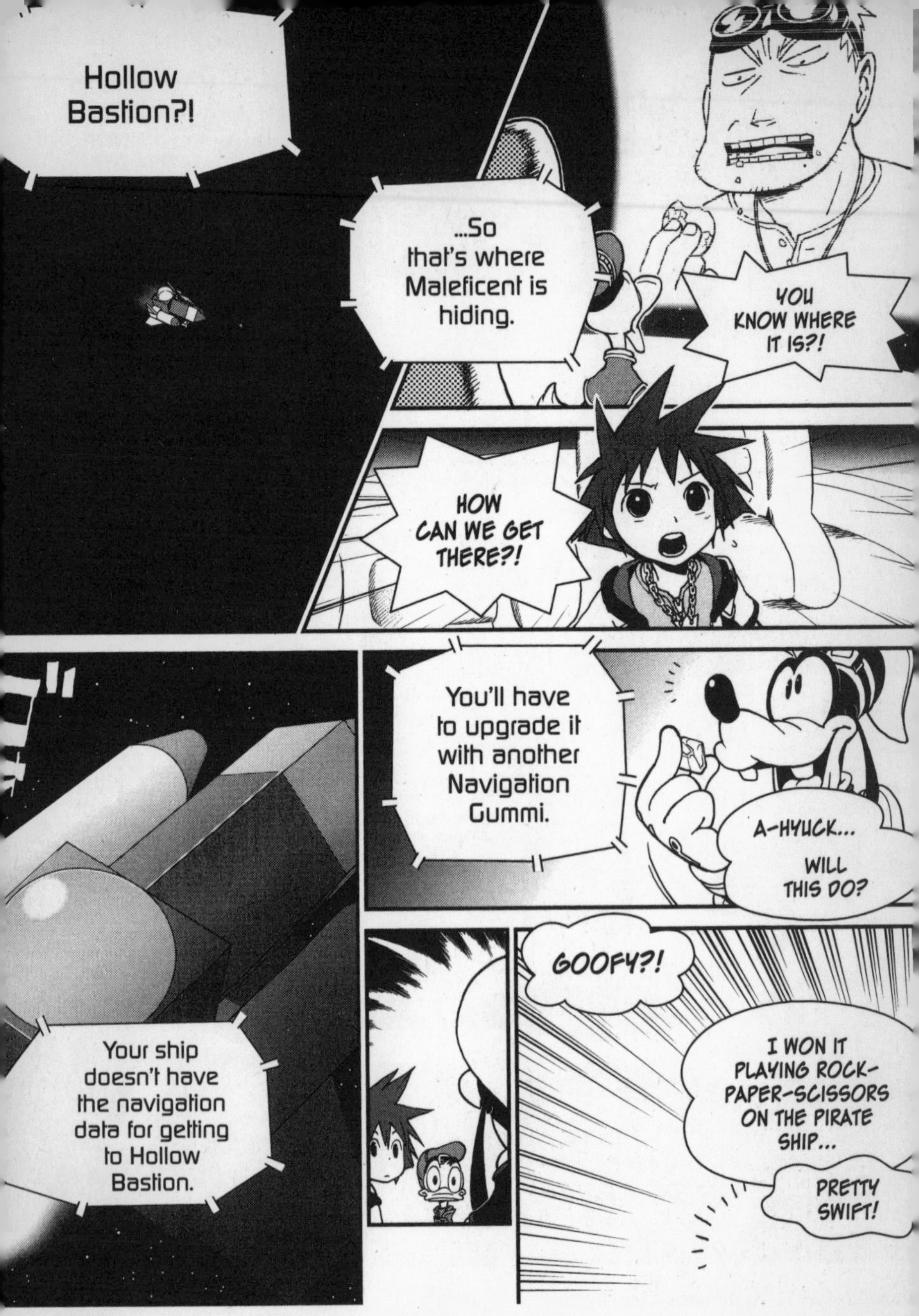
Hollow Bastion?!
...So that's where Maleficent is hiding.
YOU KNOW WHERE IT IS?!
HOW CAN WE GET THERE?!
Your ship doesn't have the navigation data for getting to Hollow Bastion.
You'll have to upgrade it with another Navigation Gummi.
A-HYUCK...
WILL THIS DO?
GOOFY?!
I WON IT PLAYING ROCK-PAPER-SCISSORS ON THE PIRATE SHIP...
PRETTY SWIFT!

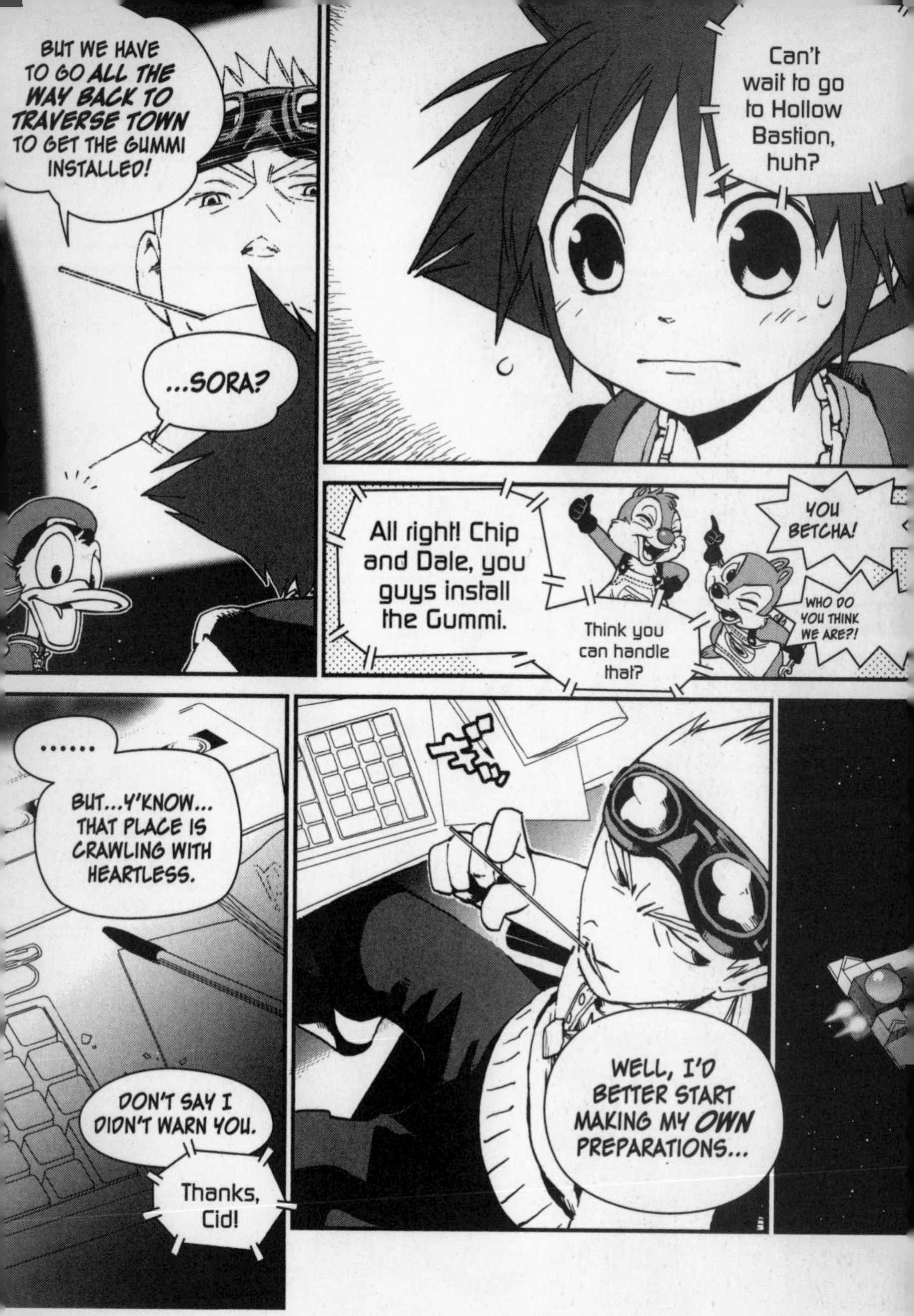
BUT WE HAVE TO GO ALL THE WAY BACK TO TRAVERSE TOWN TO GET THE GUMMI INSTALLED!
...SORA?
Can't wait to go to Hollow Bastion, huh?
All right! Chip and Dale, you guys install the Gummi.
Think you can handle that?
YOU BETCHA!
WHO DO YOU THINK WE ARE?!
......
BUT...Y'KNOW... THAT PLACE IS CRAWLING WITH HEARTLESS.
DON'T SAY I DIDN'T WARN YOU.
Thanks, Cid!
WELL, I'D BETTER START MAKING MY OWN PREPARATIONS...

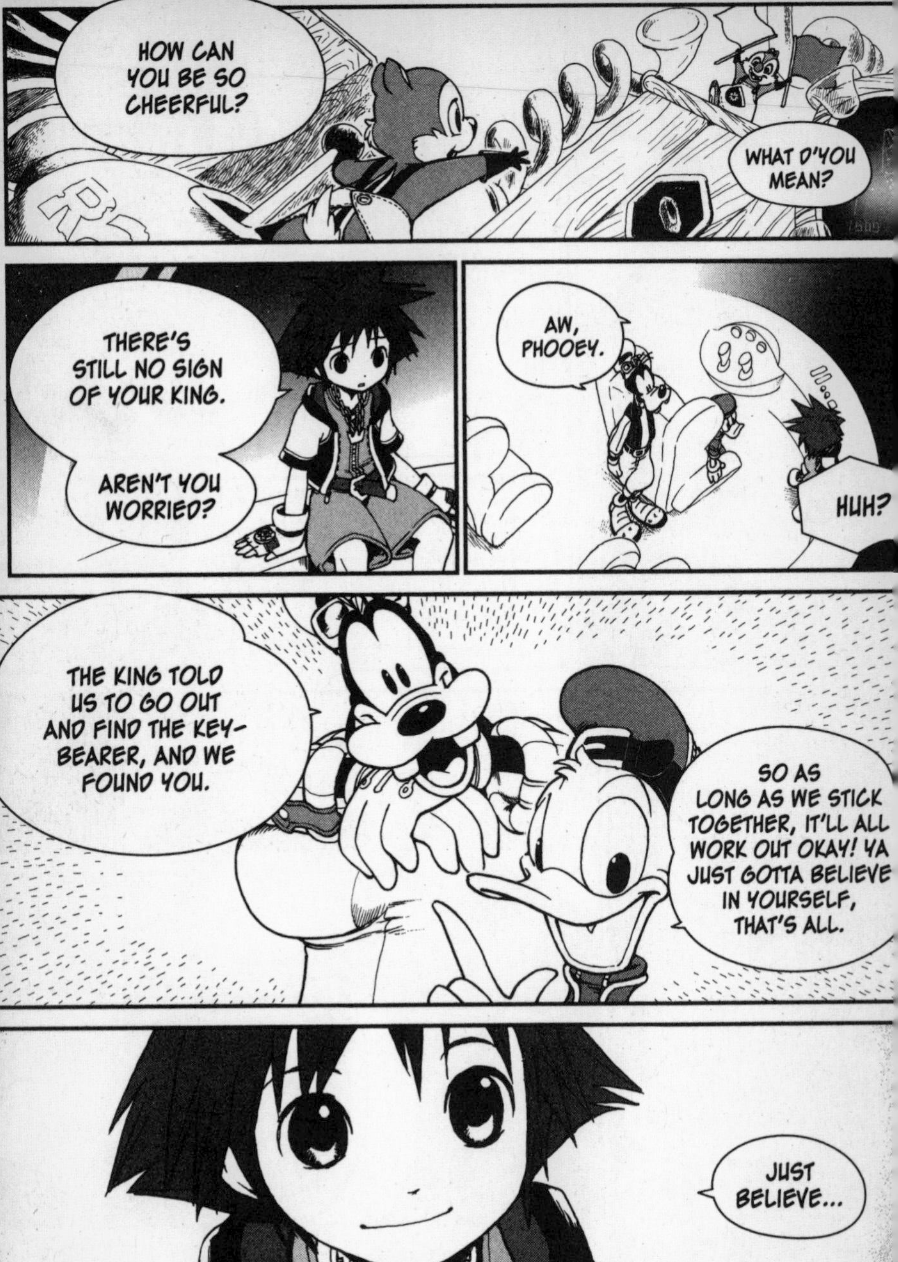
HOW CAN YOU BE SO CHEERFUL?
WHAT D'YOU MEAN?
THERE'S STILL NO SIGN OF YOUR KING.
AREN'T YOU WORRIED?
AW, PHOOEY.
HUH?
THE KING TOLD US TO GO OUT AND FIND THE KEY-BEARER, AND WE FOUND YOU.
SO AS LONG AS WE STICK TOGETHER, IT'LL ALL WORK OUT OKAY! YA JUST GOTTA BELIEVE IN YOURSELF, THAT'S ALL.
JUST BELIEVE...

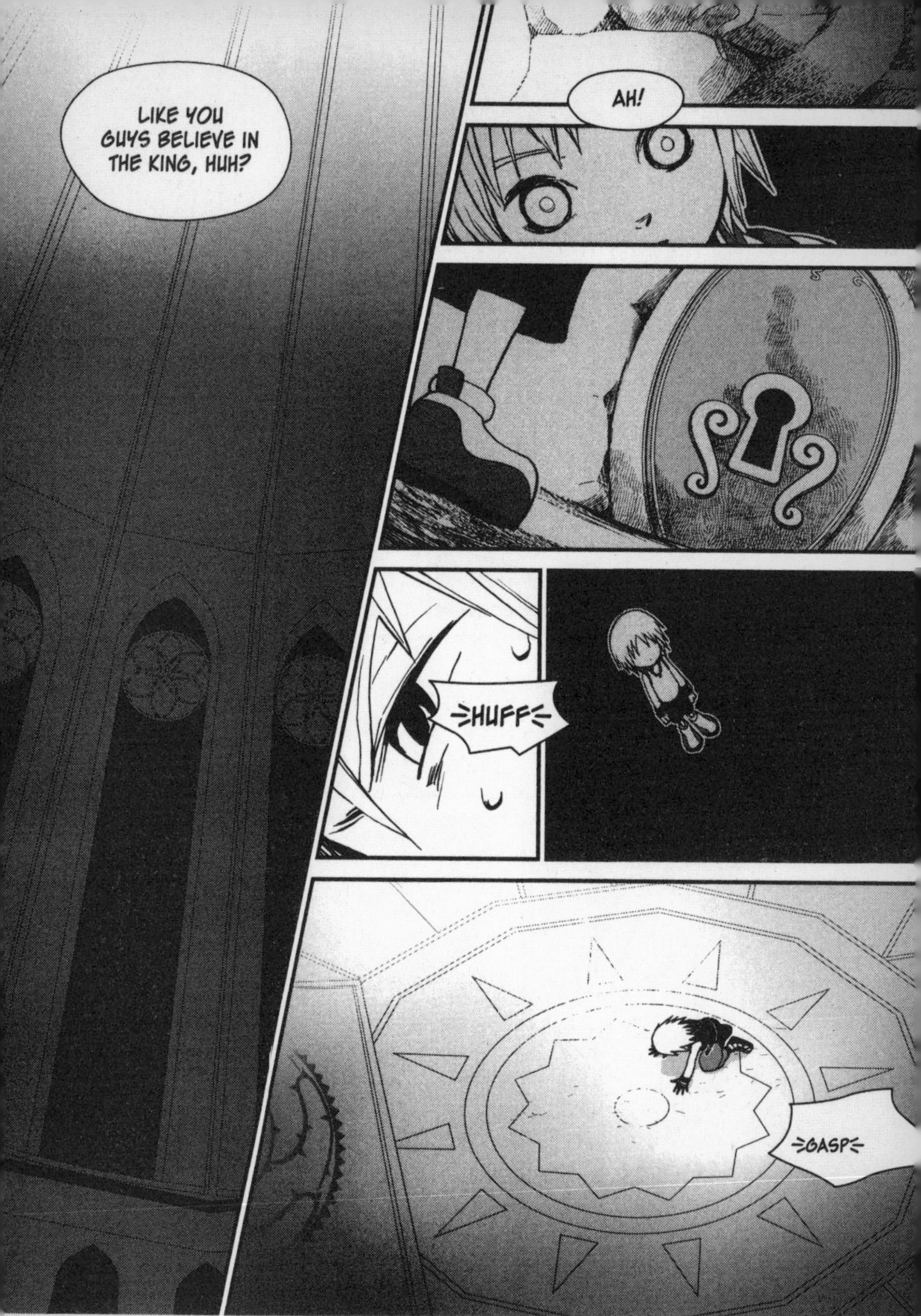
LIKE YOU GUYS BELIEVE IN THE KING, HUH?
AH!
HUFF
GASP

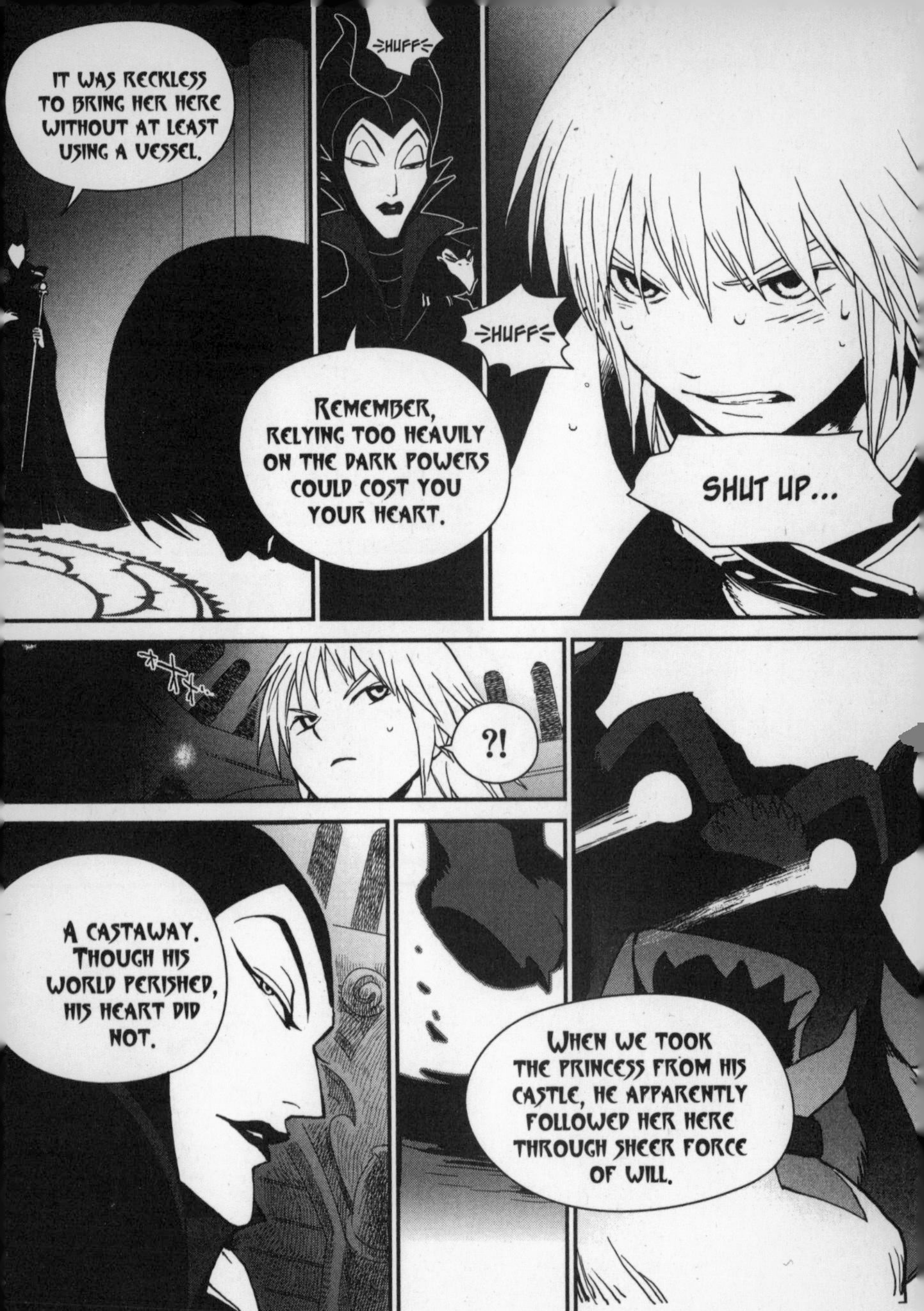
IT WAS RECKLESS TO BRING HER HERE WITHOUT AT LEAST USING A VESSEL.
HUFF
HUFF
REMEMBER, RELYING TOO HEAVILY ON THE DARK POWERS COULD COST YOU YOUR HEART.
SHUT UP...
?!
A CASTAWAY. THOUGH HIS WORLD PERISHED, HIS HEART DID NOT.
WHEN WE TOOK THE PRINCESS FROM HIS CASTLE, HE APPARENTLY FOLLOWED HER HERE THROUGH SHEER FORCE OF WILL.

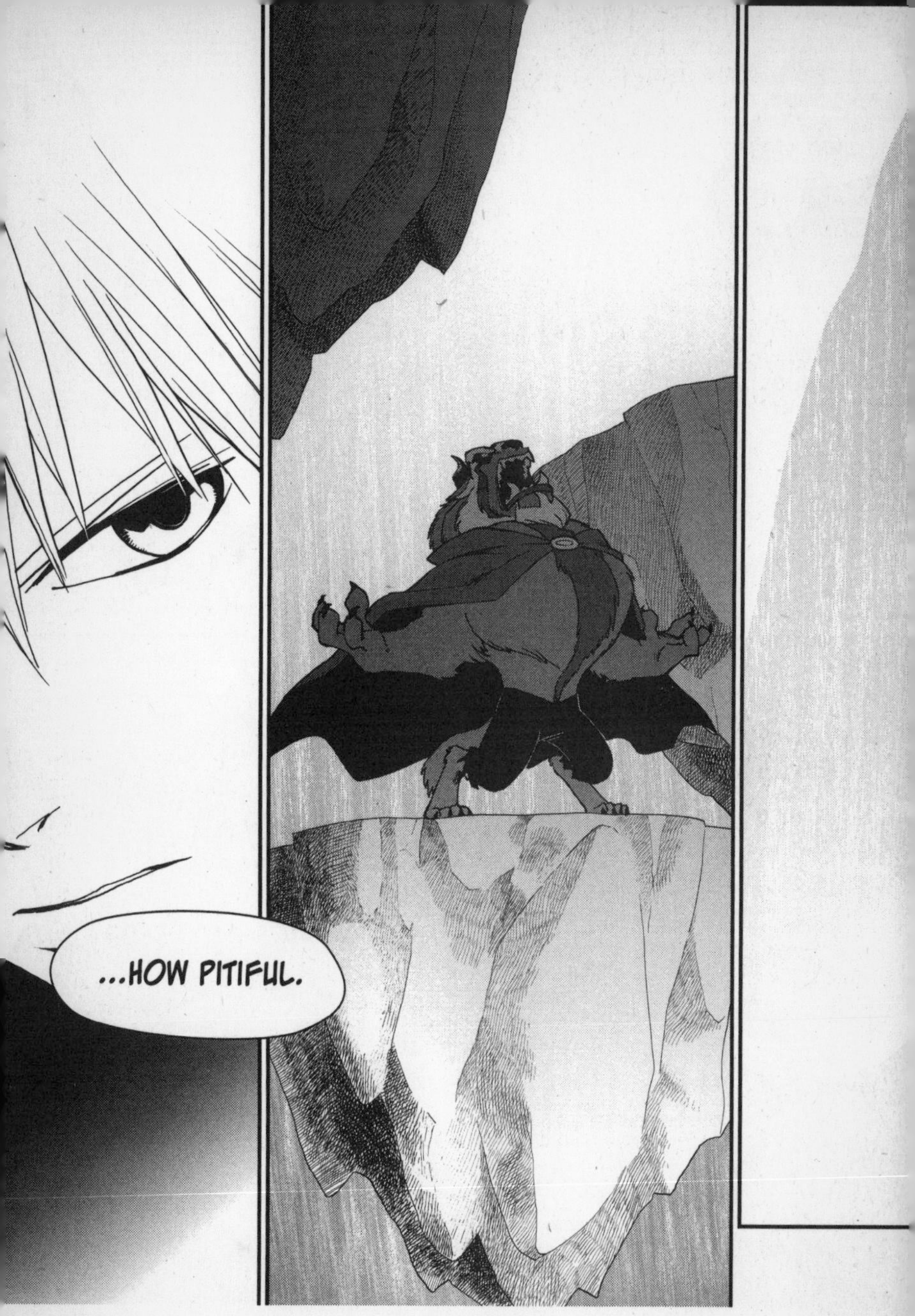
...HOW PITIFUL.

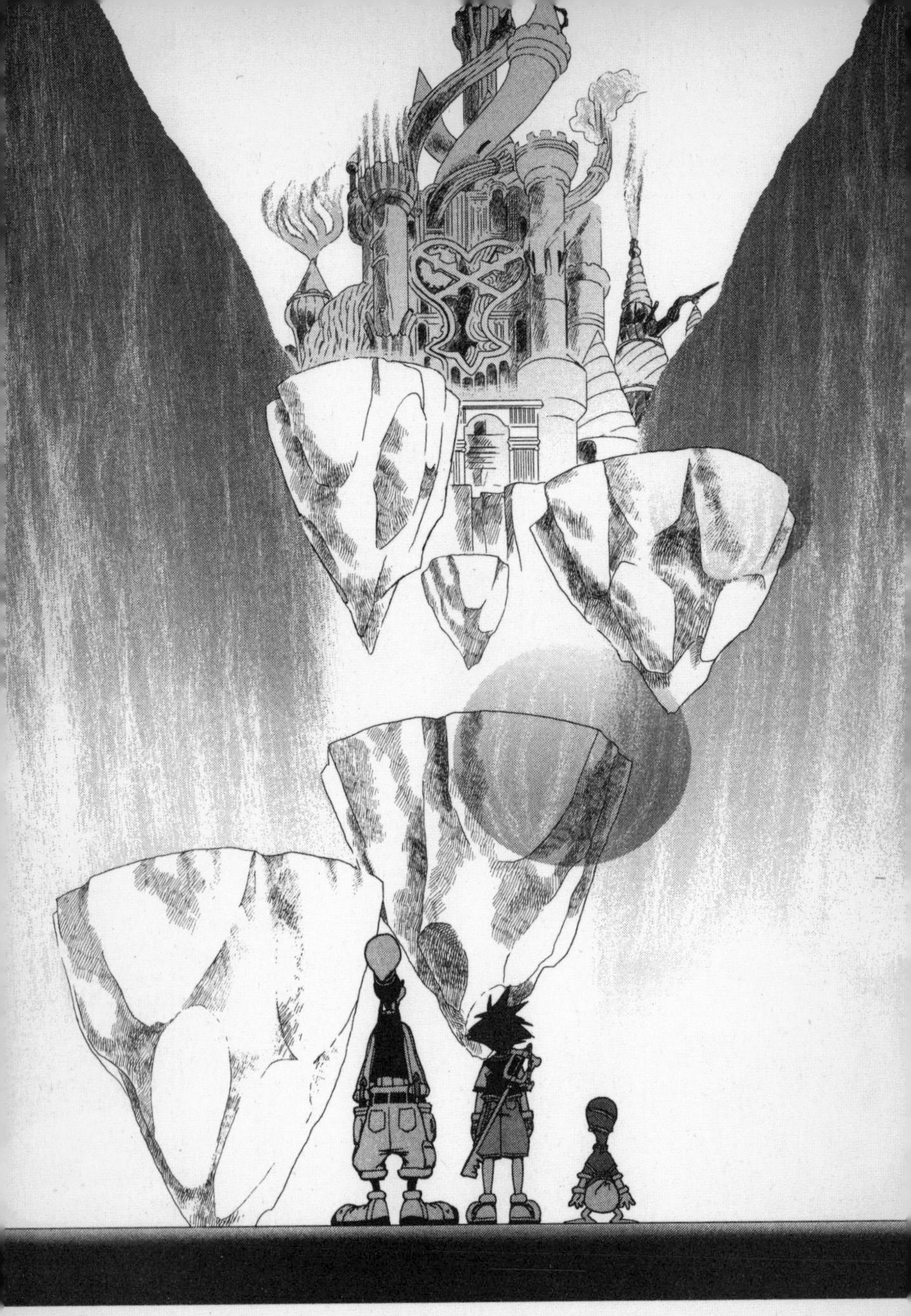

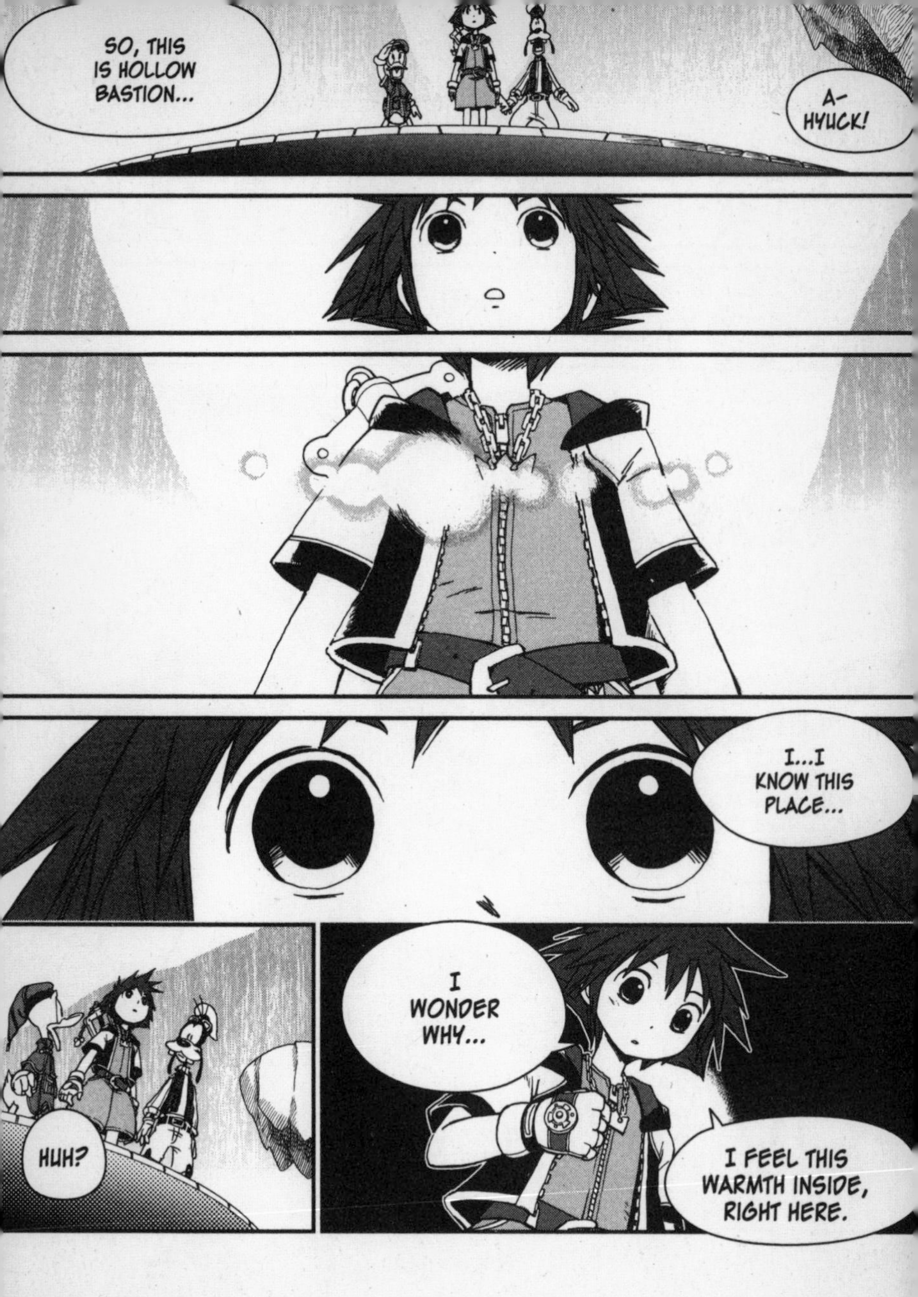
SO, THIS IS HOLLOW BASTION...
A-HYUCK!
I...I KNOW THIS PLACE...
HUH?
I WONDER WHY...
I FEEL THIS WARMTH INSIDE, RIGHT HERE.

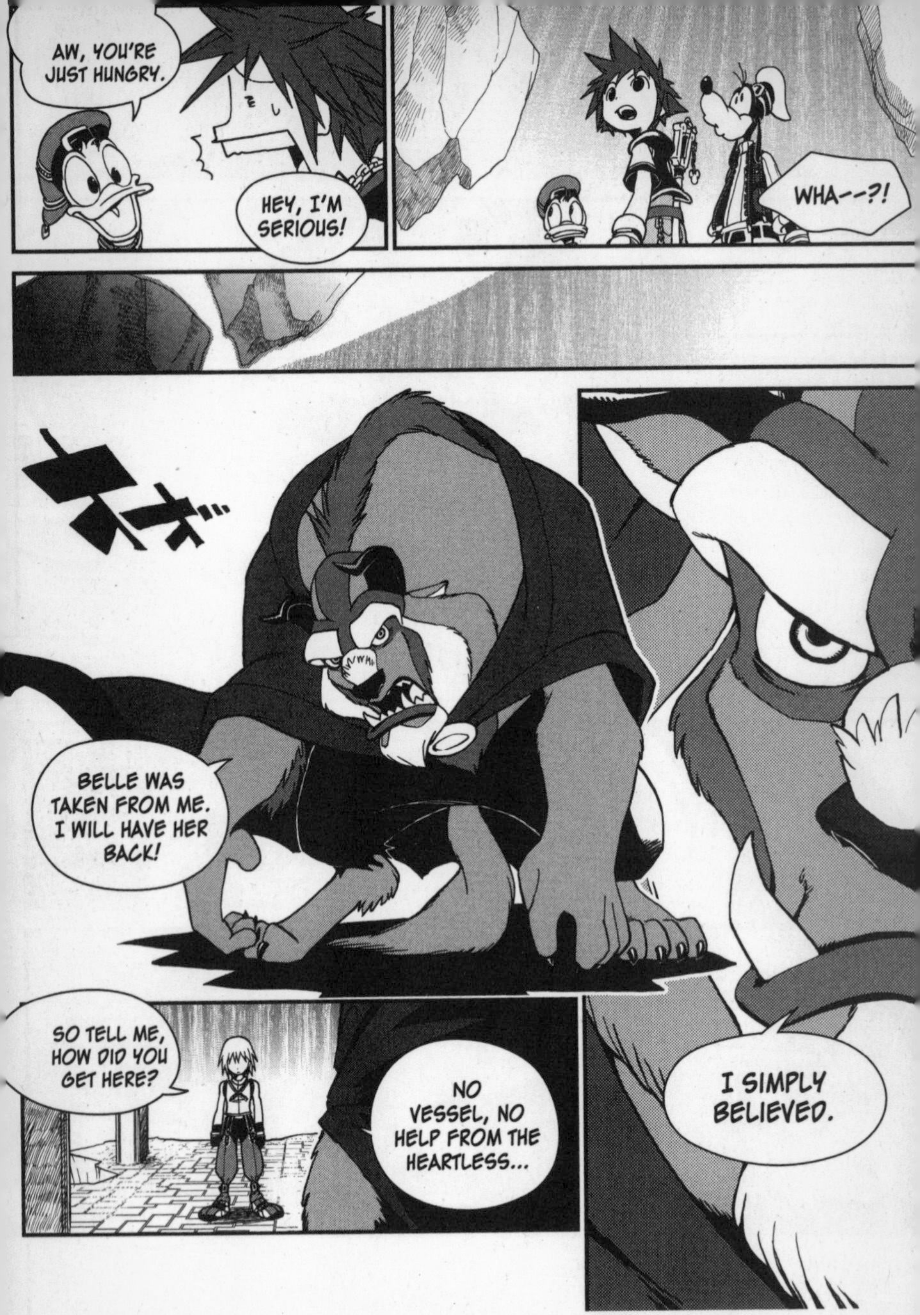
AW, YOU'RE JUST HUNGRY.
HEY, I'M SERIOUS!
WHA--?!
BELLE WAS TAKEN FROM ME. I WILL HAVE HER BACK!
SO TELL ME, HOW DID YOU GET HERE?
NO VESSEL, NO HELP FROM THE HEARTLESS...
I SIMPLY BELIEVED.

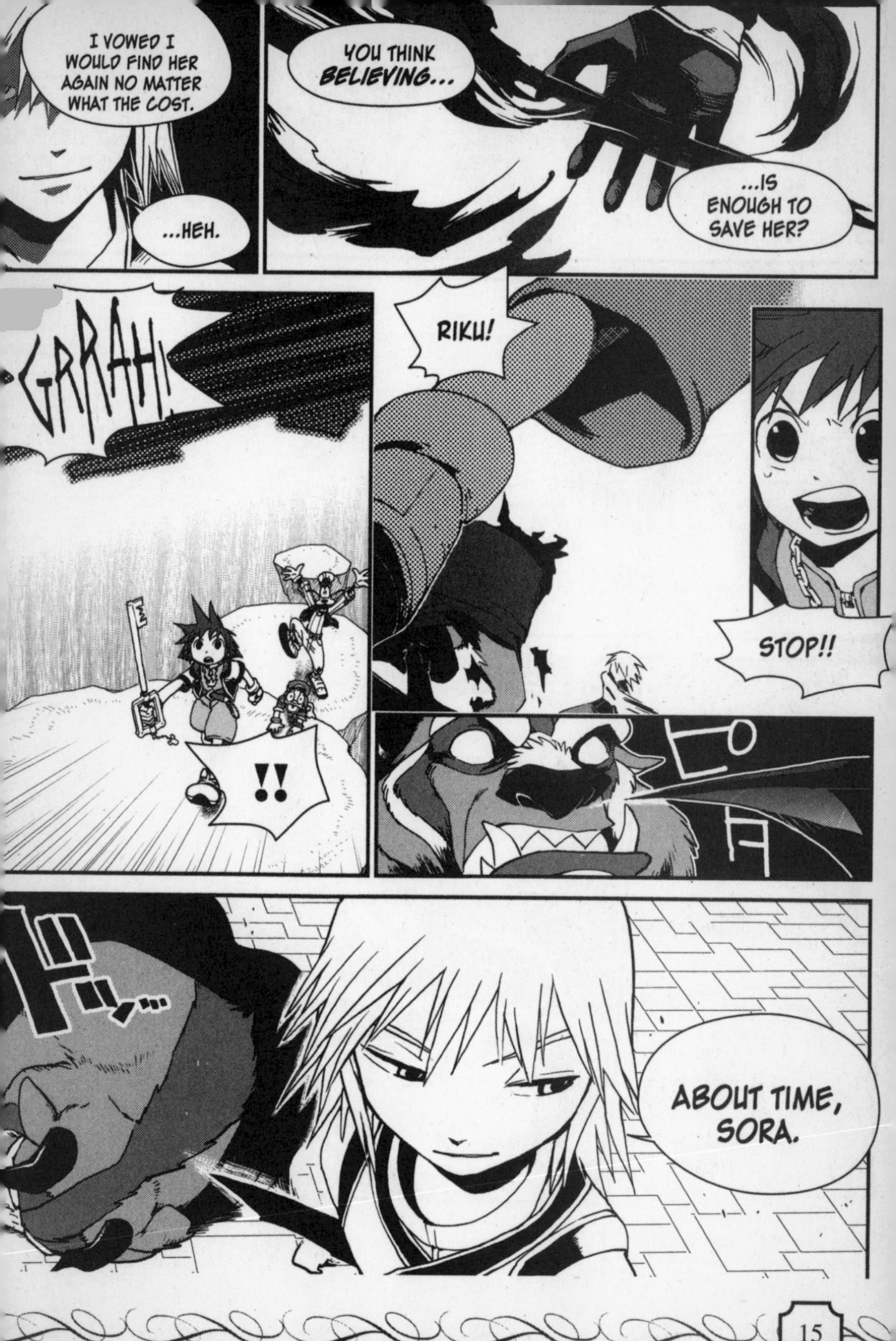

I VOWED I WOULD FIND HER AGAIN NO MATTER WHAT THE COST.
...HEH.
YOU THINK BELIEVING...
...IS ENOUGH TO SAVE HER?
GRAAH!!
!!
RIKU!
STOP!!
ABOUT TIME, SORA.

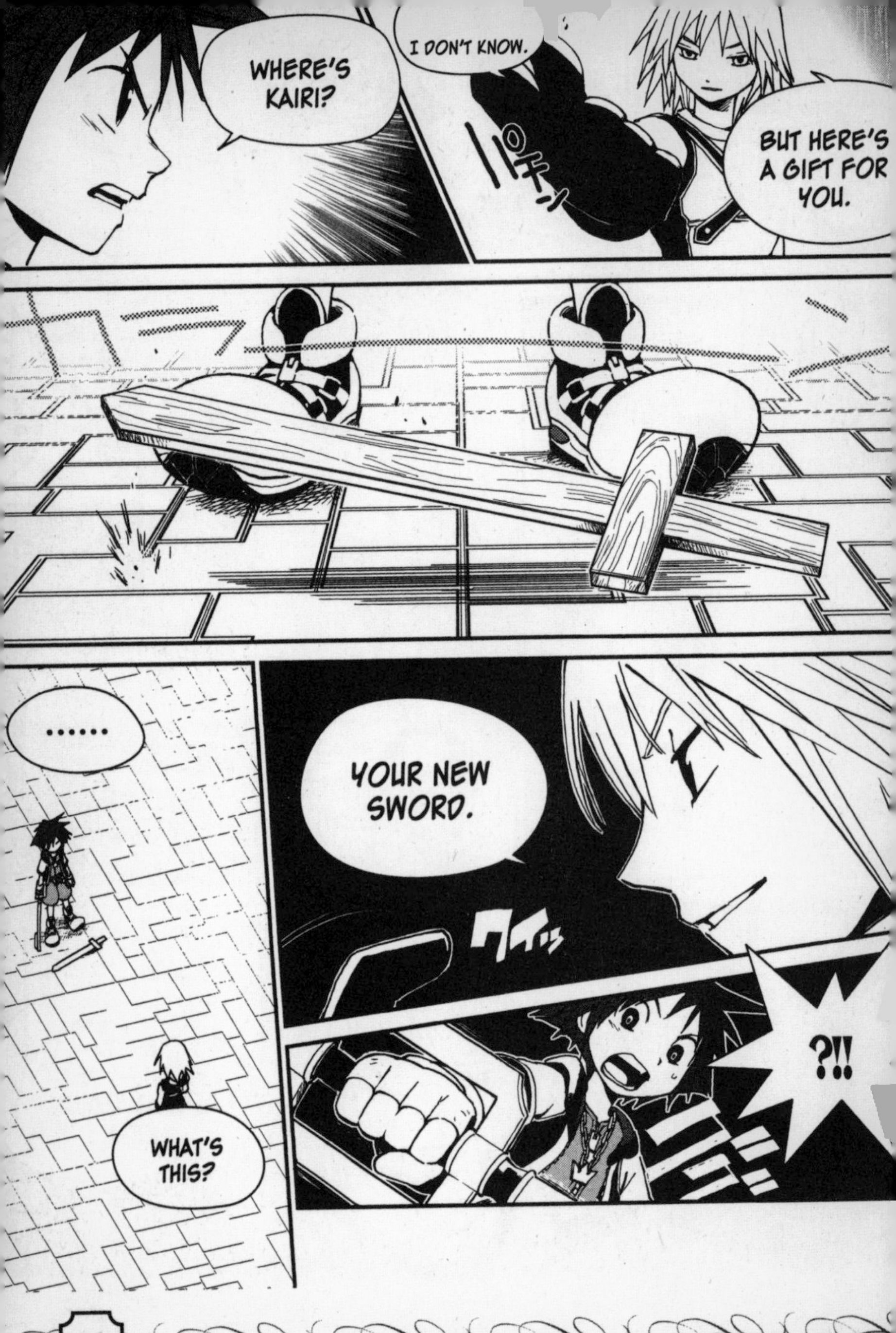
WHERE'S KAIRI?
I DON'T KNOW.
BUT HERE'S A GIFT FOR YOU.
......
WHAT'S THIS?
YOUR NEW SWORD.
?!!

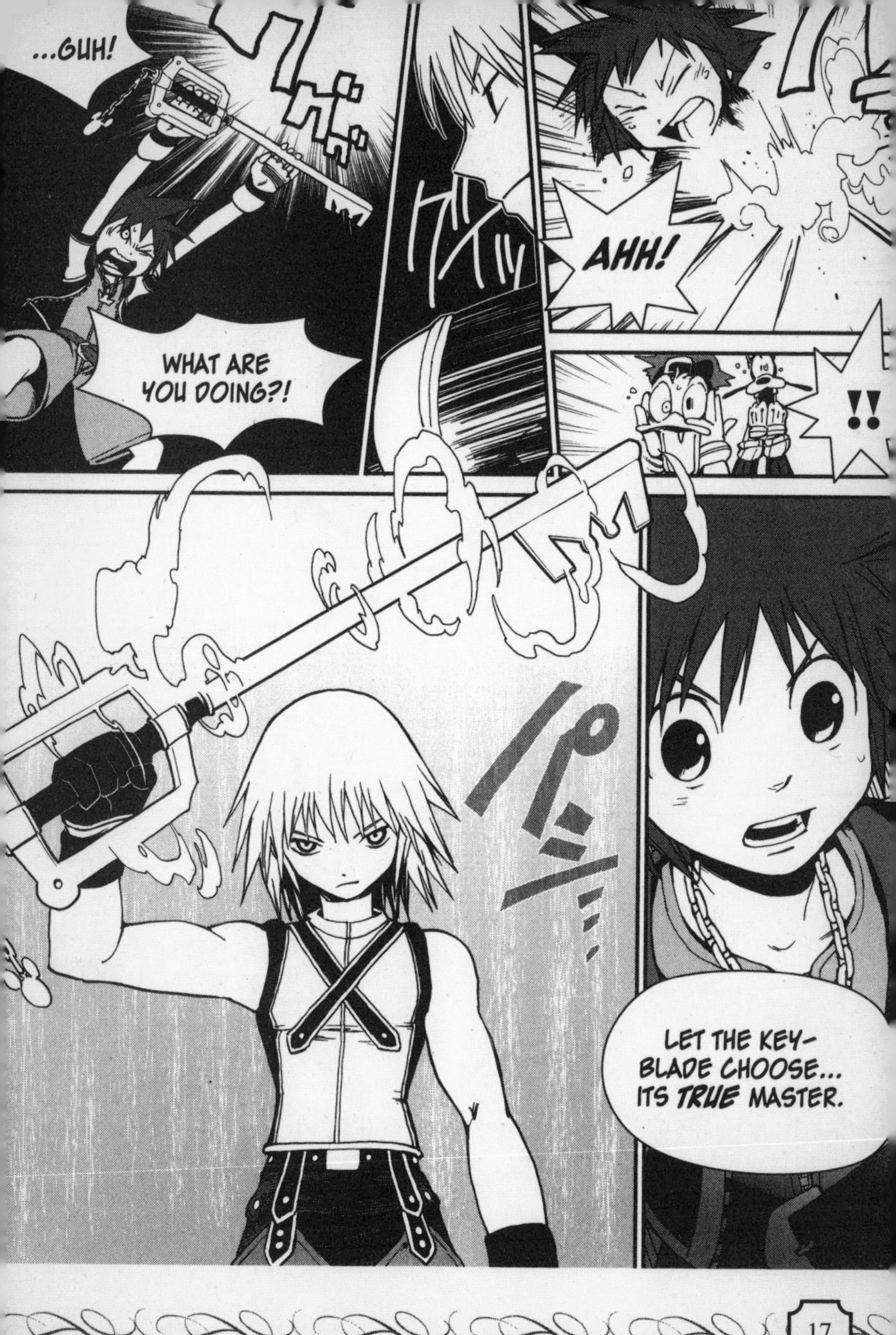
...GUH!
WHAT ARE YOU DOING?!
AHH!
!!
LET THE KEY-BLADE CHOOSE... ITS TRUE MASTER.

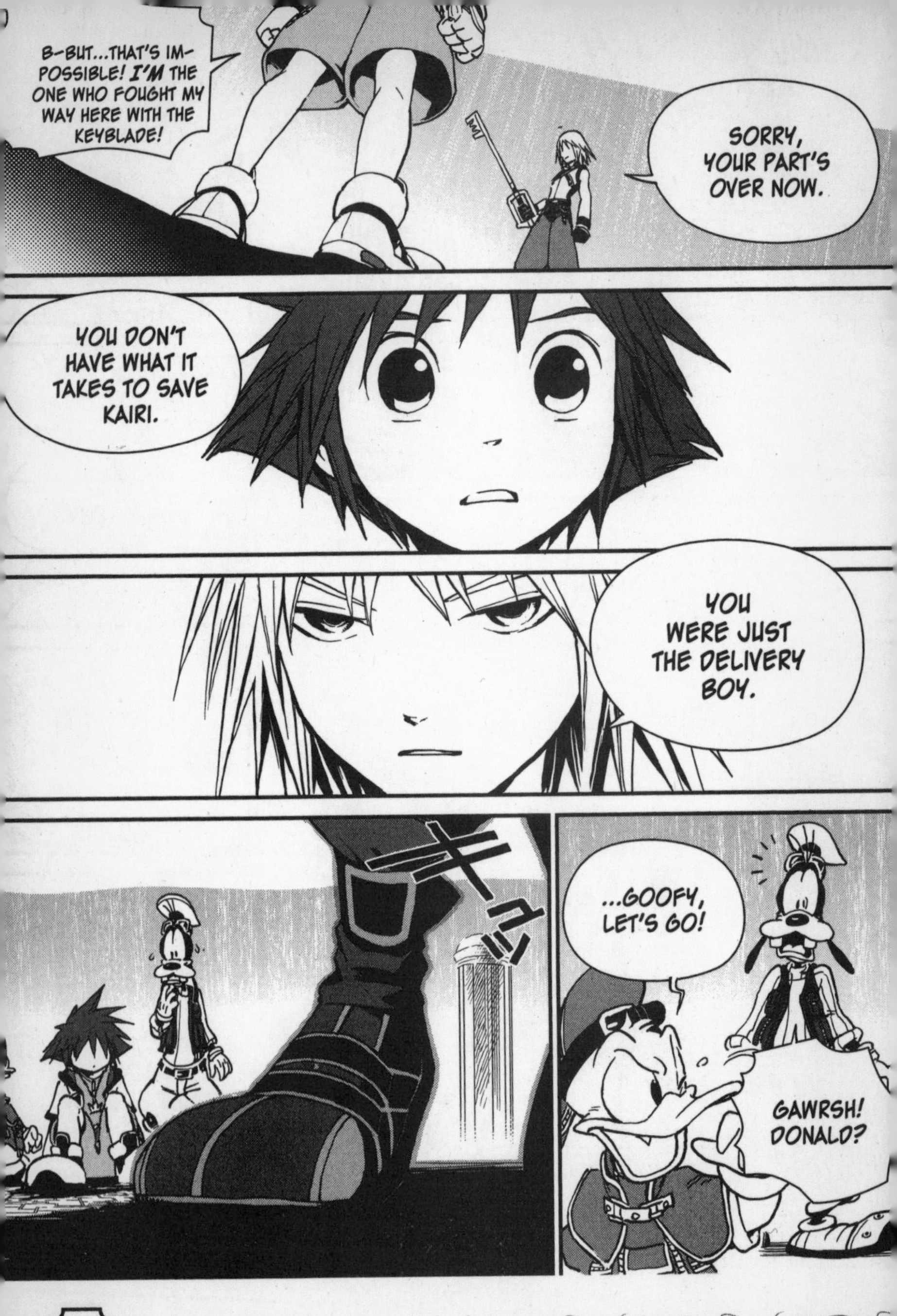
B-BUT...THAT'S IMPOSSIBLE! *I'M* THE ONE WHO FOUGHT MY WAY HERE WITH THE KEYBLADE!
SORRY, YOUR PART'S OVER NOW.
YOU DON'T HAVE WHAT IT TAKES TO SAVE KAIRI.
YOU WERE JUST THE DELIVERY BOY.
キュッ
...GOOFY, LET'S GO!
GAWRSH! DONALD?

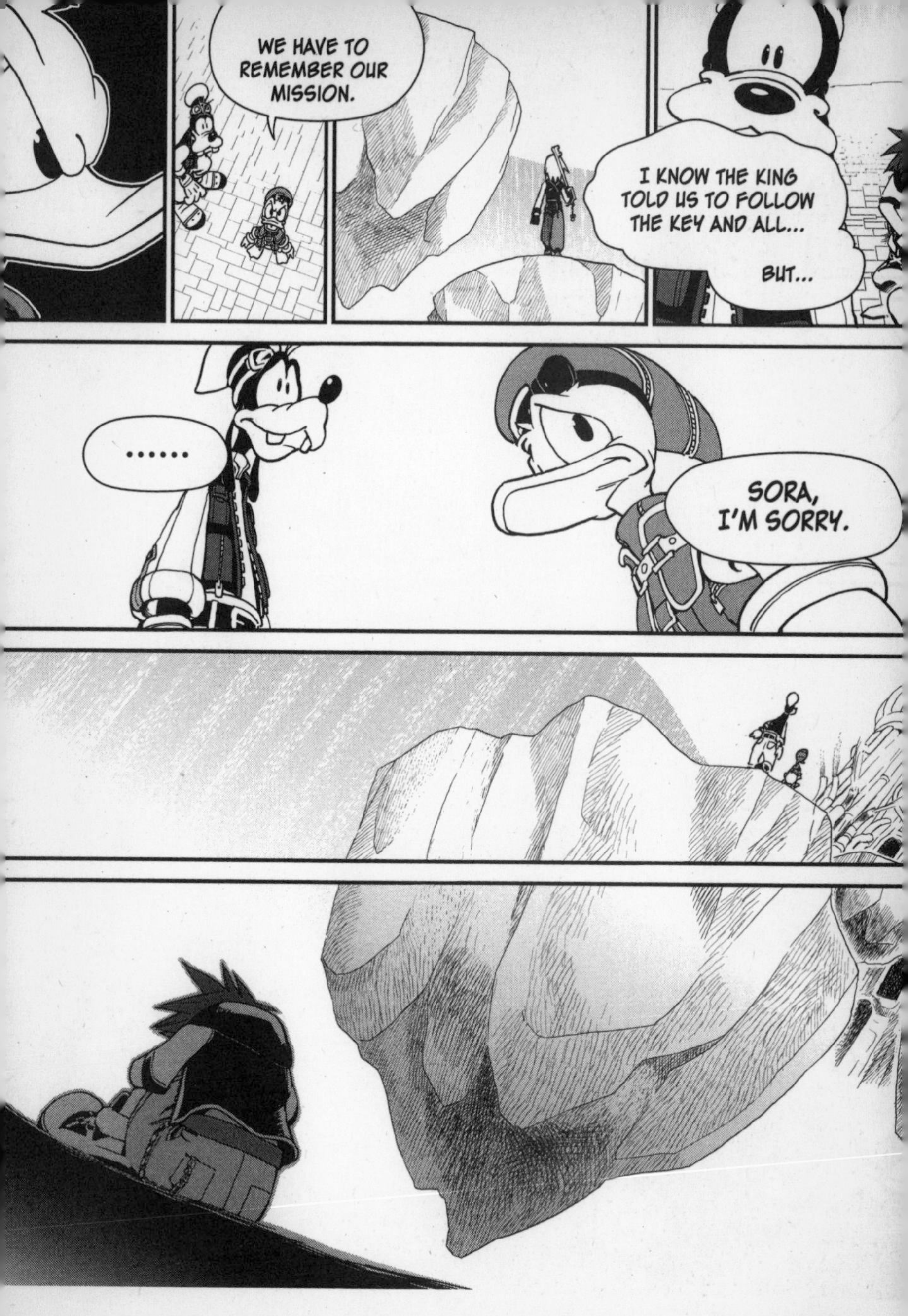
WE HAVE TO REMEMBER OUR MISSION.
I KNOW THE KING TOLD US TO FOLLOW THE KEY AND ALL...
BUT...
......
SORA, I'M SORRY.

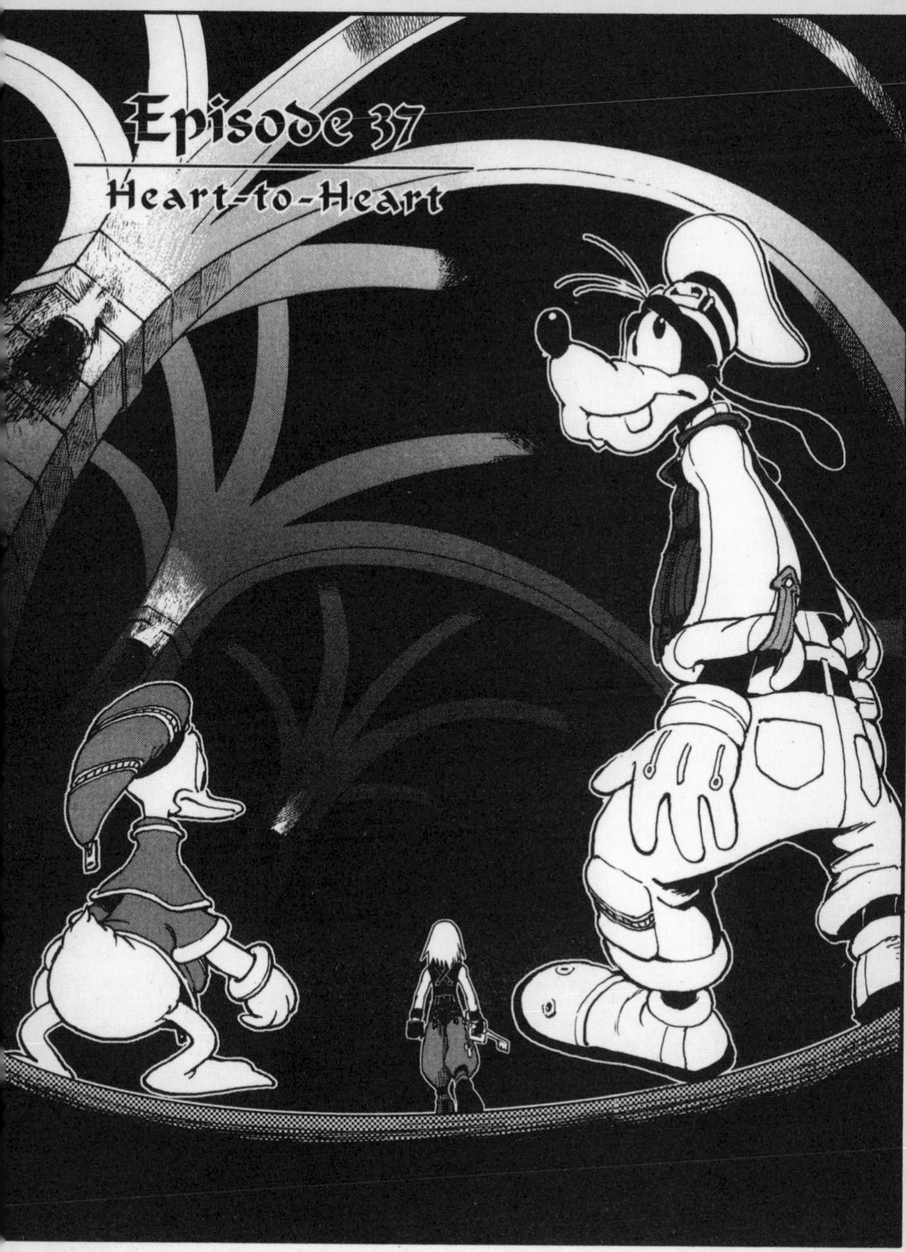
Episode 37
Heart-to-Heart

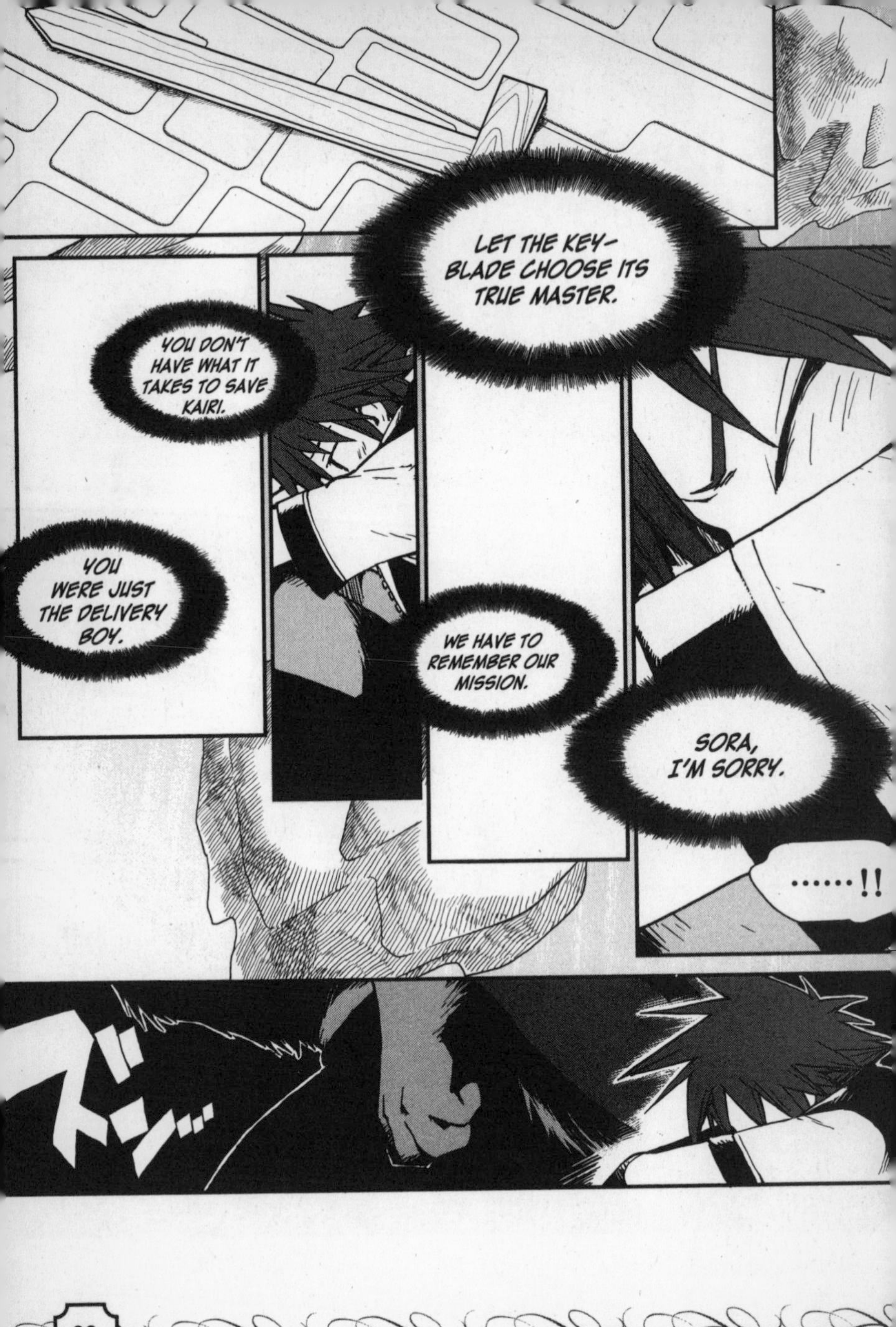
LET THE KEY-BLADE CHOOSE ITS TRUE MASTER.
YOU DON'T HAVE WHAT IT TAKES TO SAVE KAIRI.
YOU WERE JUST THE DELIVERY BOY.
WE HAVE TO REMEMBER OUR MISSION.
SORA, I'M SORRY.
......!!
ズン…

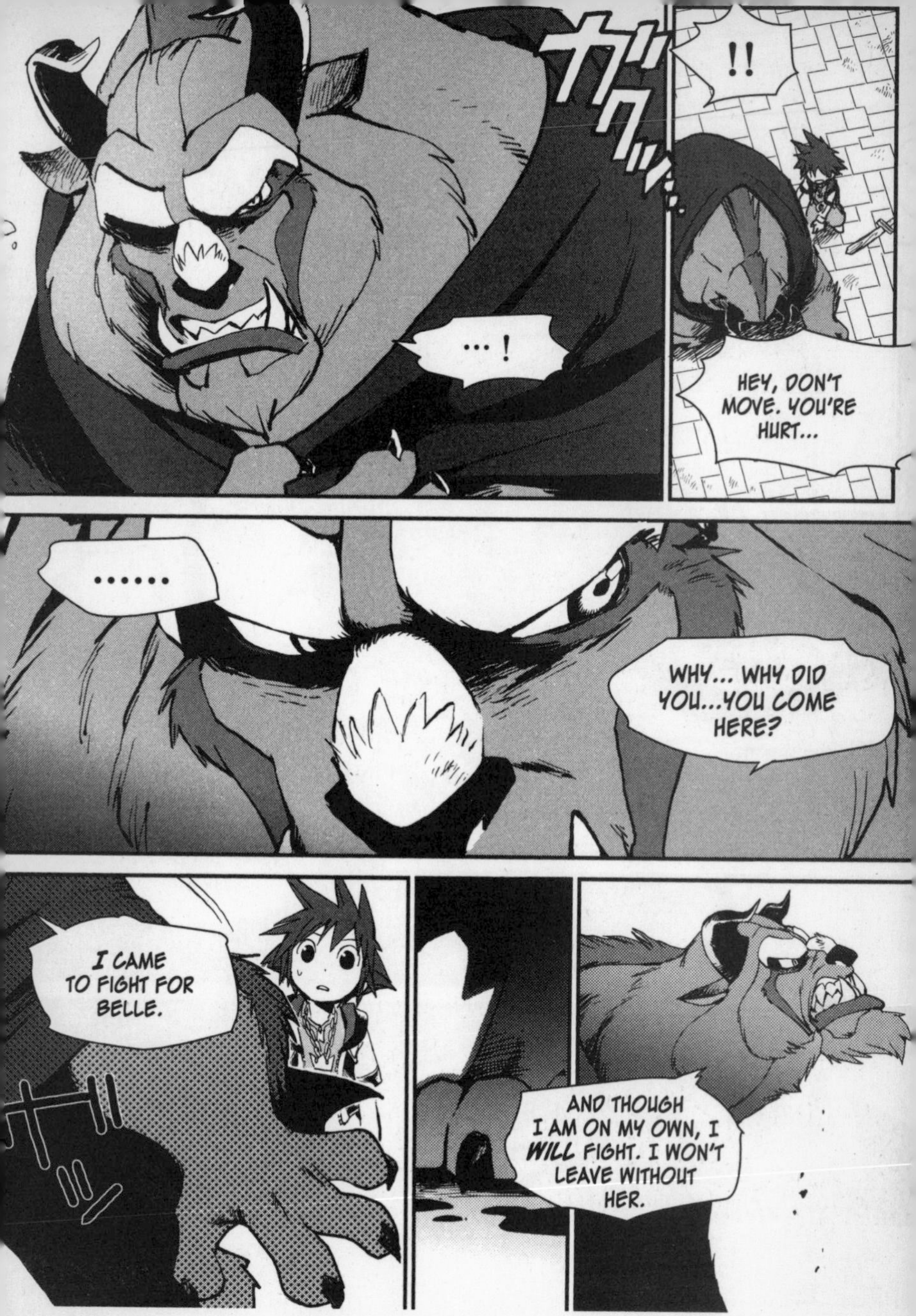
...!
!!
HEY, DON'T MOVE. YOU'RE HURT...
......
WHY... WHY DID YOU...YOU COME HERE?
I CAME TO FIGHT FOR BELLE.
AND THOUGH I AM ON MY OWN, I WILL FIGHT. I WON'T LEAVE WITHOUT HER.

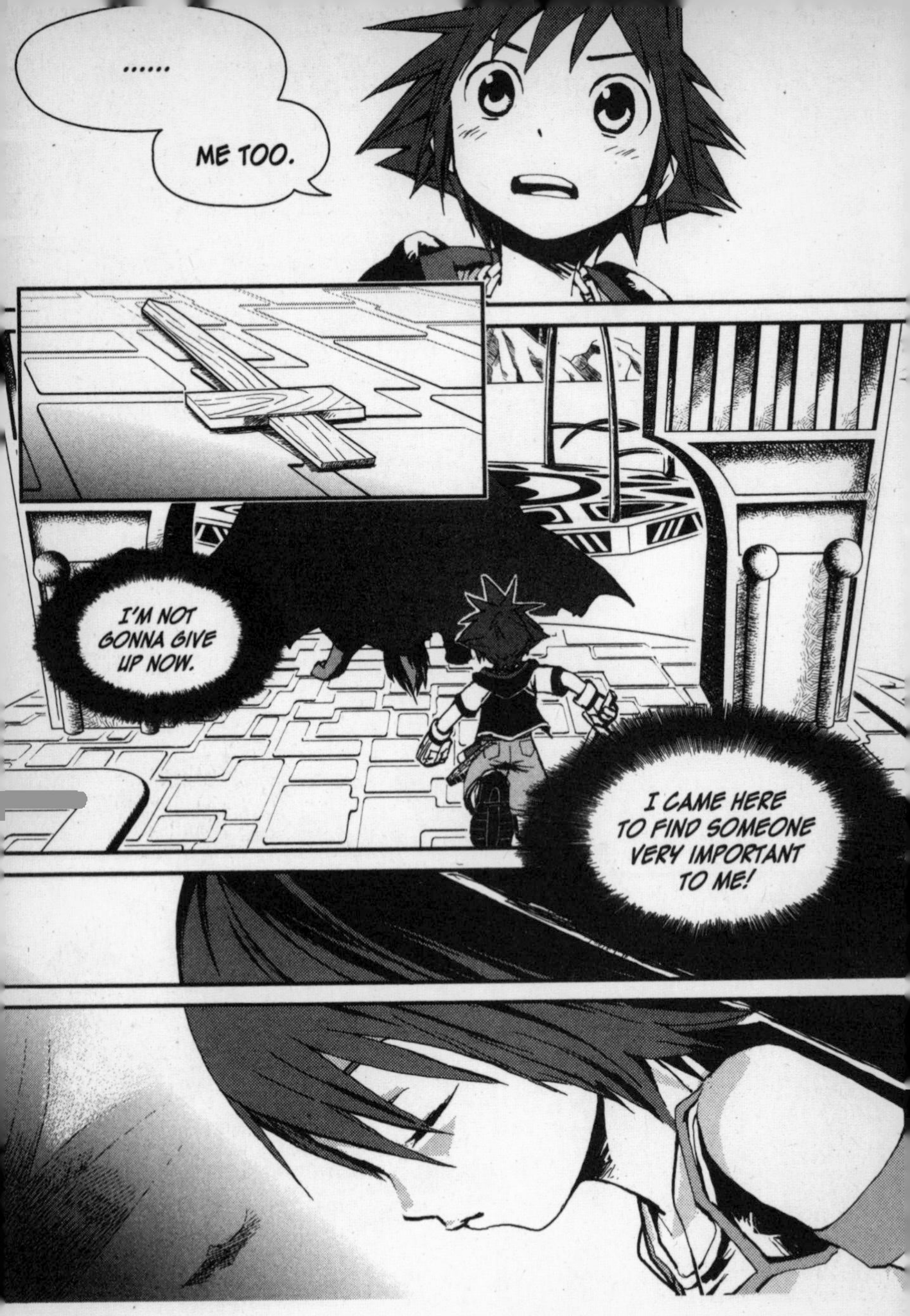
......
ME TOO.
I'M NOT GONNA GIVE UP NOW.
I CAME HERE TO FIND SOMEONE VERY IMPORTANT TO ME!

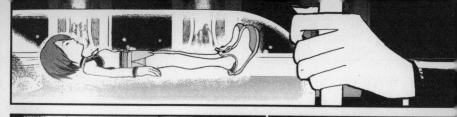

O PUREST OF HEARTS!

REVEAL TO ME THE KEYHOLE!

WAIT! I *SAID*, WAIT!

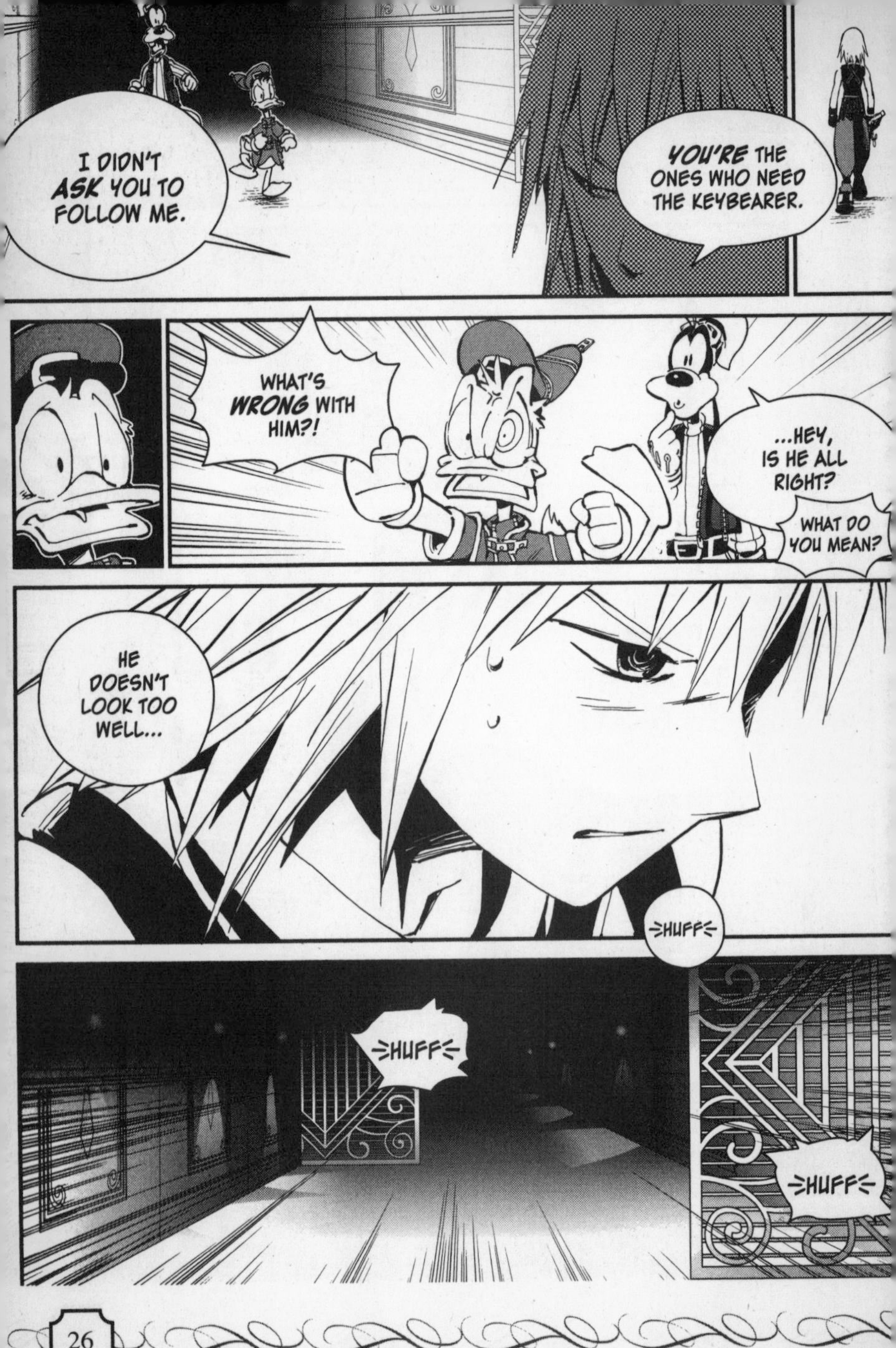

I DIDN'T ASK YOU TO FOLLOW ME.
YOU'RE THE ONES WHO NEED THE KEYBEARER.
WHAT'S WRONG WITH HIM?!
...HEY, IS HE ALL RIGHT?
WHAT DO YOU MEAN?
HE DOESN'T LOOK TOO WELL...
HUFF
HUFF
HUFF

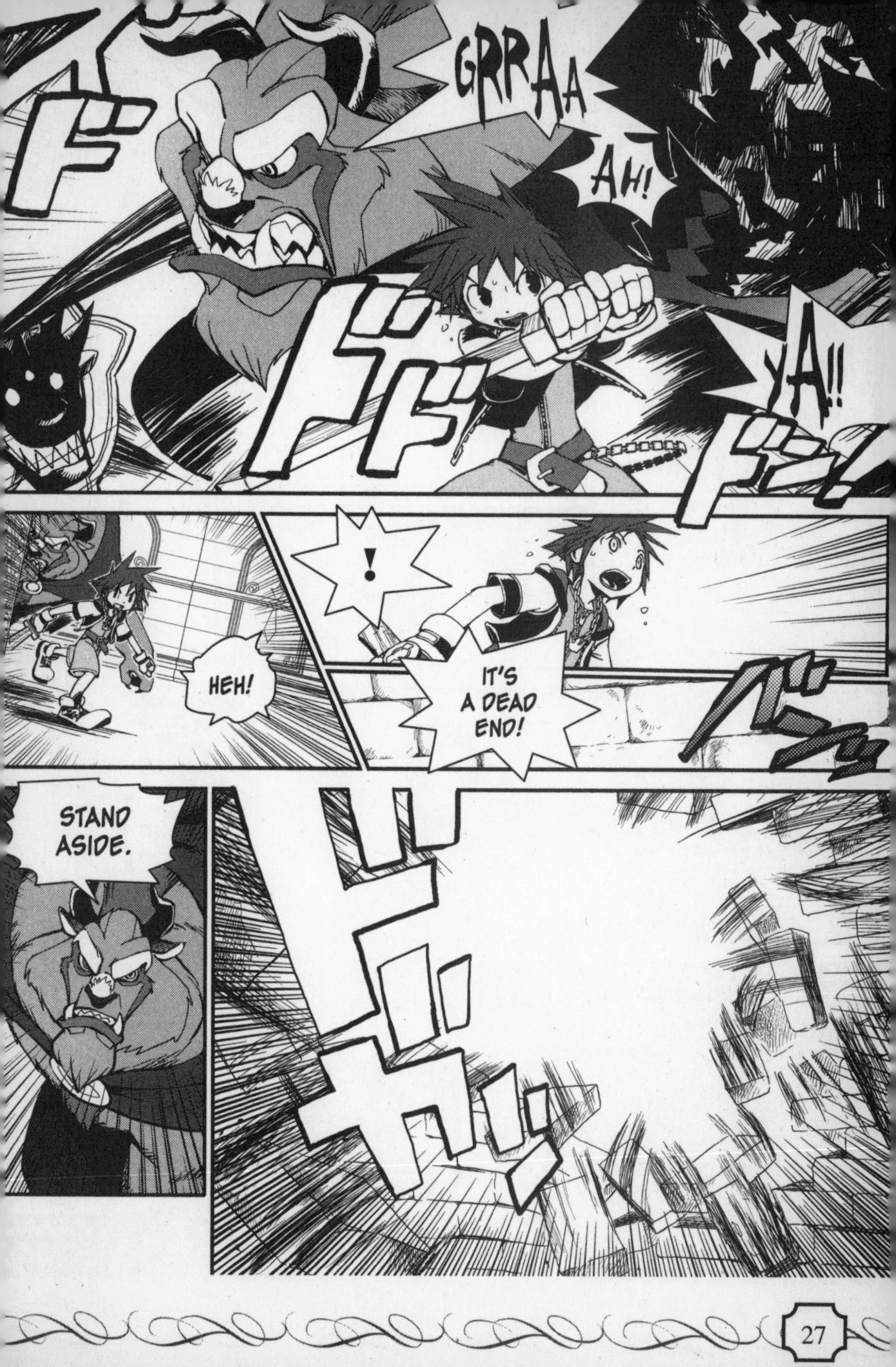
GRRAA
AH!
YA!!
HEH!
!
IT'S A DEAD END!
STAND ASIDE.

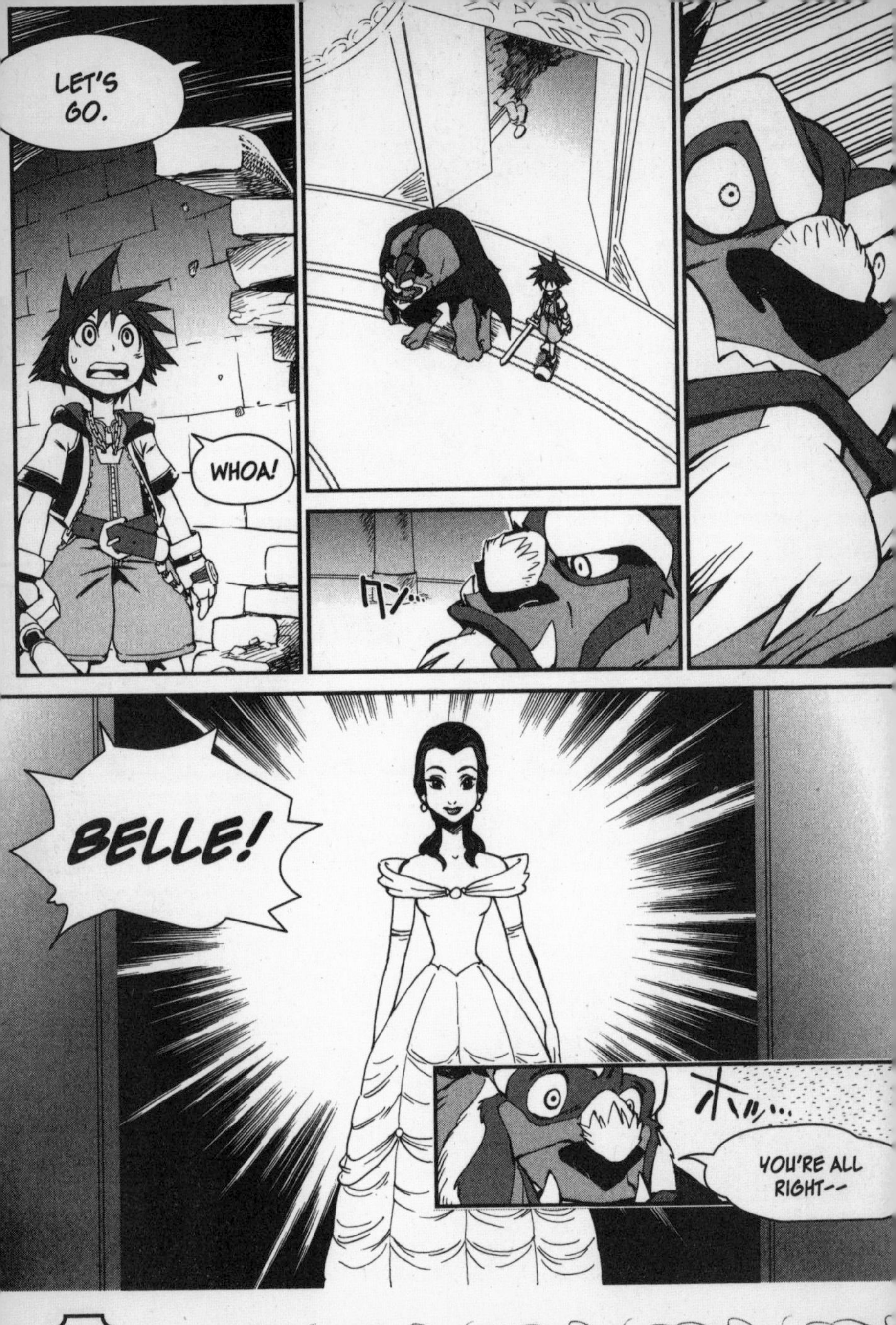
LET'S GO.
WHOA!
クン…
BELLE!
ホッ…
YOU'RE ALL RIGHT--

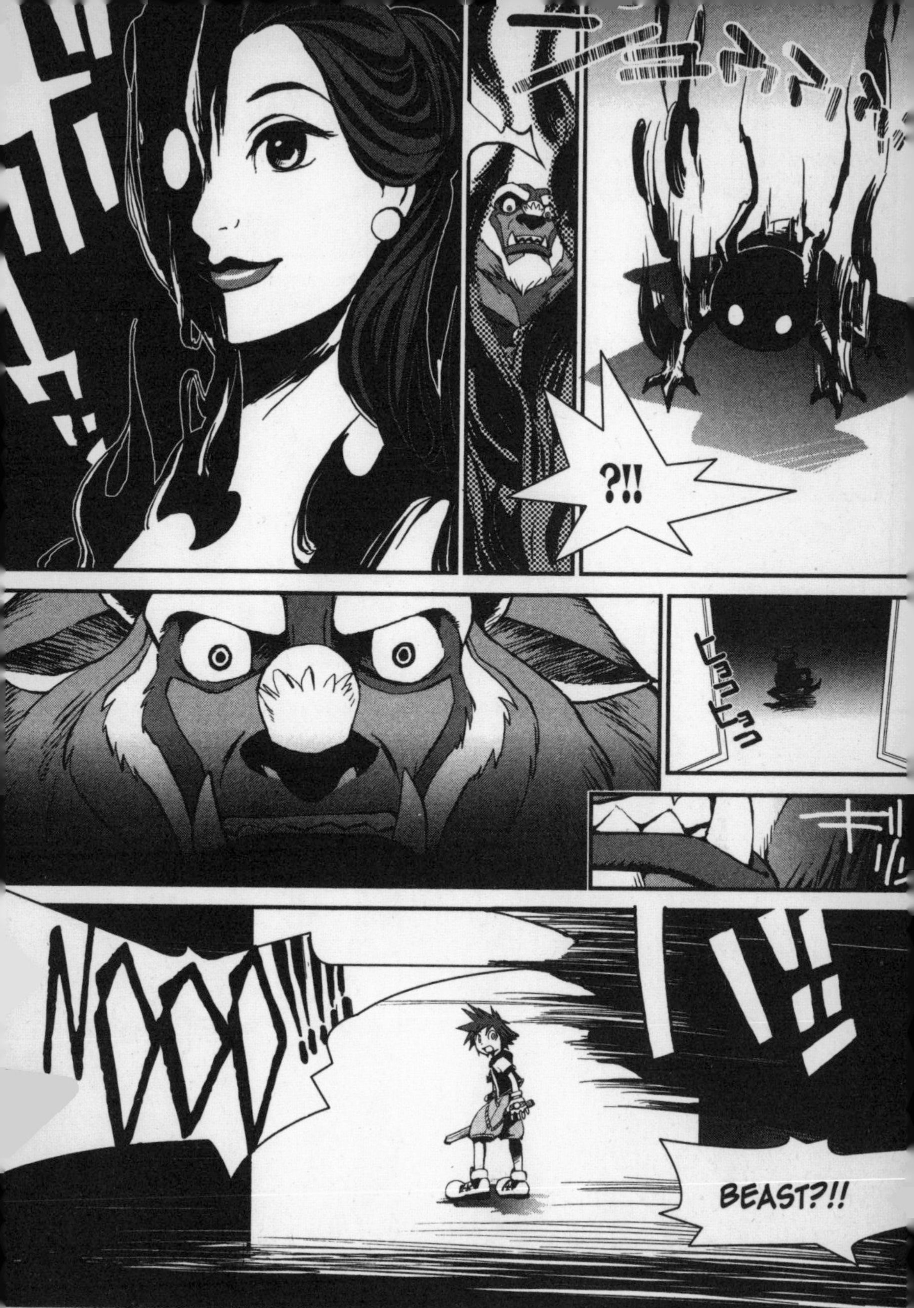
?!!
NOOO!!!
BEAST?!!

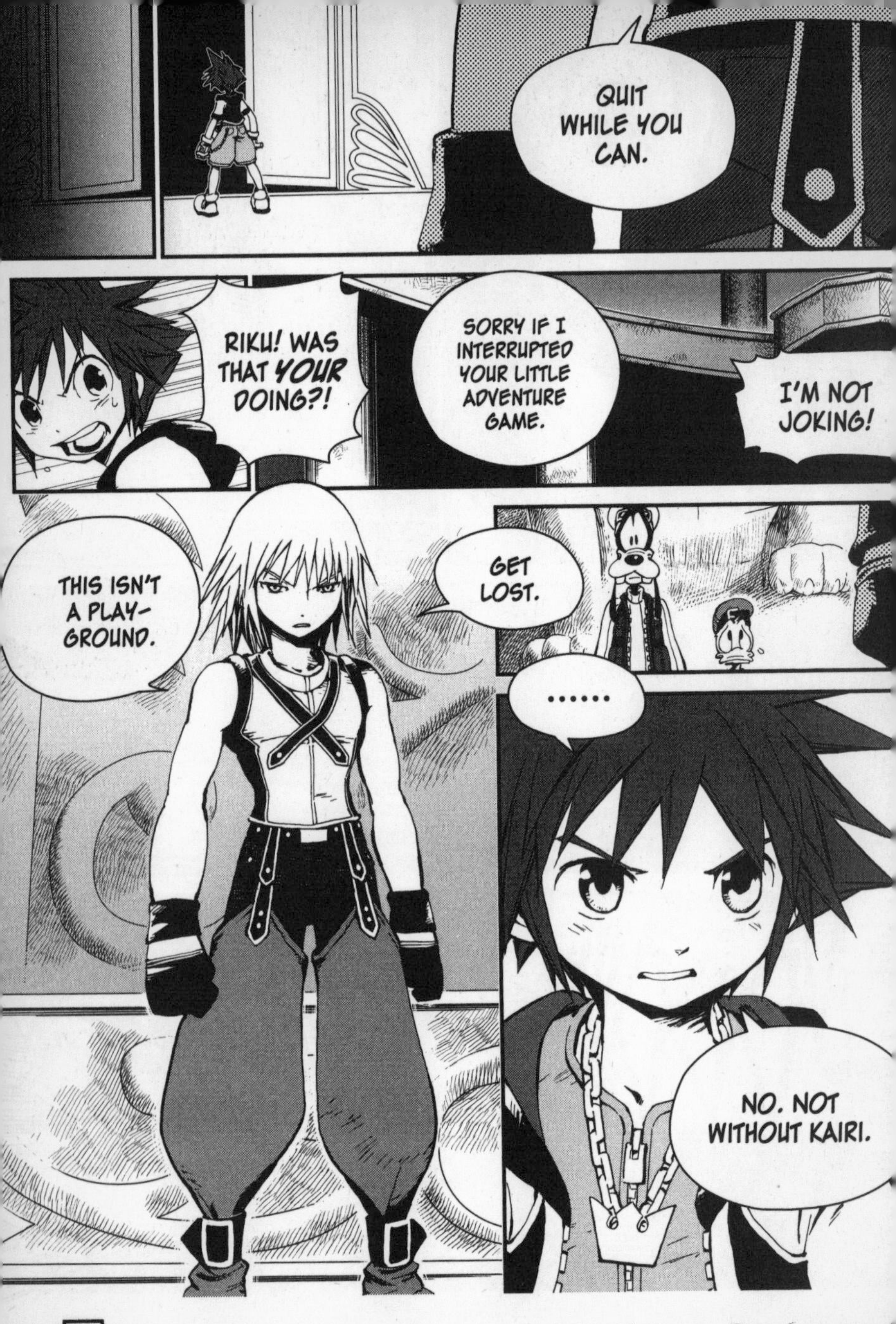
QUIT WHILE YOU CAN.
RIKU! WAS THAT YOUR DOING?!
SORRY IF I INTERRUPTED YOUR LITTLE ADVENTURE GAME.
I'M NOT JOKING!
THIS ISN'T A PLAY-GROUND.
GET LOST.
......
NO. NOT WITHOUT KAIRI.

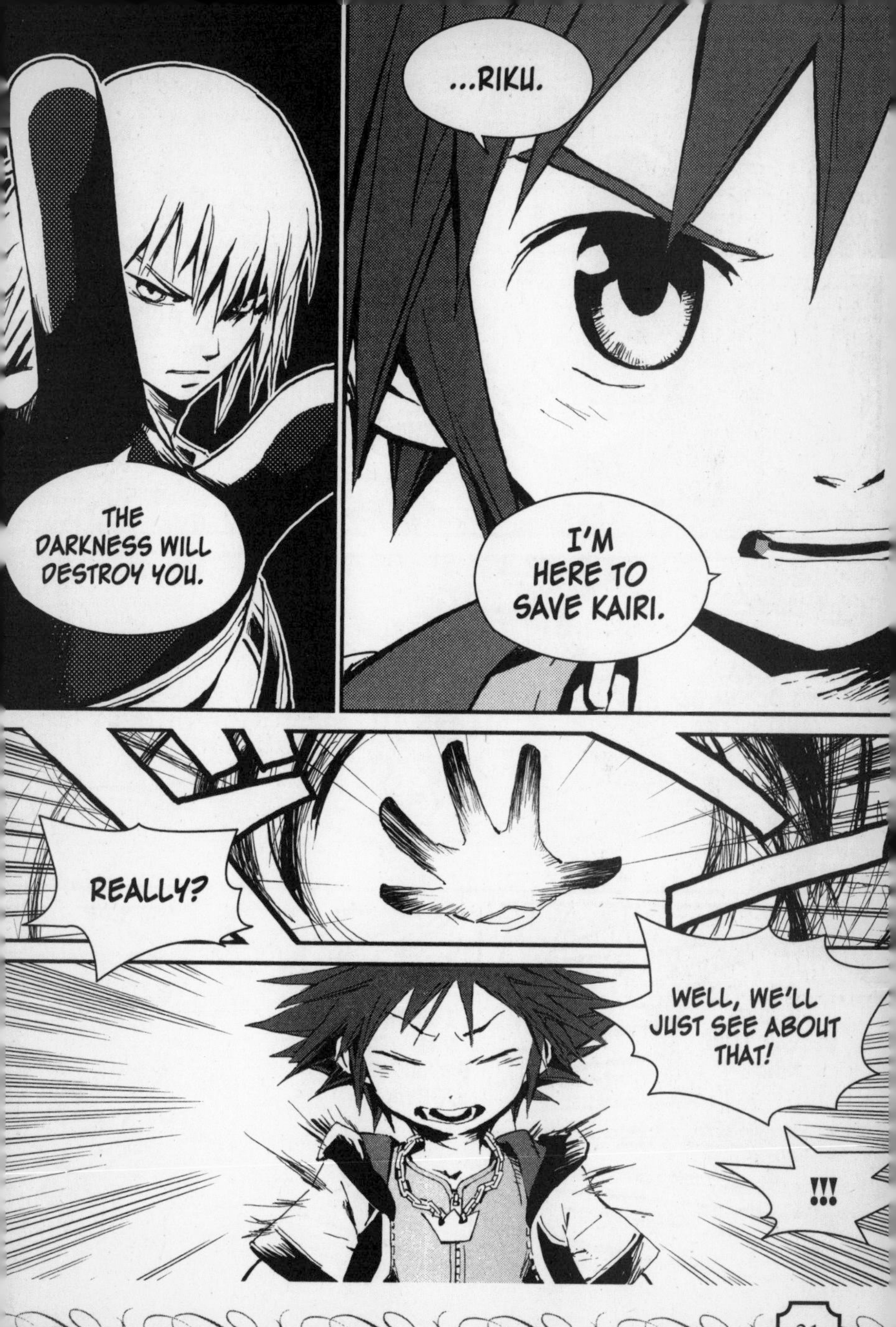
THE DARKNESS WILL DESTROY YOU.
...RIKU.
I'M HERE TO SAVE KAIRI.
REALLY?
WELL, WE'LL JUST SEE ABOUT THAT!
!!!

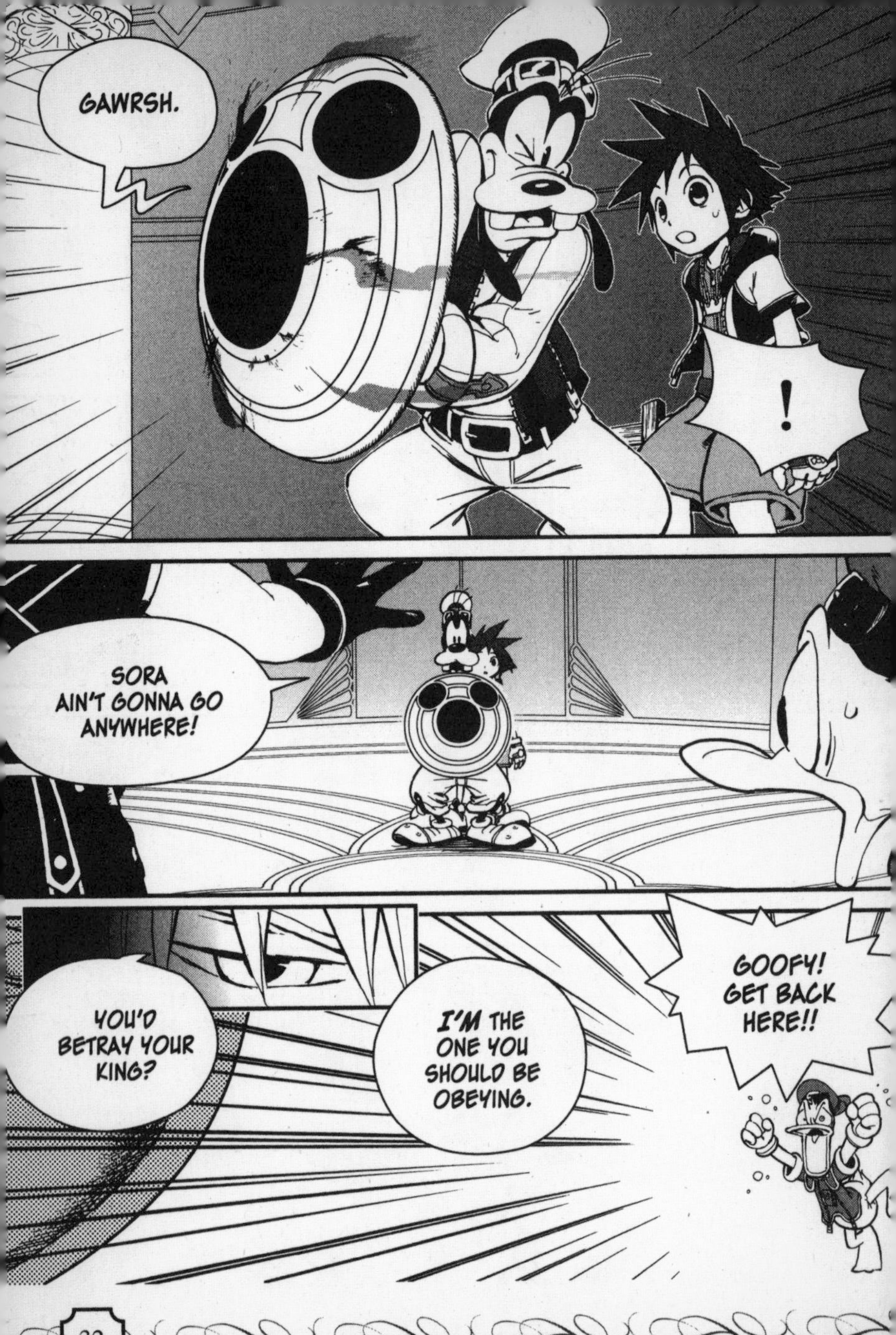
GAWRSH.
!
SORA AIN'T GONNA GO ANYWHERE!
YOU'D BETRAY YOUR KING?
I'M THE ONE YOU SHOULD BE OBEYING.
GOOFY! GET BACK HERE!!

BUT I'M NOT GONNA BETRAY SORA, EITHER.

HE'S BECOME ONE OF MY BEST BUDDIES, AFTER ALL.

SEE YA LATER, DONALD.

COULD YA TELL THE KING I'M REALLY SORRY?

WHAT?!

I'M GOING TO STICK WITH SORA.

GOOFY!

WAIT!

THAT'S NOT FAIR!!

YOU DO WHAT YOU FEEL YOU HAVE TO DO, DONALD.

A-HYUCK!

タッ, タッ, タッ,

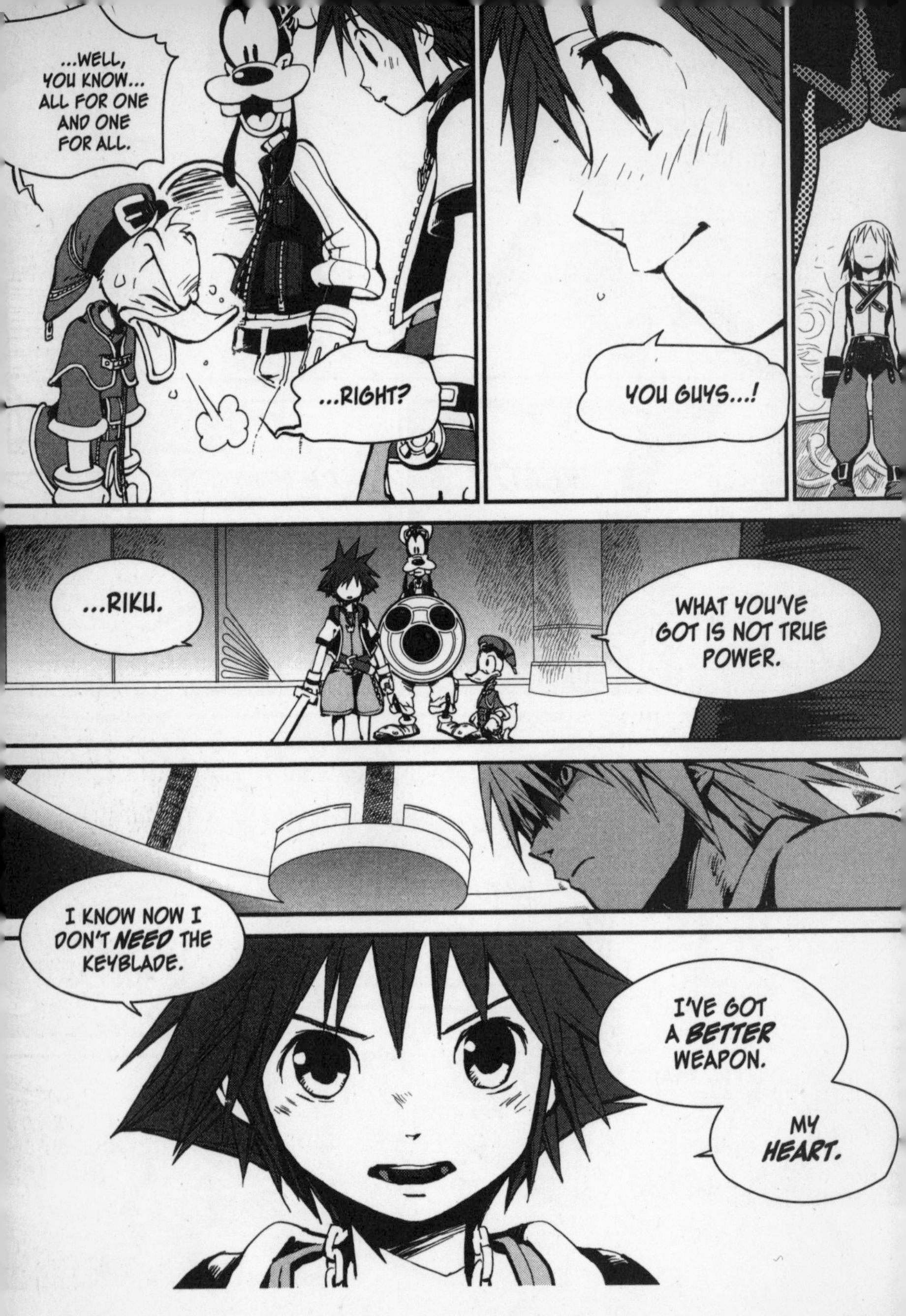
...WELL, YOU KNOW... ALL FOR ONE AND ONE FOR ALL.
...RIGHT?
YOU GUYS...!
...RIKU.
WHAT YOU'VE GOT IS NOT TRUE POWER.
I KNOW NOW I DON'T NEED THE KEYBLADE.
I'VE GOT A BETTER WEAPON.
MY HEART.

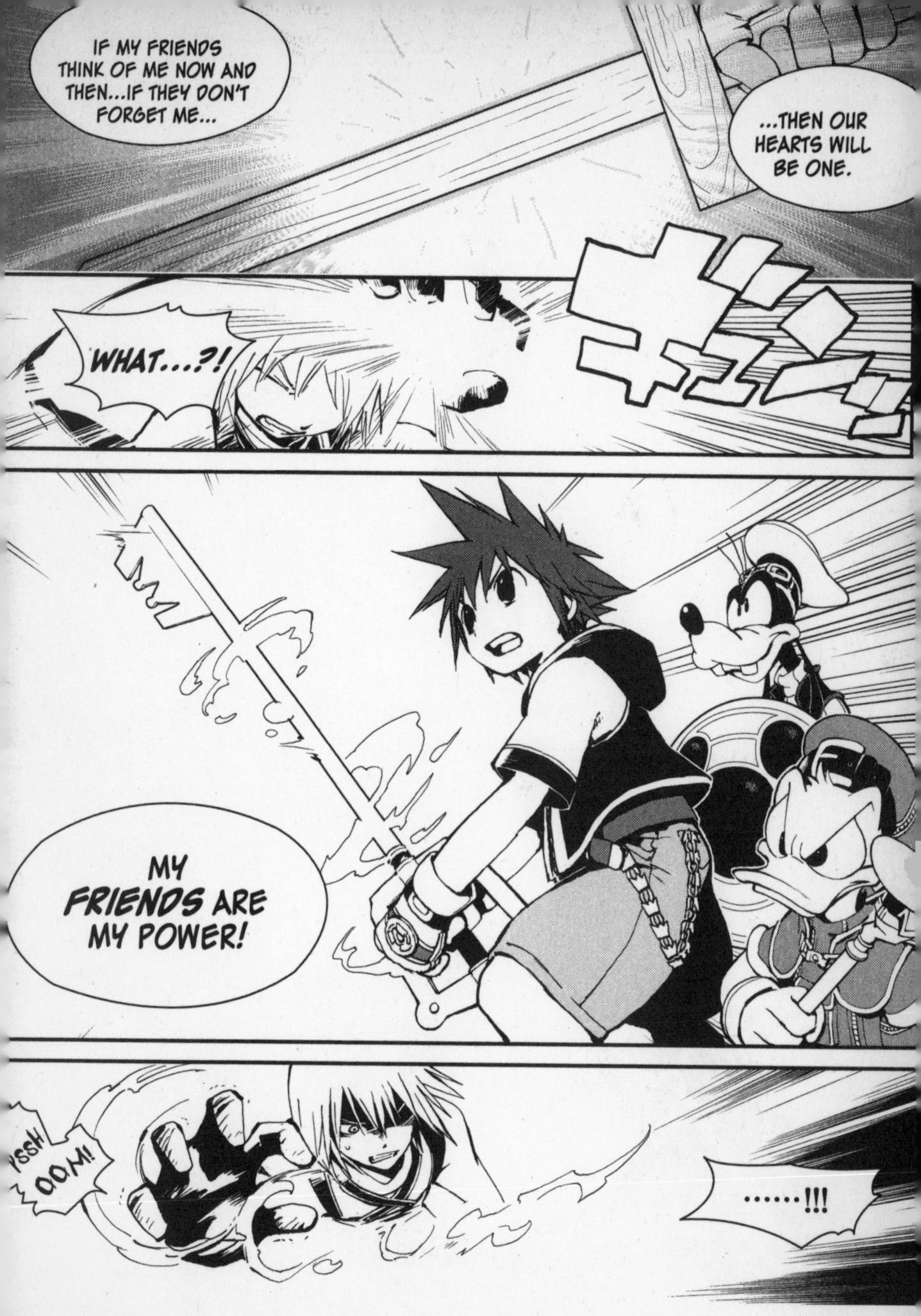
IF MY FRIENDS THINK OF ME NOW AND THEN...IF THEY DON'T FORGET ME...
...THEN OUR HEARTS WILL BE ONE.
WHAT...?!
MY *FRIENDS* ARE MY POWER!
YSSH OOM!
......!!!

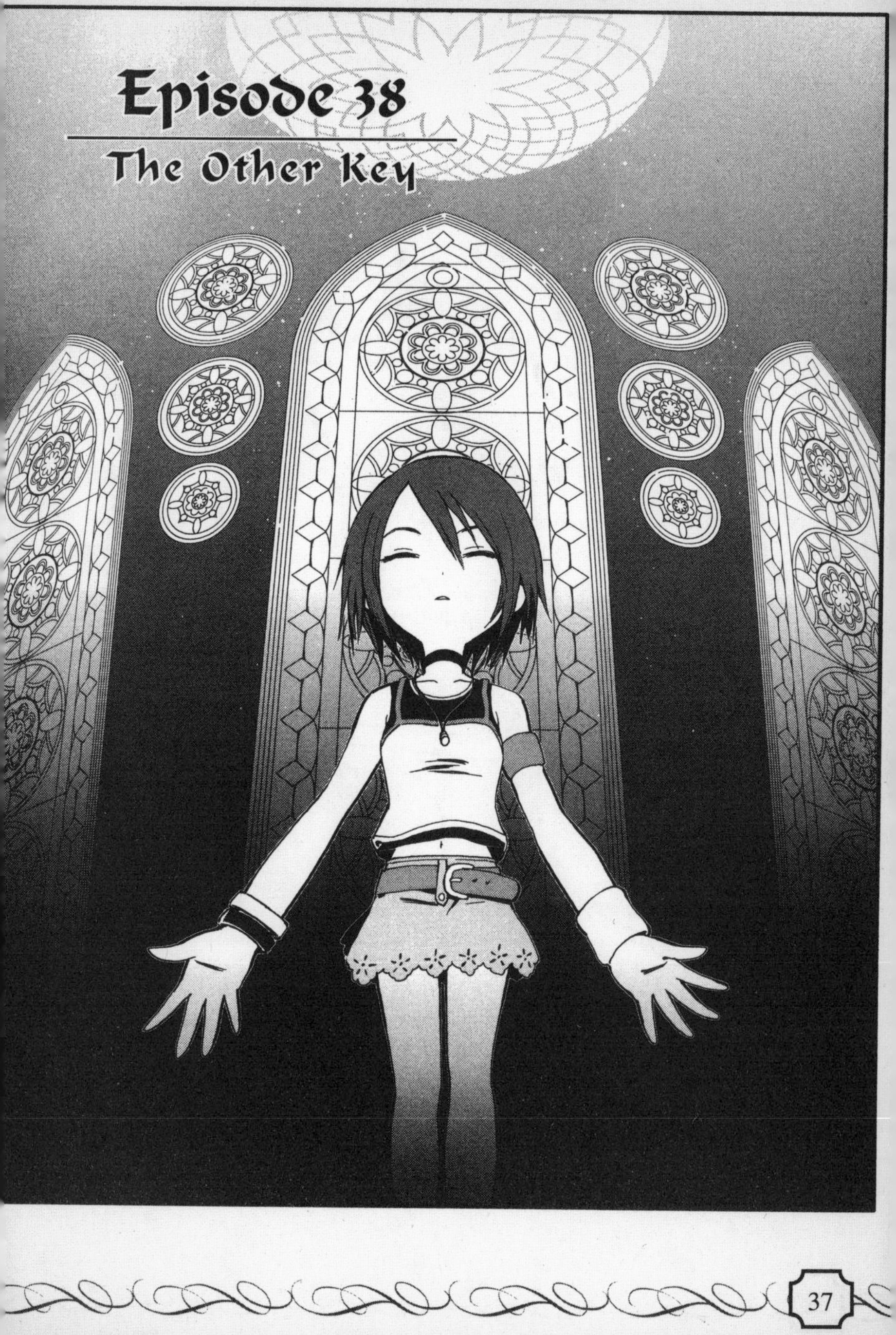
Episode 38
The Other Key

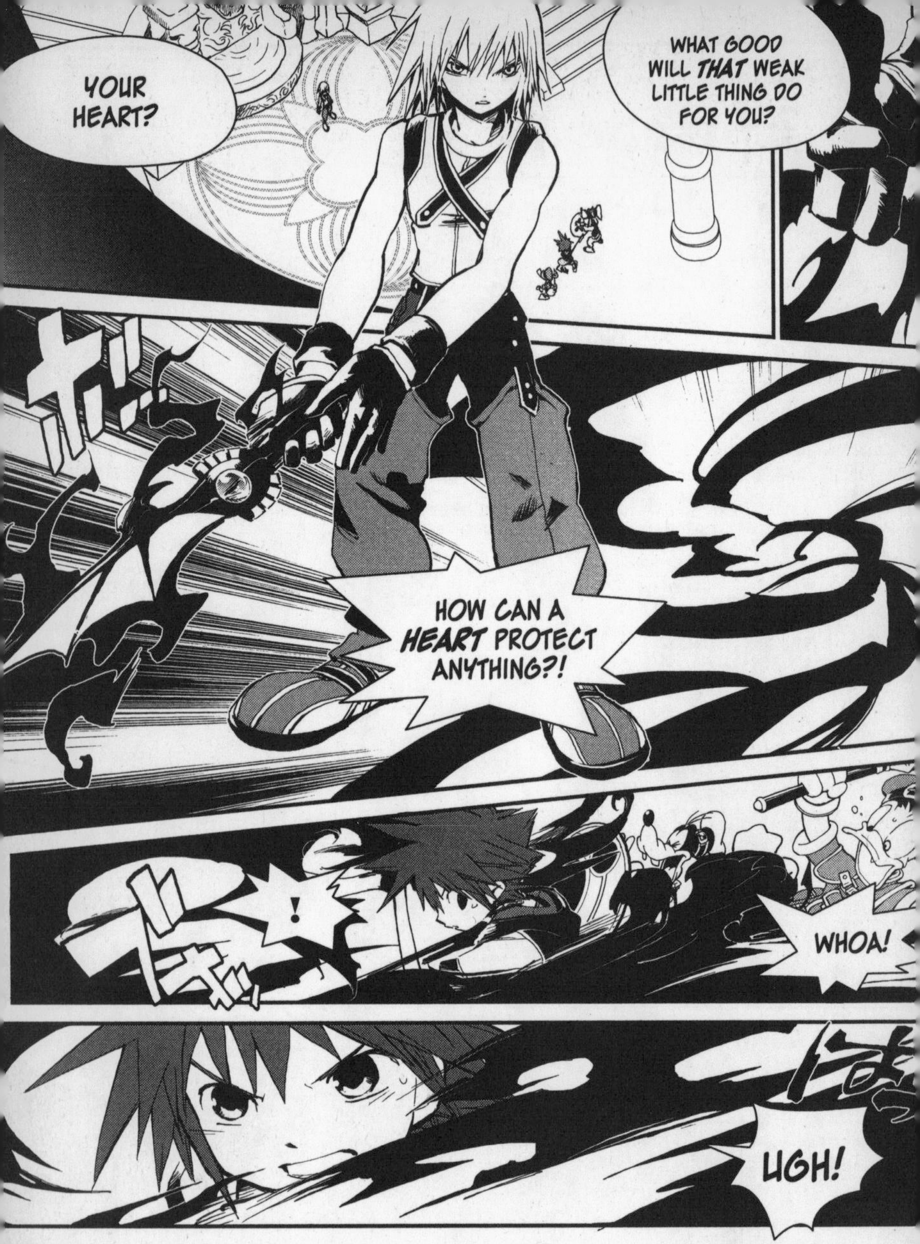
YOUR HEART?
WHAT GOOD WILL THAT WEAK LITTLE THING DO FOR YOU?
HOW CAN A HEART PROTECT ANYTHING?!
!
WHOA!
UGH!

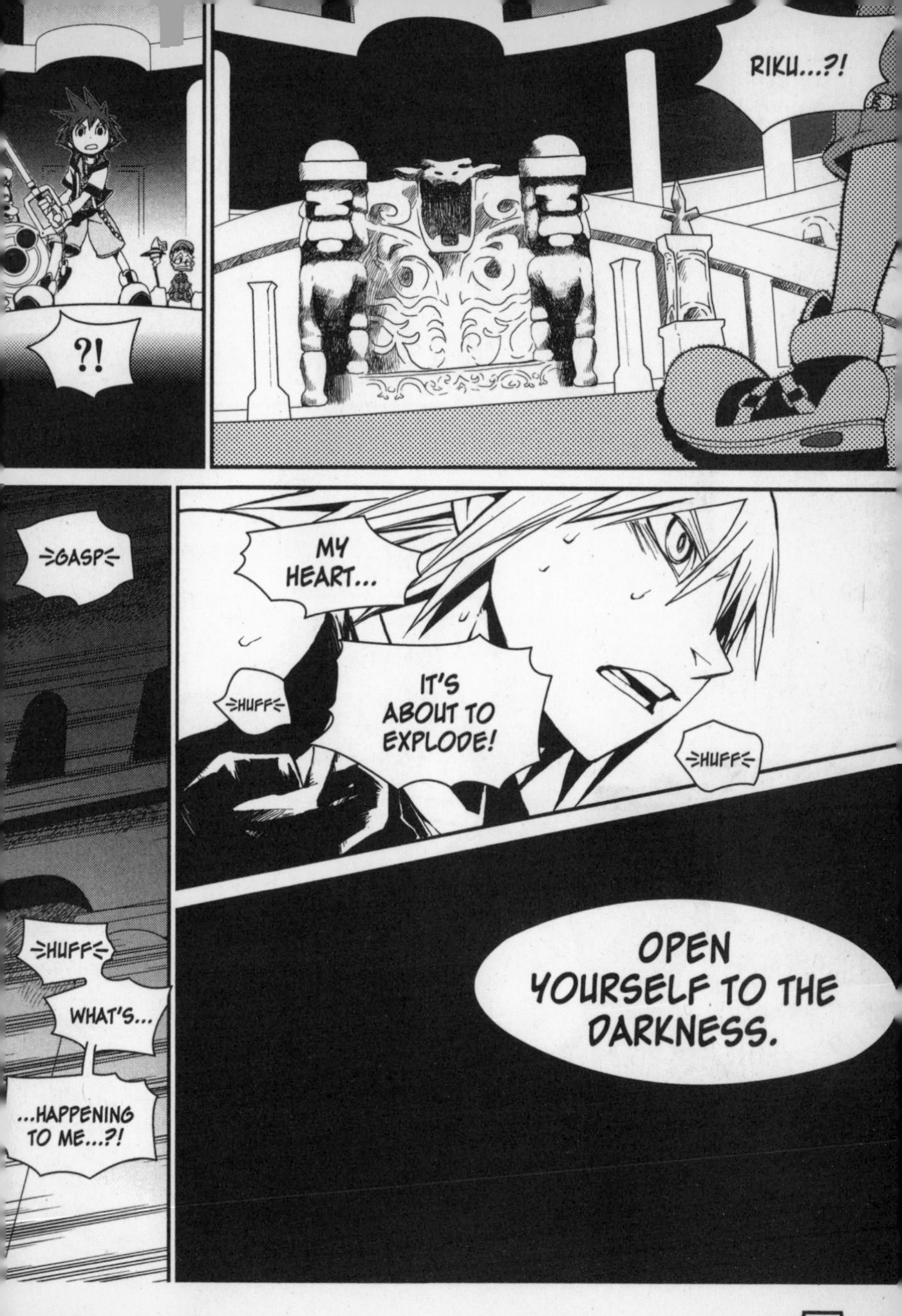
?!
RIKU...?!
=GASP=
=HUFF=
WHAT'S...
...HAPPENING TO ME...?!
MY HEART...
=HUFF=
IT'S ABOUT TO EXPLODE!
=HUFF=
OPEN YOURSELF TO THE DARKNESS.

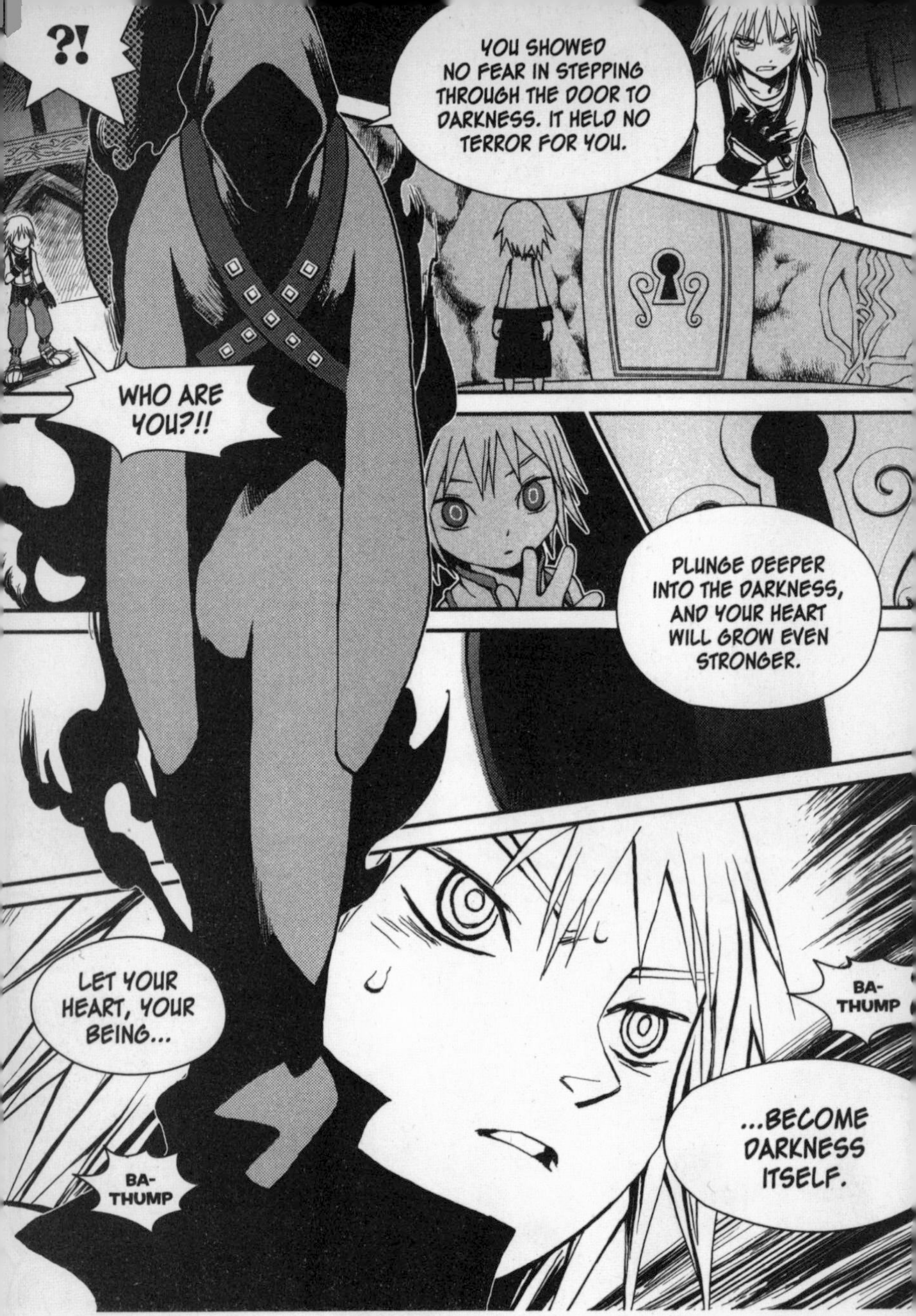
?!
WHO ARE YOU?!!
YOU SHOWED NO FEAR IN STEPPING THROUGH THE DOOR TO DARKNESS. IT HELD NO TERROR FOR YOU.
PLUNGE DEEPER INTO THE DARKNESS, AND YOUR HEART WILL GROW EVEN STRONGER.
LET YOUR HEART, YOUR BEING...
BA-THUMP
BA-THUMP
...BECOME DARKNESS ITSELF.

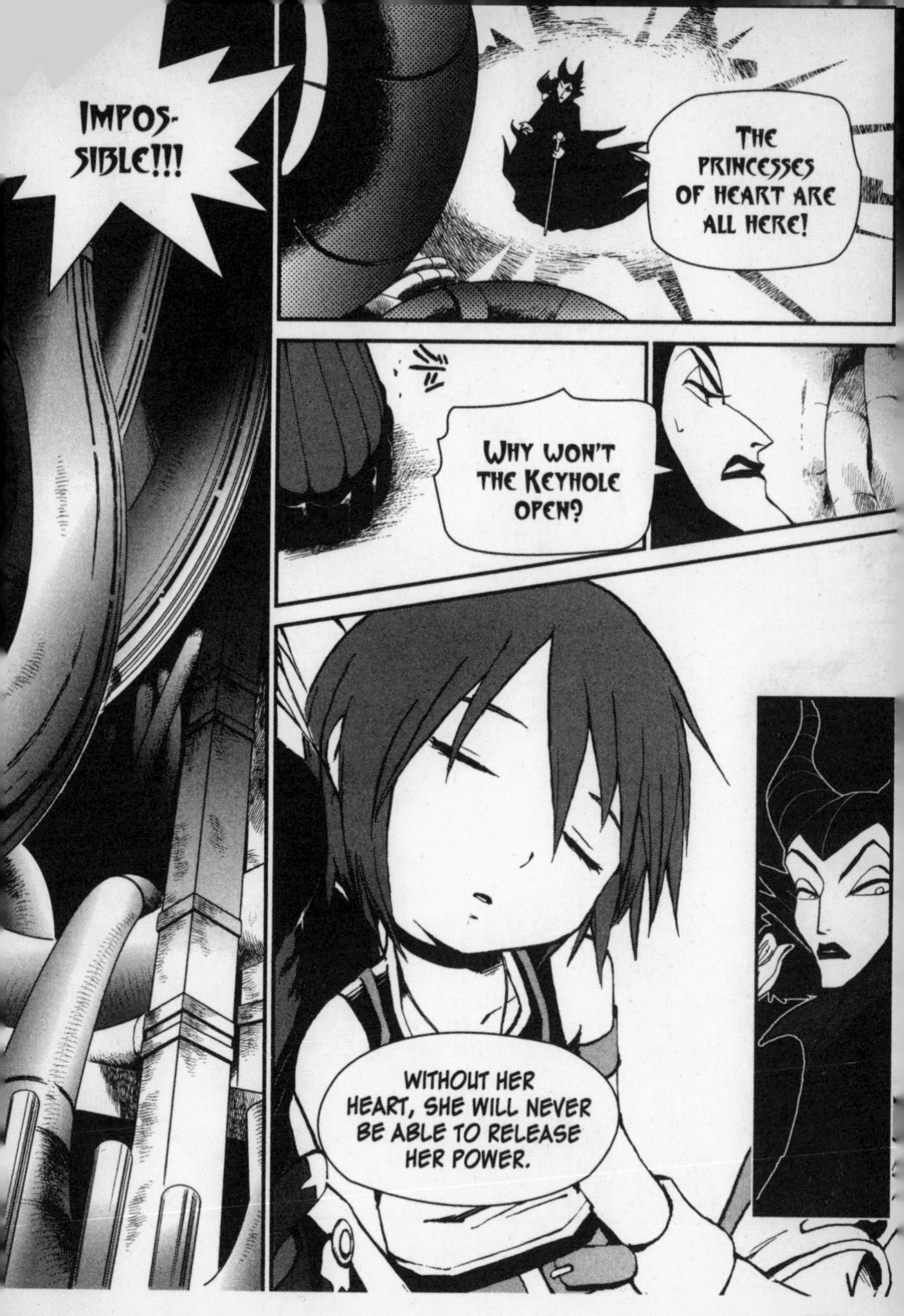
IMPOS-SIBLE!!!
THE PRINCESSES OF HEART ARE ALL HERE!
WHY WON'T THE KEYHOLE OPEN?
WITHOUT HER HEART, SHE WILL NEVER BE ABLE TO RELEASE HER POWER.

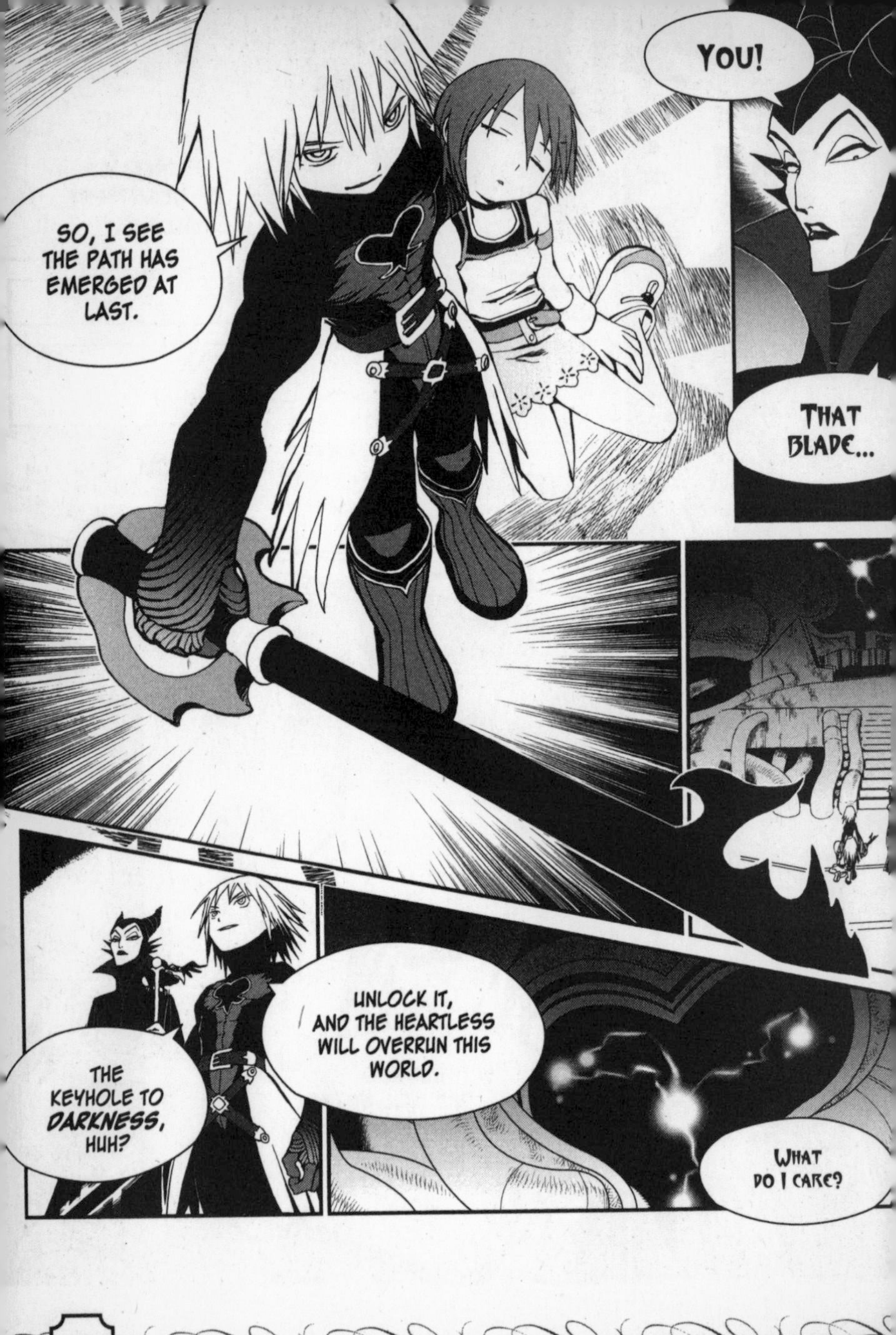
SO, I SEE THE PATH HAS EMERGED AT LAST.
YOU!
THAT BLADE...
THE KEYHOLE TO DARKNESS, HUH?
UNLOCK IT, AND THE HEARTLESS WILL OVERRUN THIS WORLD.
WHAT DO I CARE?

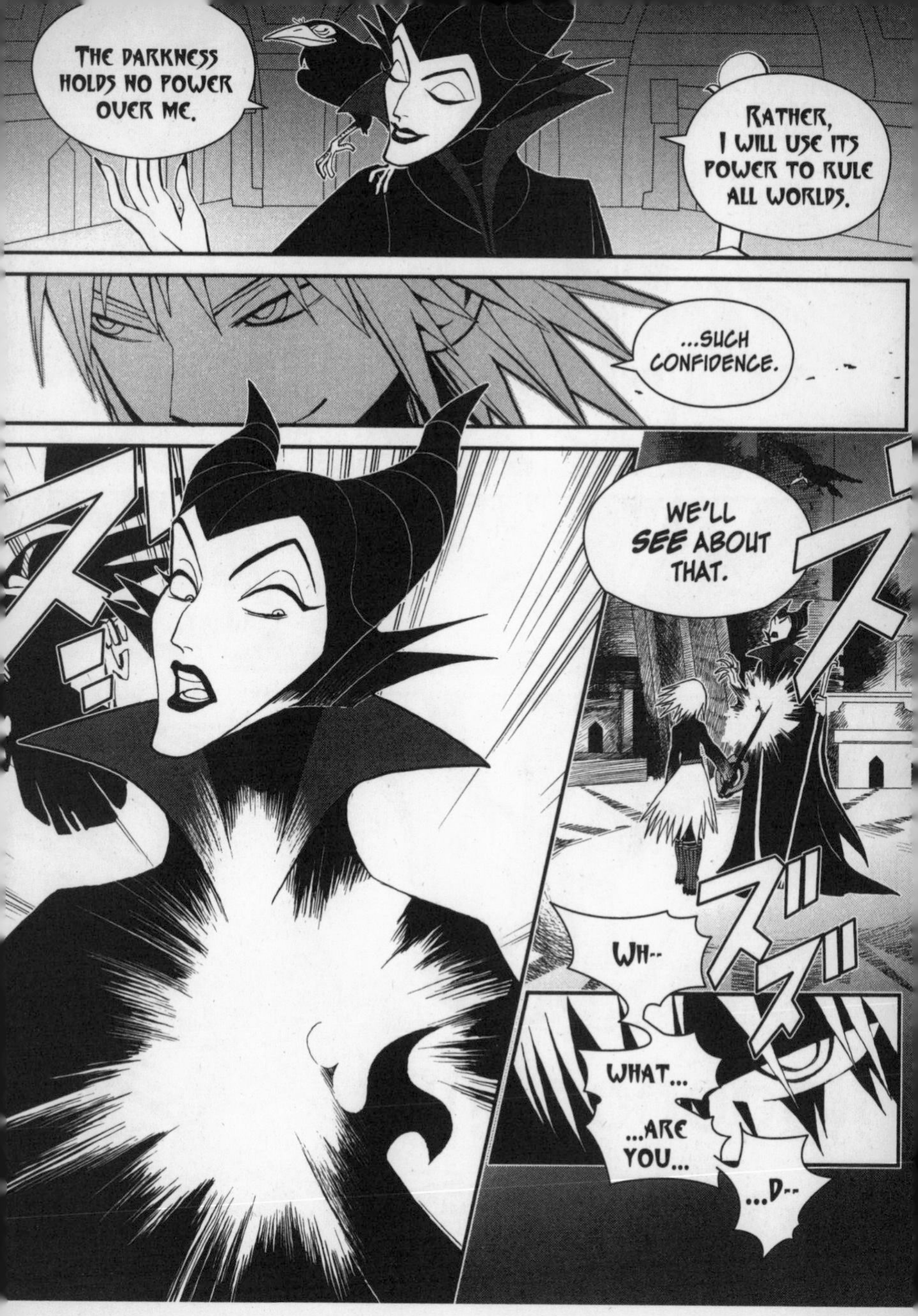

THE DARKNESS HOLDS NO POWER OVER ME.
RATHER, I WILL USE ITS POWER TO RULE ALL WORLDS.
...SUCH CONFIDENCE.
WE'LL SEE ABOUT THAT.
WH--
WHAT...
...ARE YOU...
...D--

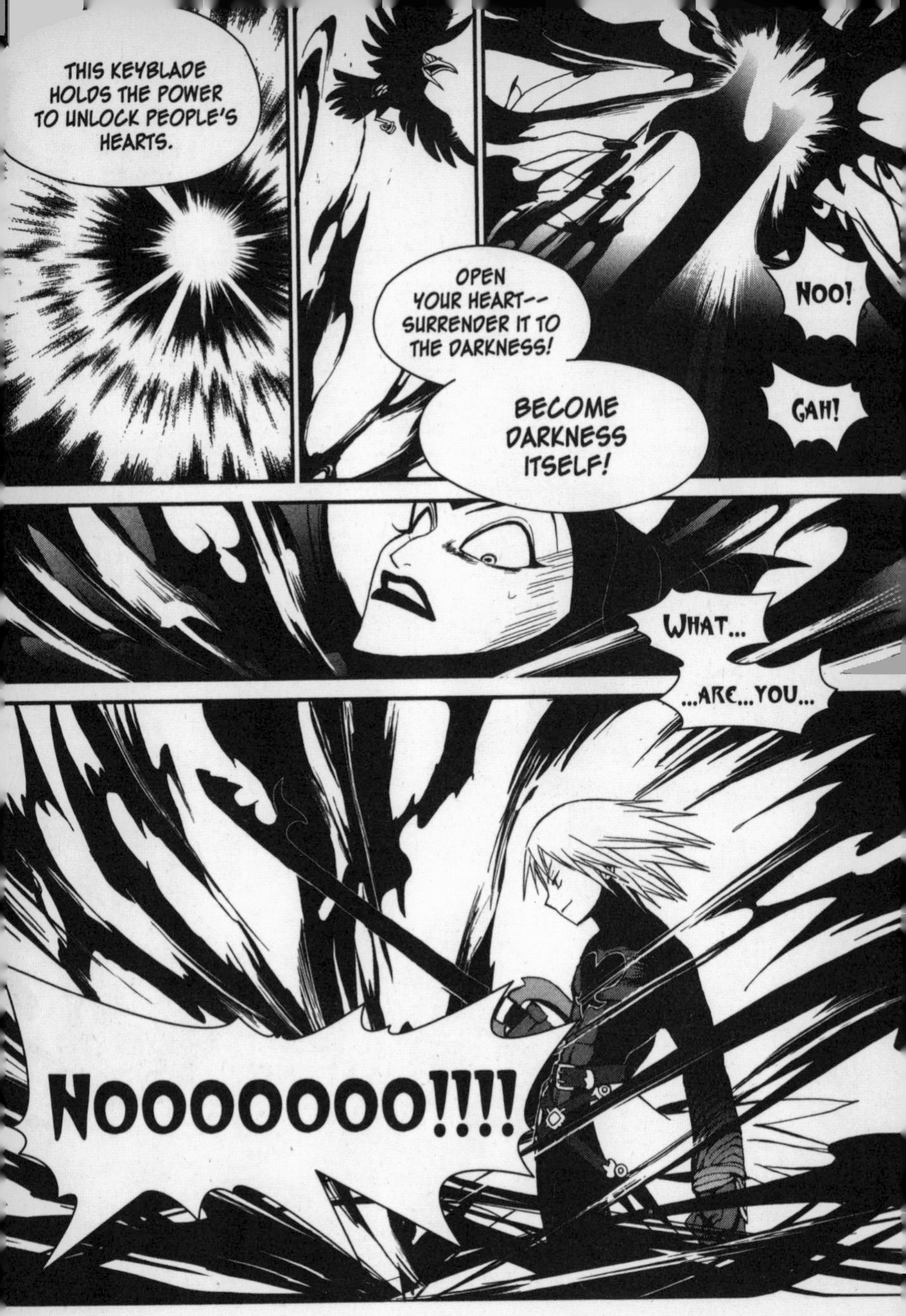
THIS KEYBLADE HOLDS THE POWER TO UNLOCK PEOPLE'S HEARTS.
OPEN YOUR HEART-- SURRENDER IT TO THE DARKNESS!
BECOME DARKNESS ITSELF!
NOO!
GAH!
WHAT...
...ARE...YOU...
NOOOOOOO!!!!

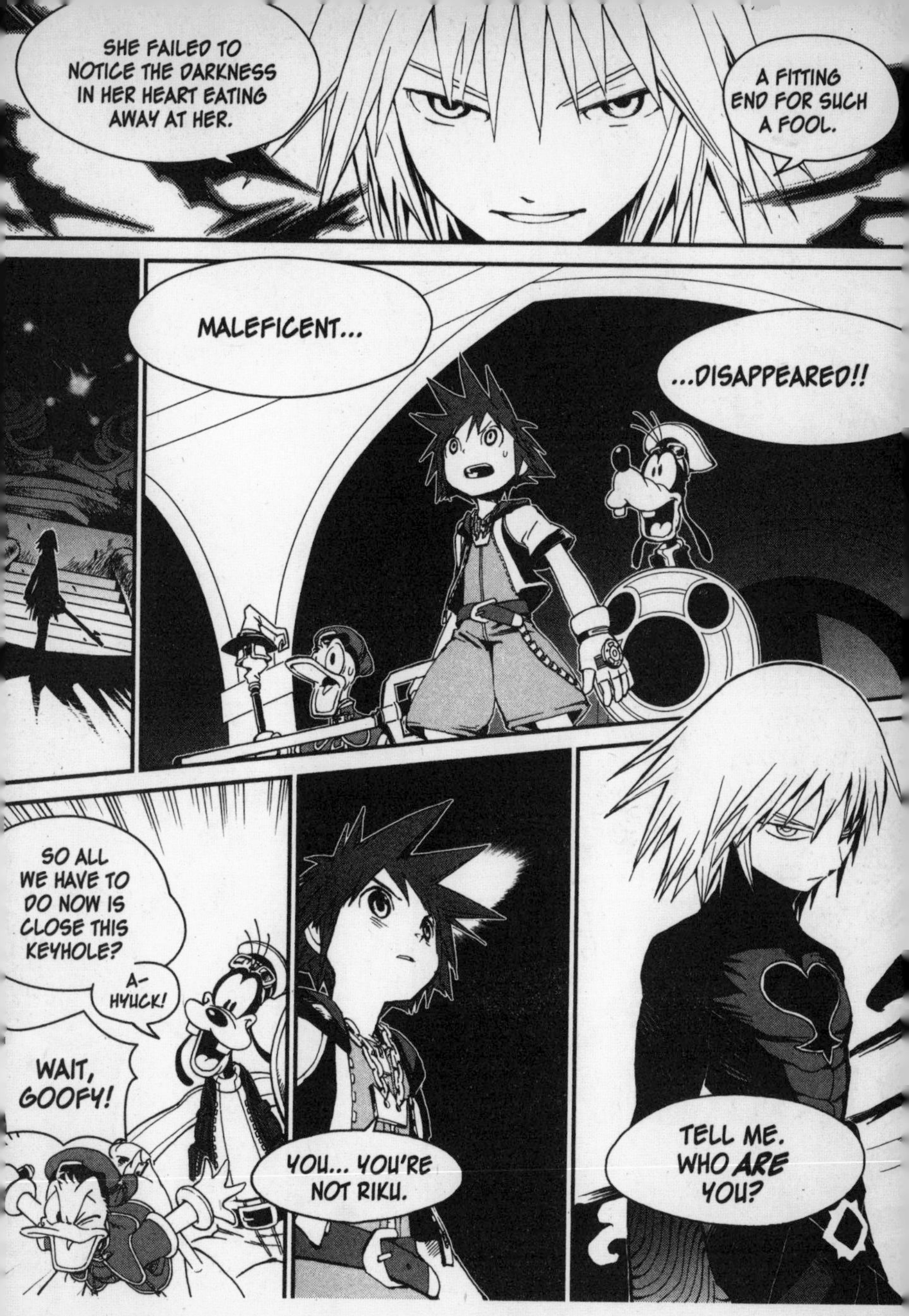
SHE FAILED TO NOTICE THE DARKNESS IN HER HEART EATING AWAY AT HER.
A FITTING END FOR SUCH A FOOL.
MALEFICENT...
...DISAPPEARED!!
SO ALL WE HAVE TO DO NOW IS CLOSE THIS KEYHOLE?
A-HYUCK!
WAIT, GOOFY!
YOU... YOU'RE NOT RIKU.
TELL ME. WHO ARE YOU?

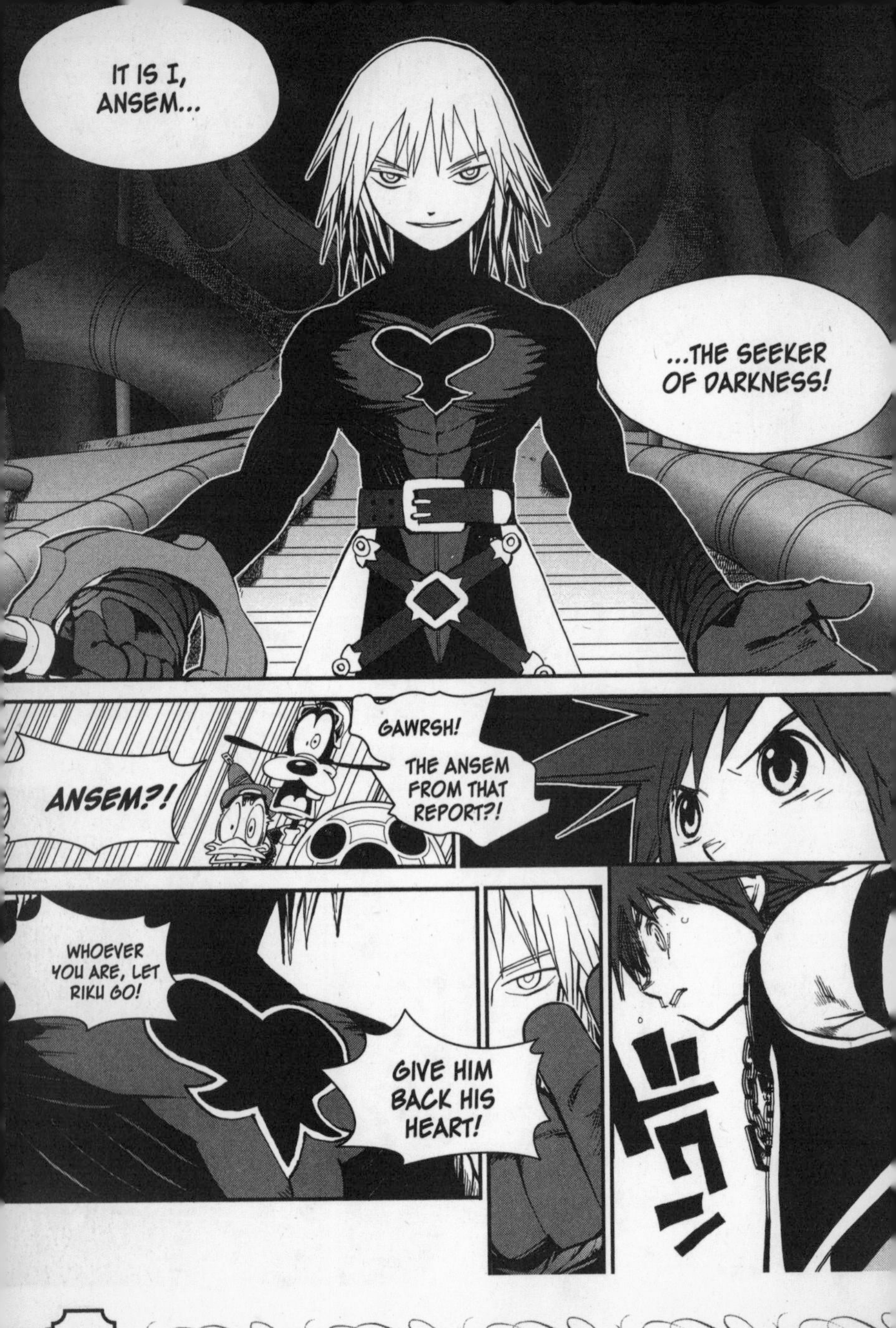
IT IS I, ANSEM...
...THE SEEKER OF DARKNESS!
ANSEM?!
GAWRSH!
THE ANSEM FROM THAT REPORT?!
WHOEVER YOU ARE, LET RIKU GO!
GIVE HIM BACK HIS HEART!

=GASP=

FIRST, YOU MUST GIVE THE PRINCESS BACK HER HEART.

WHAT'S--

DON'T YOU SEE YET? KAIRI'S HEART RESTS WITHIN YOU!

KAIRI?

THE KEYHOLE CANNOT BE COMPLETED SO LONG AS THE LAST PRINCESS OF HEART STILL SLEEPS.

KAIRI'S INSIDE OF ME?!

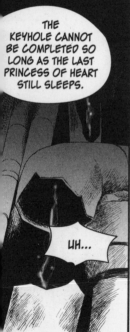

UH...

FORGET IT! THERE'S NO *WAY* YOU'RE TAKING KAIRI'S HEART!

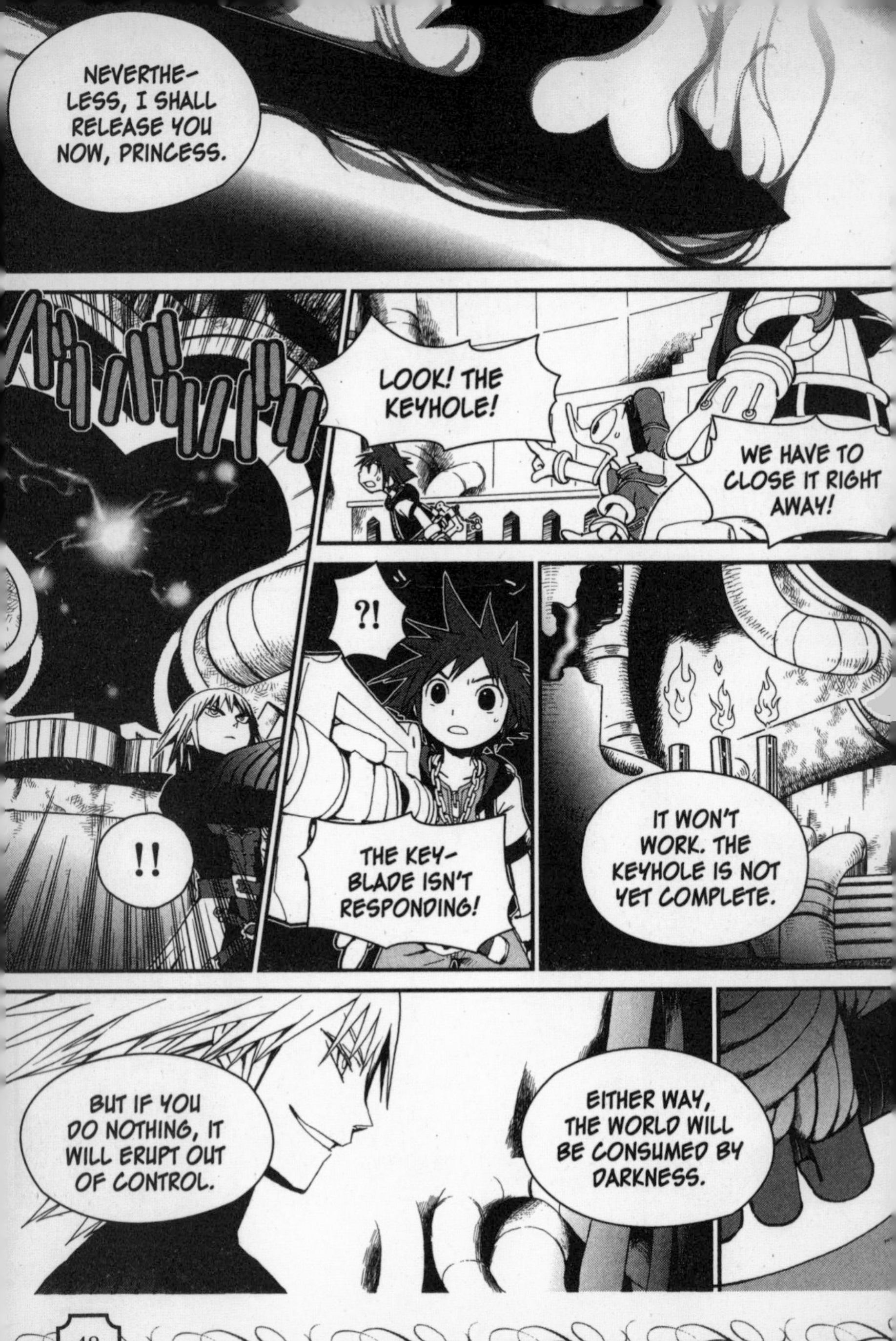
NEVERTHE-LESS, I SHALL RELEASE YOU NOW, PRINCESS.
!!
LOOK! THE KEYHOLE!
WE HAVE TO CLOSE IT RIGHT AWAY!
?!
THE KEY-BLADE ISN'T RESPONDING!
IT WON'T WORK. THE KEYHOLE IS NOT YET COMPLETE.
BUT IF YOU DO NOTHING, IT WILL ERUPT OUT OF CONTROL.
EITHER WAY, THE WORLD WILL BE CONSUMED BY DARKNESS.

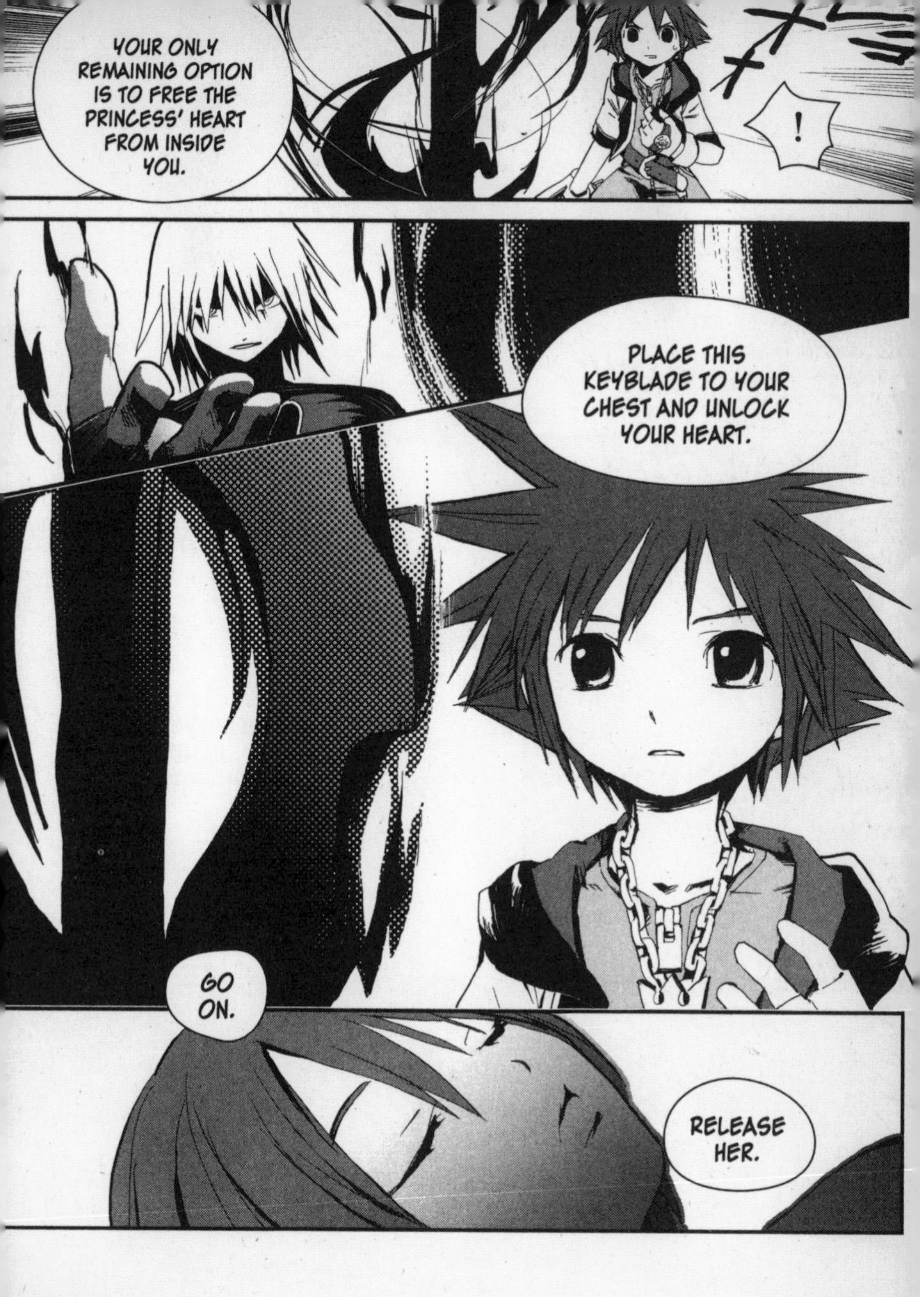
YOUR ONLY REMAINING OPTION IS TO FREE THE PRINCESS' HEART FROM INSIDE YOU.
!
PLACE THIS KEYBLADE TO YOUR CHEST AND UNLOCK YOUR HEART.
GO ON.
RELEASE HER.

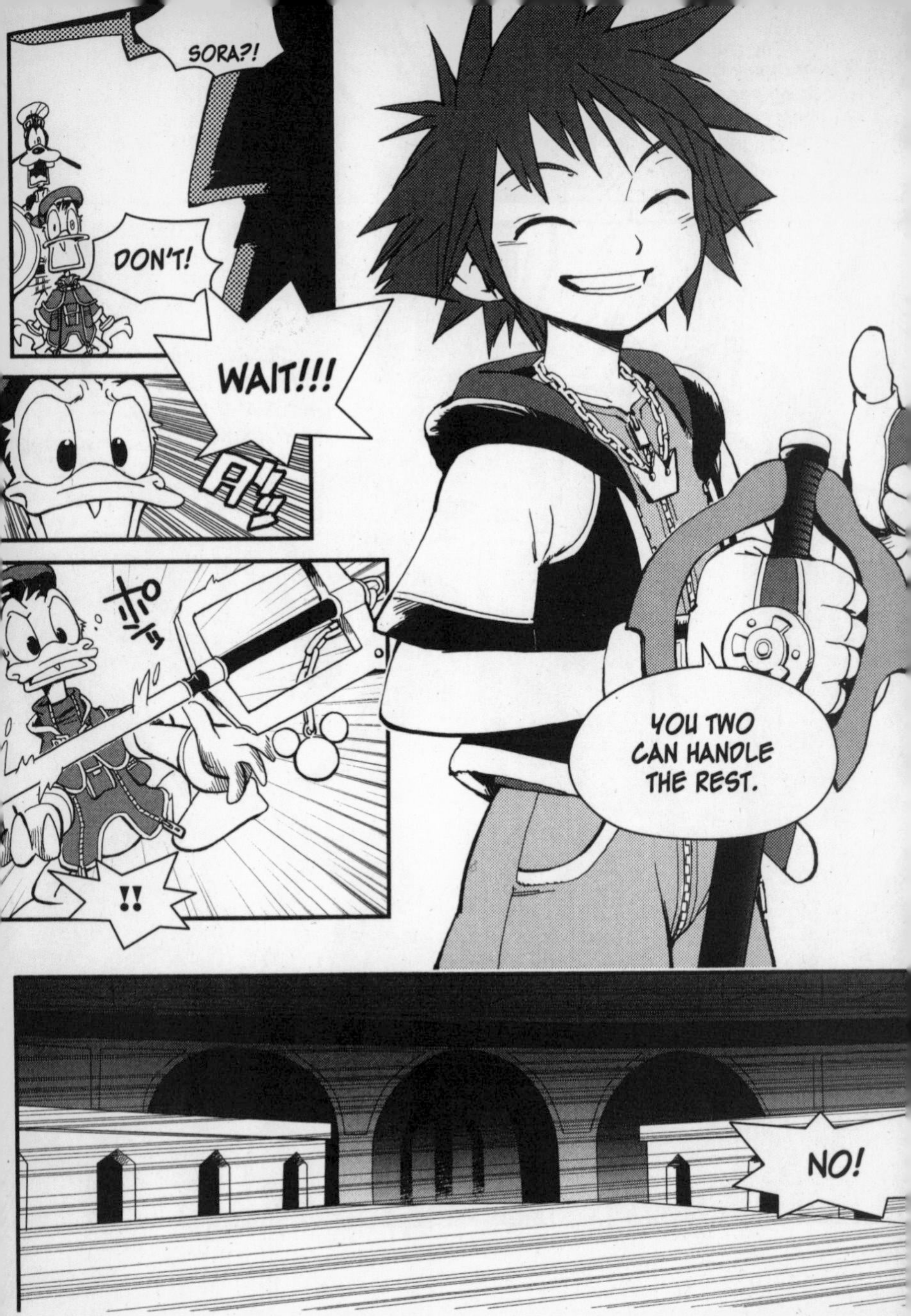
SORA?!
DON'T!
WAIT!!!
!!
YOU TWO CAN HANDLE THE REST.
NO!

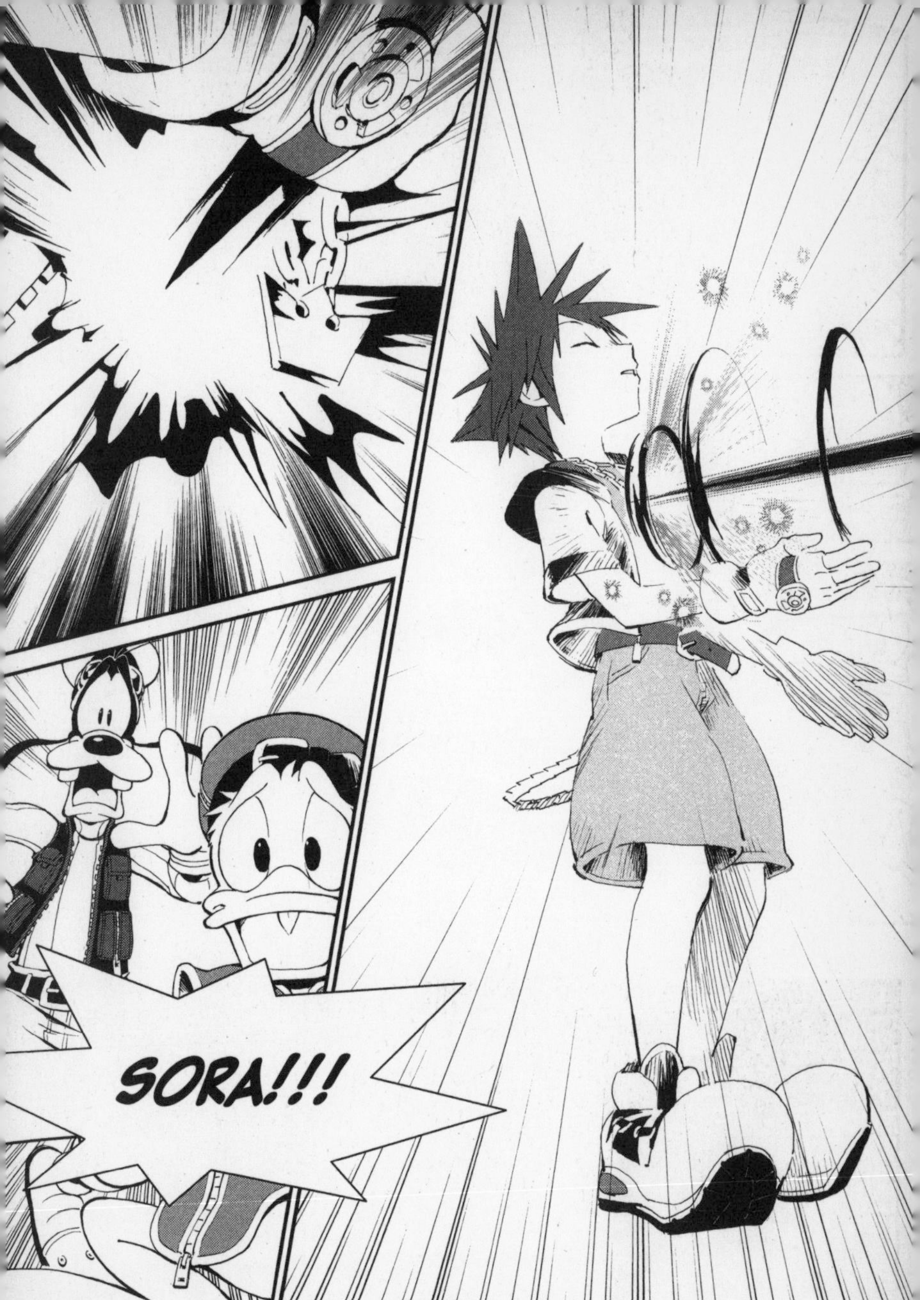
SORA!!!

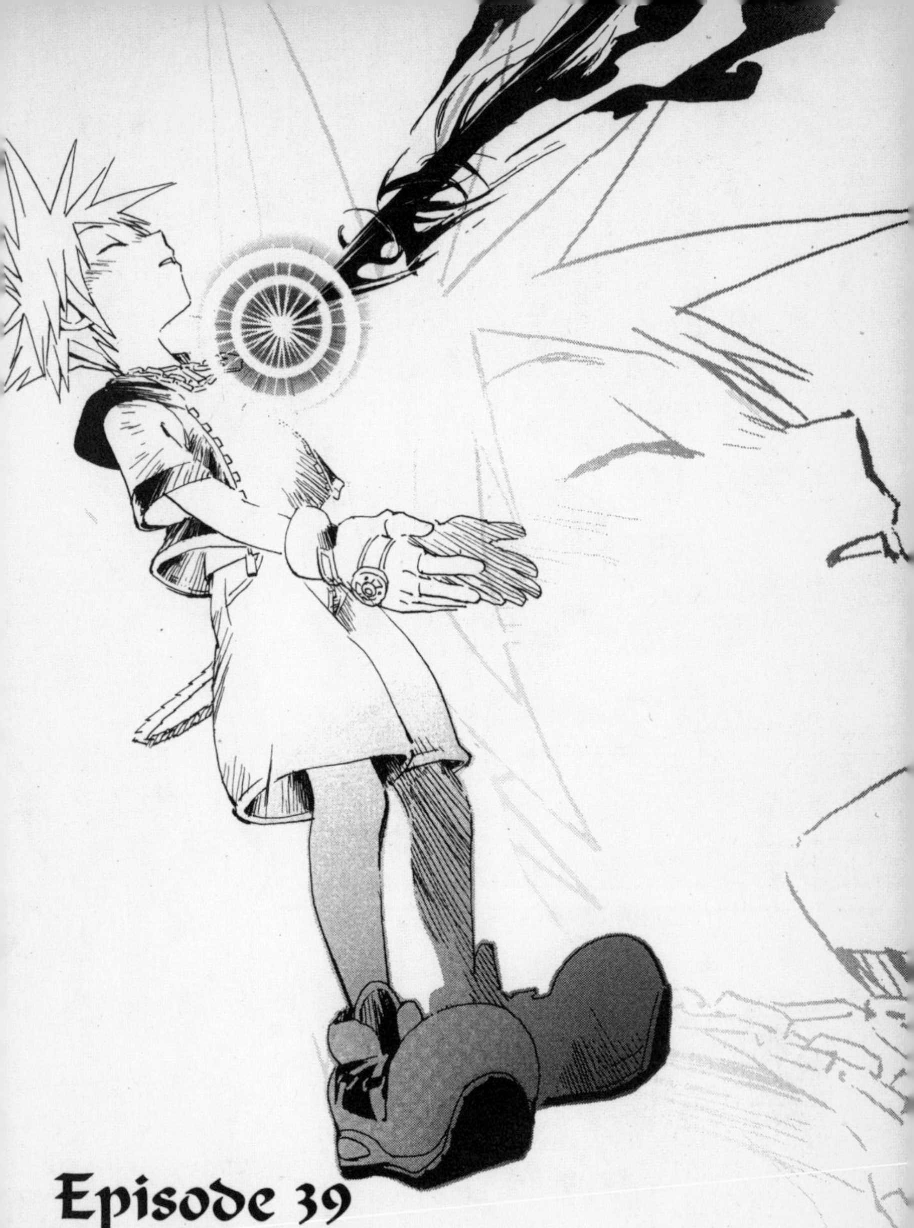

Episode 39

Man of Darkness

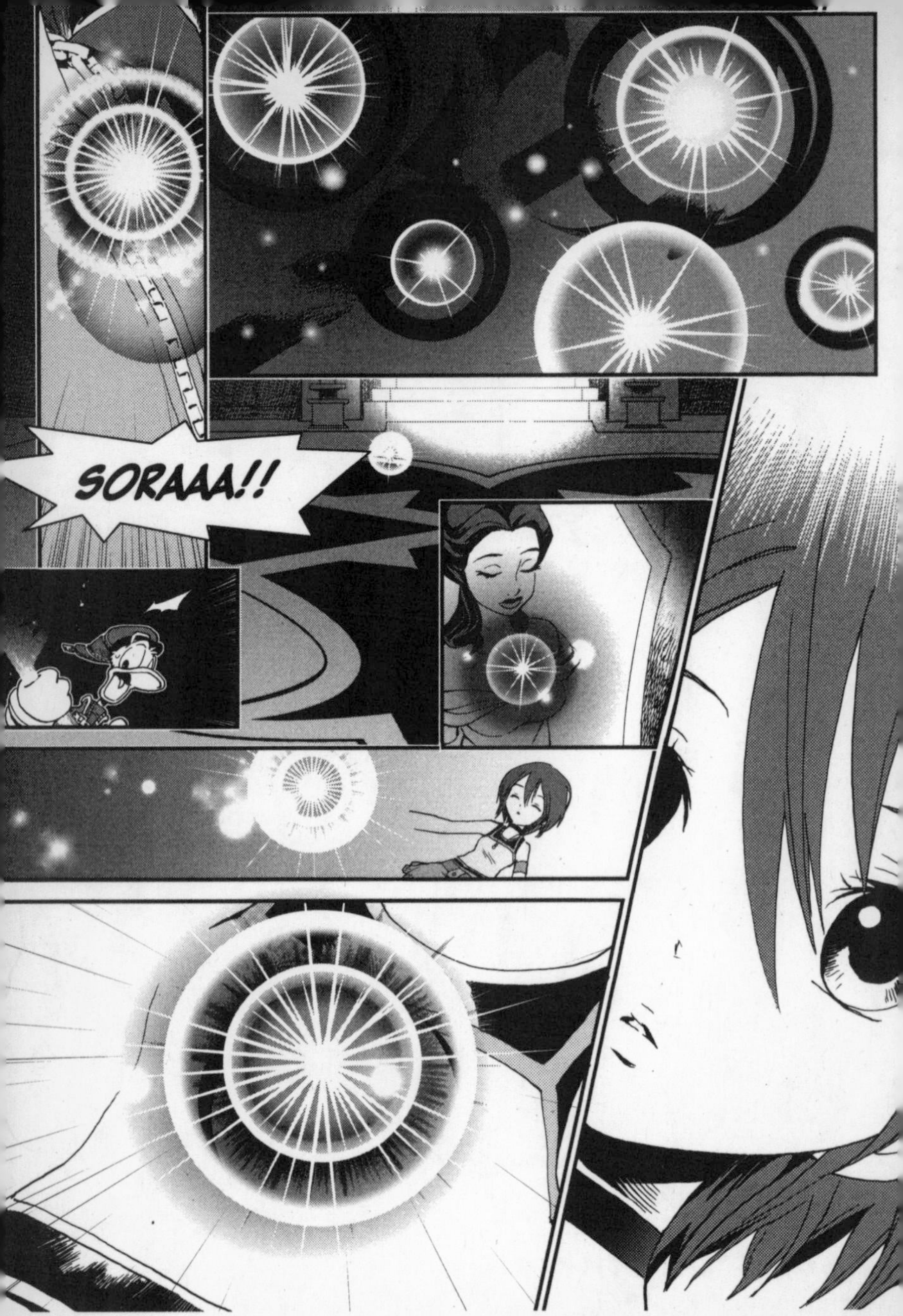
SORAAA!!

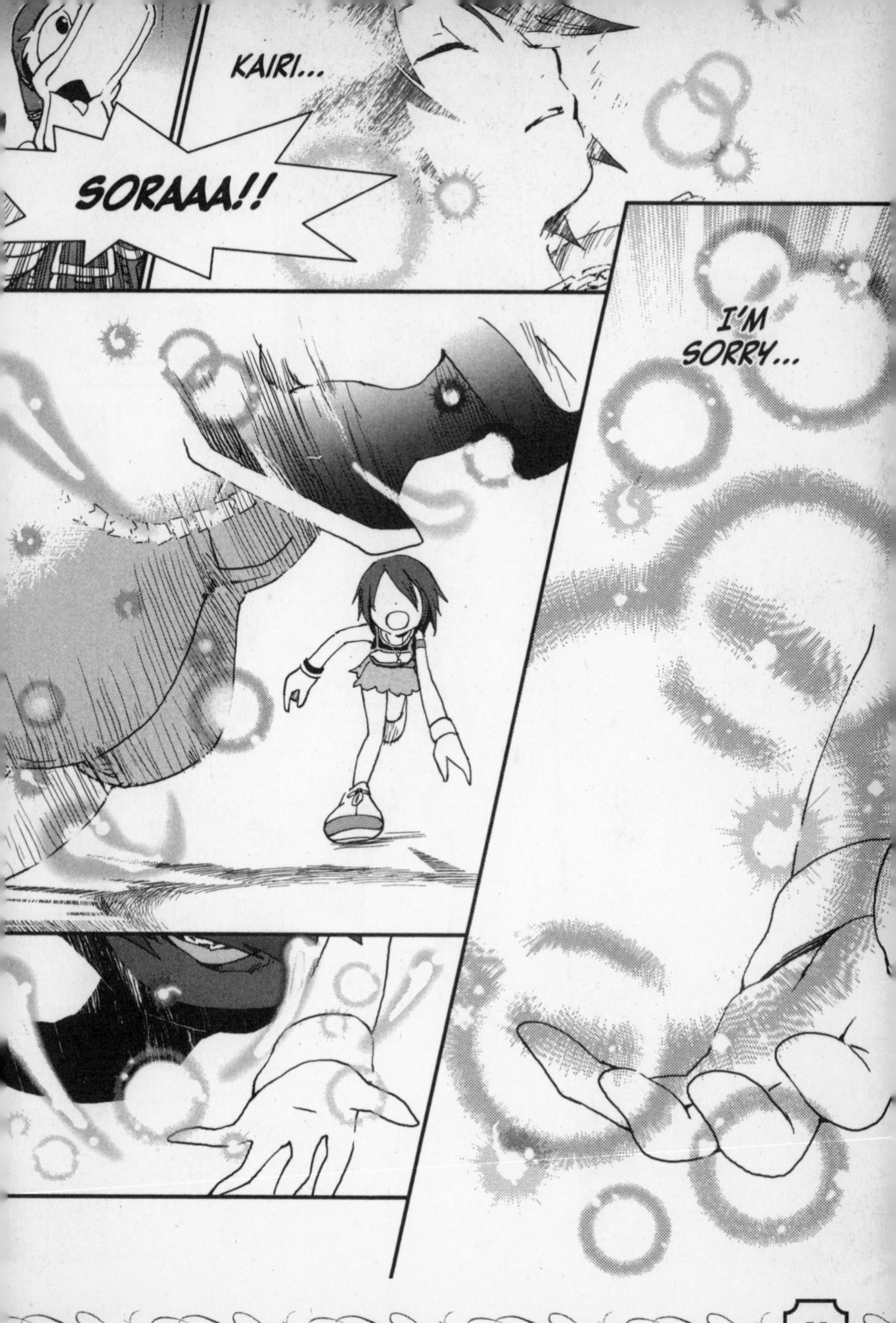
KAIRI...
SORAAA!!
I'M SORRY...

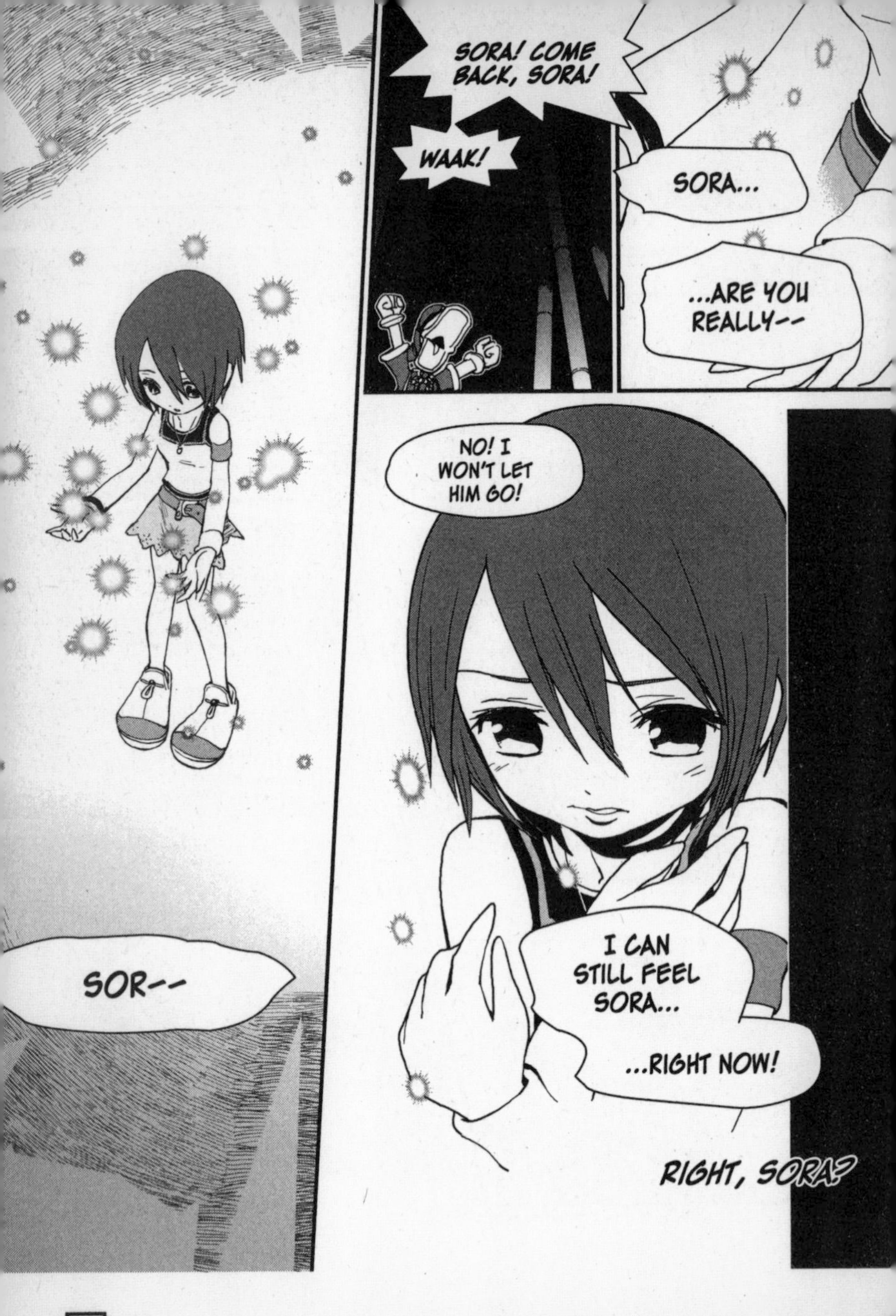
SOR--
SORA! COME BACK, SORA!
WAAK!
SORA...
...ARE YOU REALLY--
NO! I WON'T LET HIM GO!
I CAN STILL FEEL SORA...
...RIGHT NOW!
RIGHT, SORA?

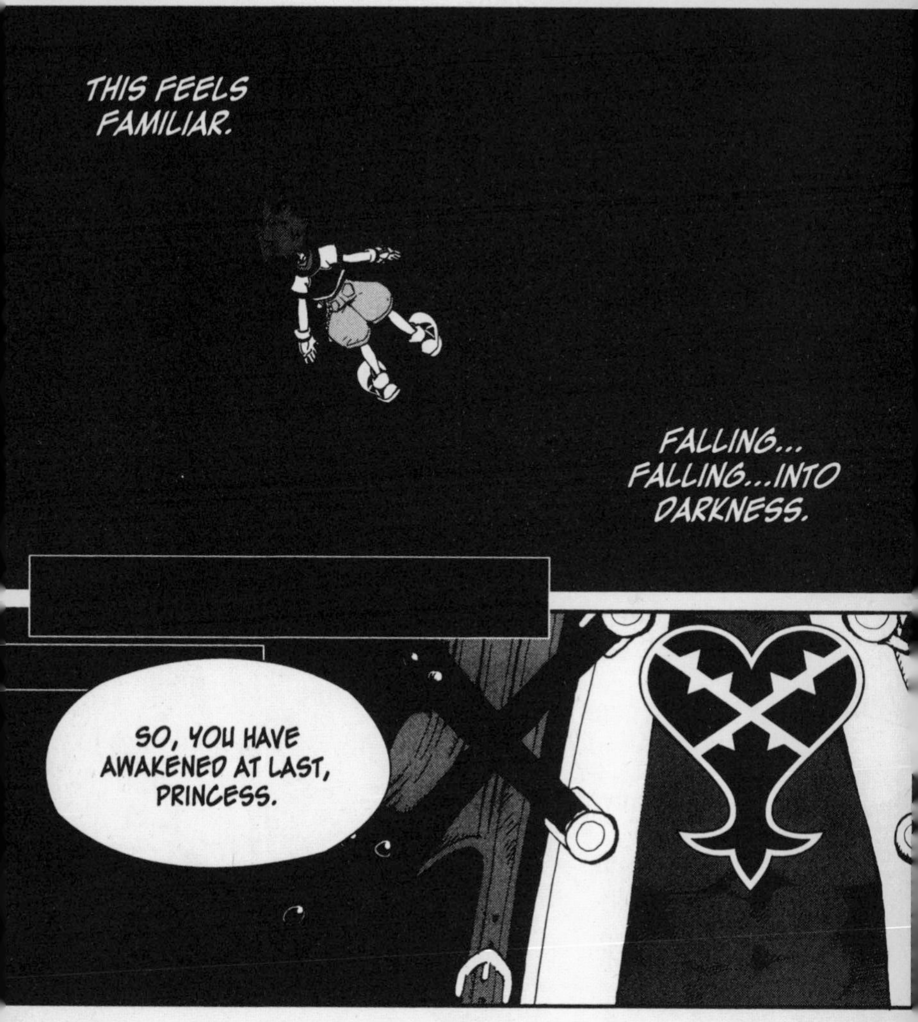
THIS FEELS FAMILIAR.
FALLING... FALLING...INTO DARKNESS.
SO, YOU HAVE AWAKENED AT LAST, PRINCESS.

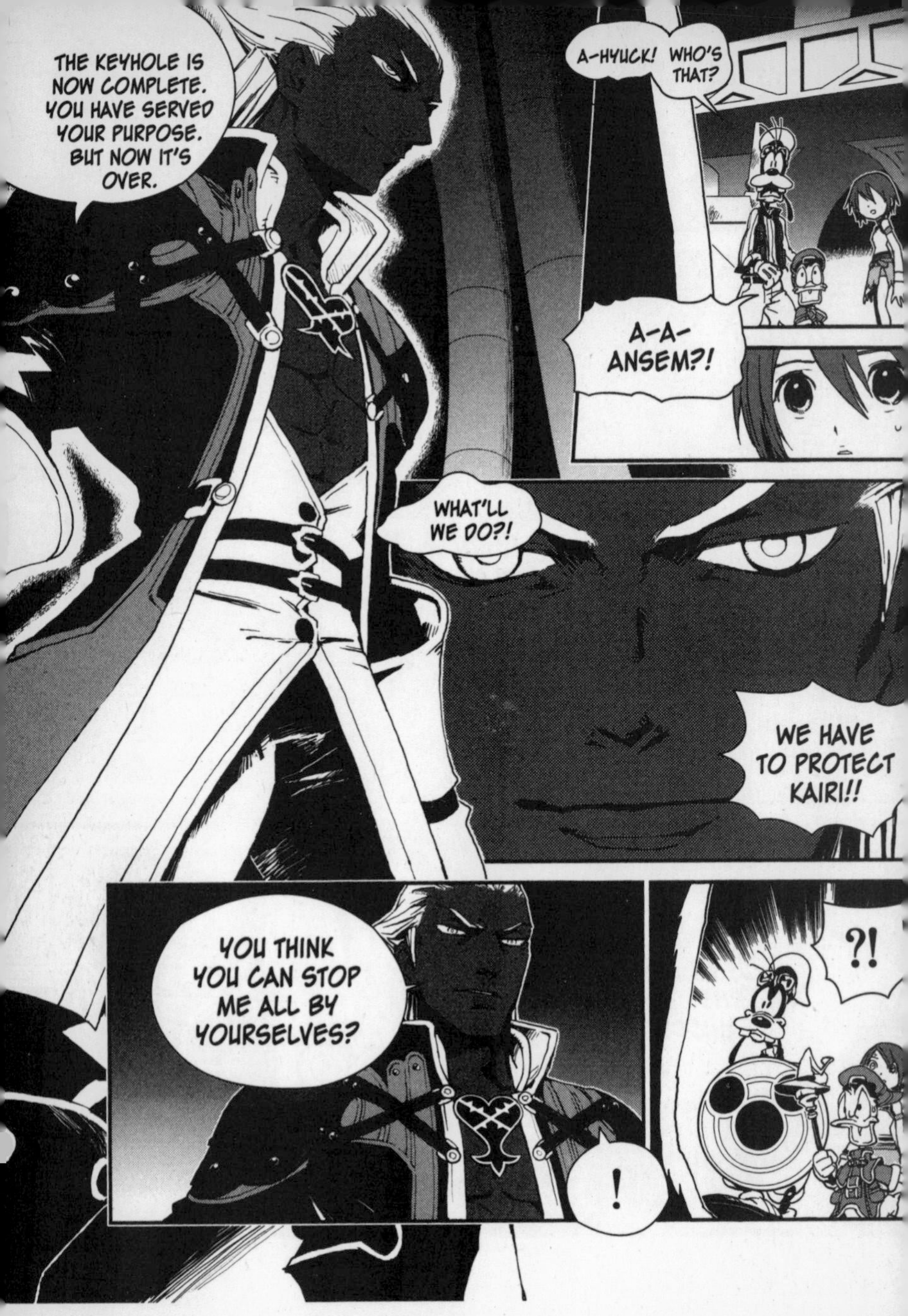
THE KEYHOLE IS NOW COMPLETE. YOU HAVE SERVED YOUR PURPOSE. BUT NOW IT'S OVER.
A-HYUCK!
WHO'S THAT?
A-A-ANSEM?!
WHAT'LL WE DO?!
WE HAVE TO PROTECT KAIRI!!
YOU THINK YOU CAN STOP ME ALL BY YOURSELVES?
!
?!

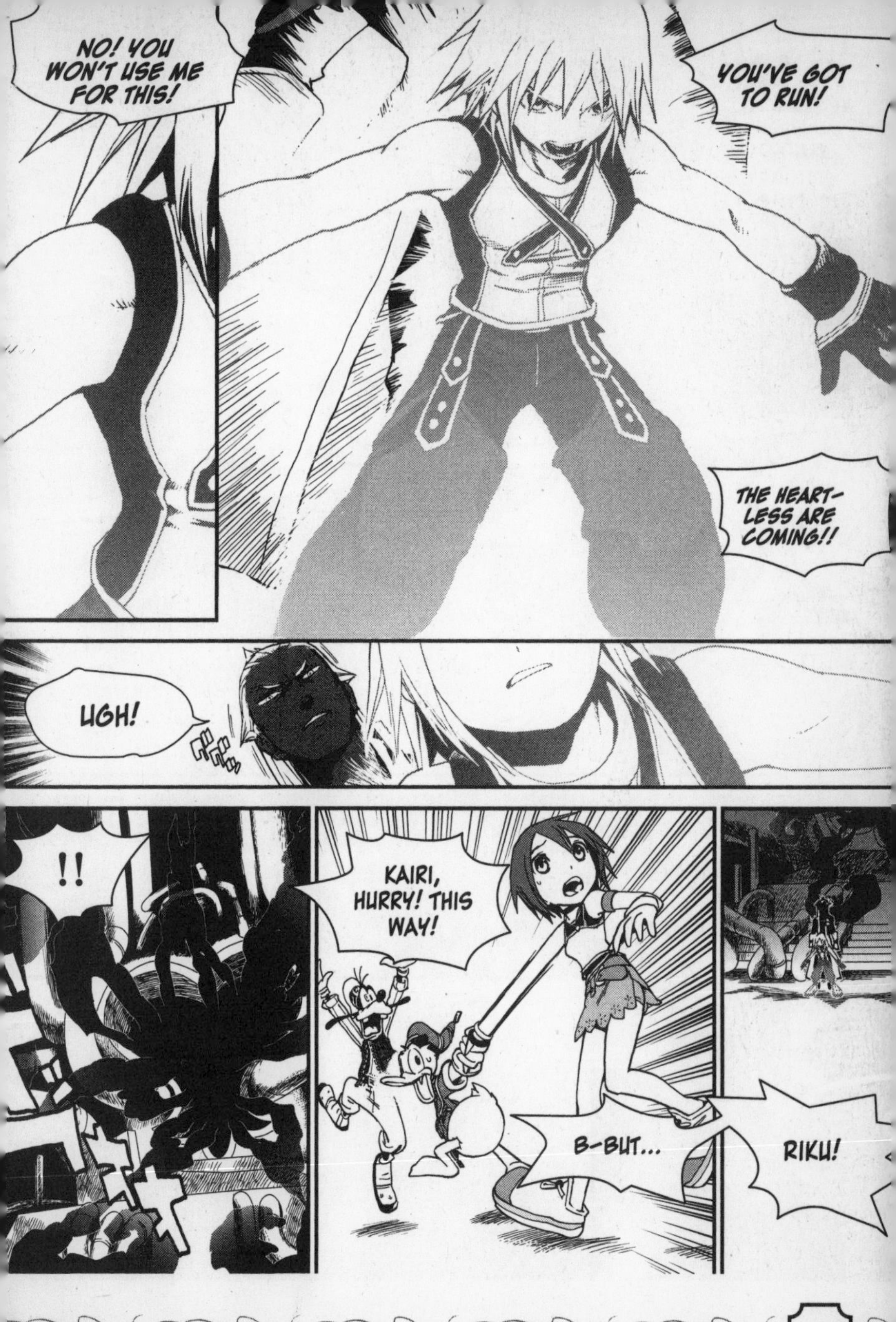
NO! YOU WON'T USE ME FOR THIS!
YOU'VE GOT TO RUN!
THE HEART-LESS ARE COMING!!
UGH!
!!
KAIRI, HURRY! THIS WAY!
B-BUT...
RIKU!

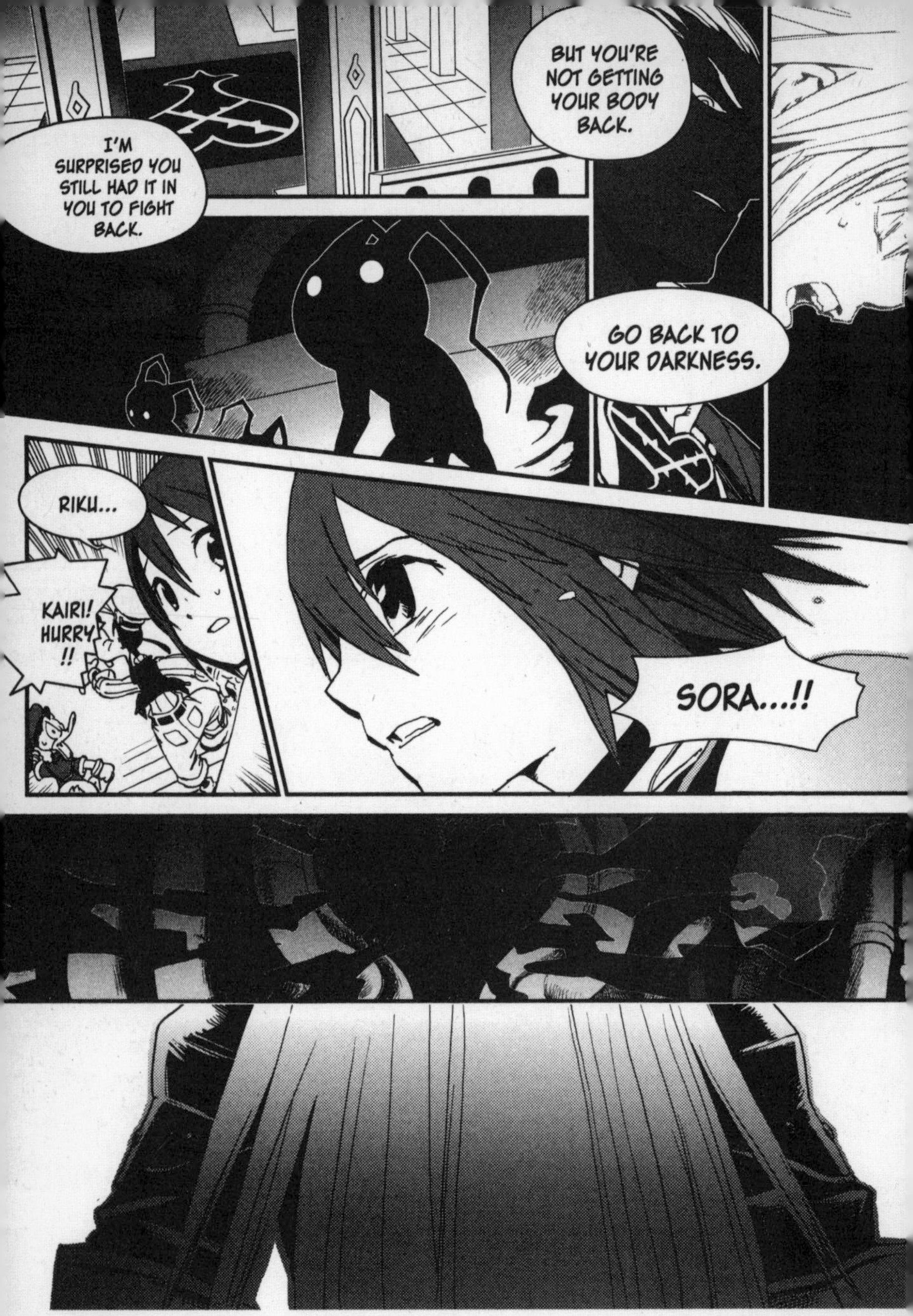
I'M SURPRISED YOU STILL HAD IT IN YOU TO FIGHT BACK.
BUT YOU'RE NOT GETTING YOUR BODY BACK.
GO BACK TO YOUR DARKNESS.
RIKU...
KAIRI! HURRY !!
SORA...!!

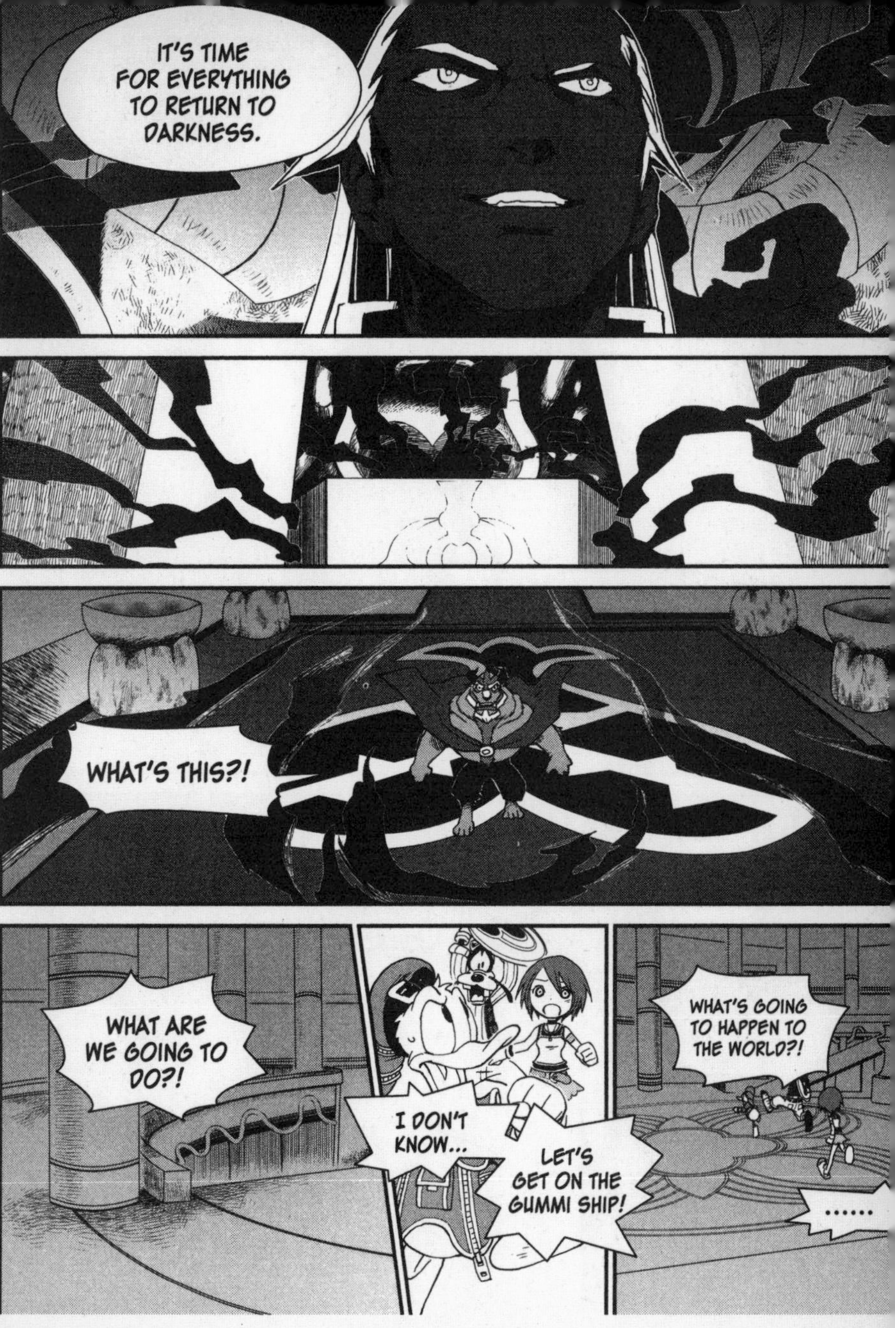
IT'S TIME FOR EVERYTHING TO RETURN TO DARKNESS.
WHAT'S THIS?!
WHAT ARE WE GOING TO DO?!
I DON'T KNOW...
LET'S GET ON THE GUMMI SHIP!
WHAT'S GOING TO HAPPEN TO THE WORLD?!
......

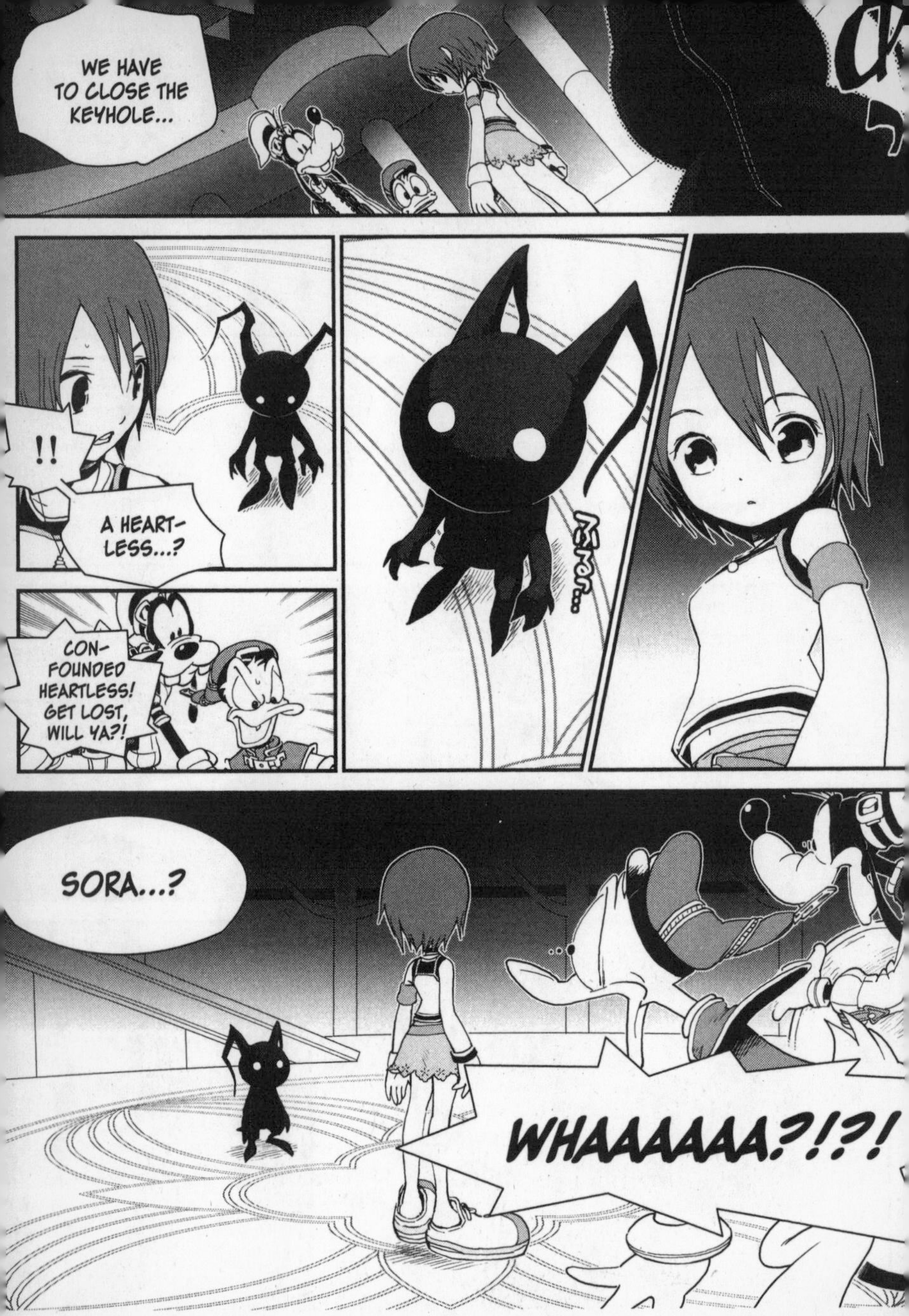
WE HAVE TO CLOSE THE KEYHOLE...
!!
A HEART-LESS...?
CON-FOUNDED HEARTLESS! GET LOST, WILL YA?!
SORA...?
WHAAAAAAA?!?!

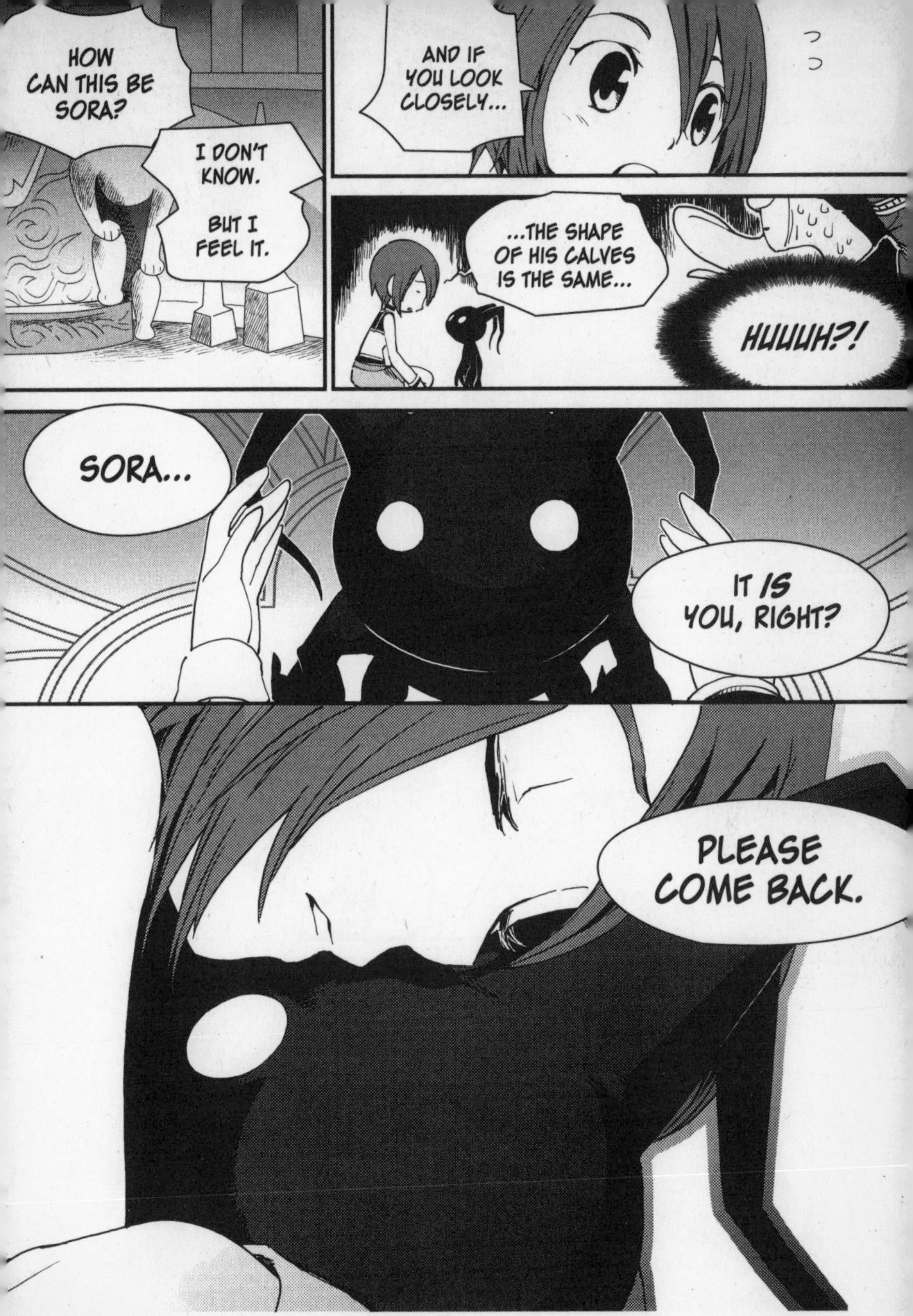
HOW CAN THIS BE SORA?
I DON'T KNOW.
BUT I FEEL IT.
AND IF YOU LOOK CLOSELY...
...THE SHAPE OF HIS CALVES IS THE SAME...
HUUUH?!
SORA...
IT IS YOU, RIGHT?
PLEASE COME BACK.

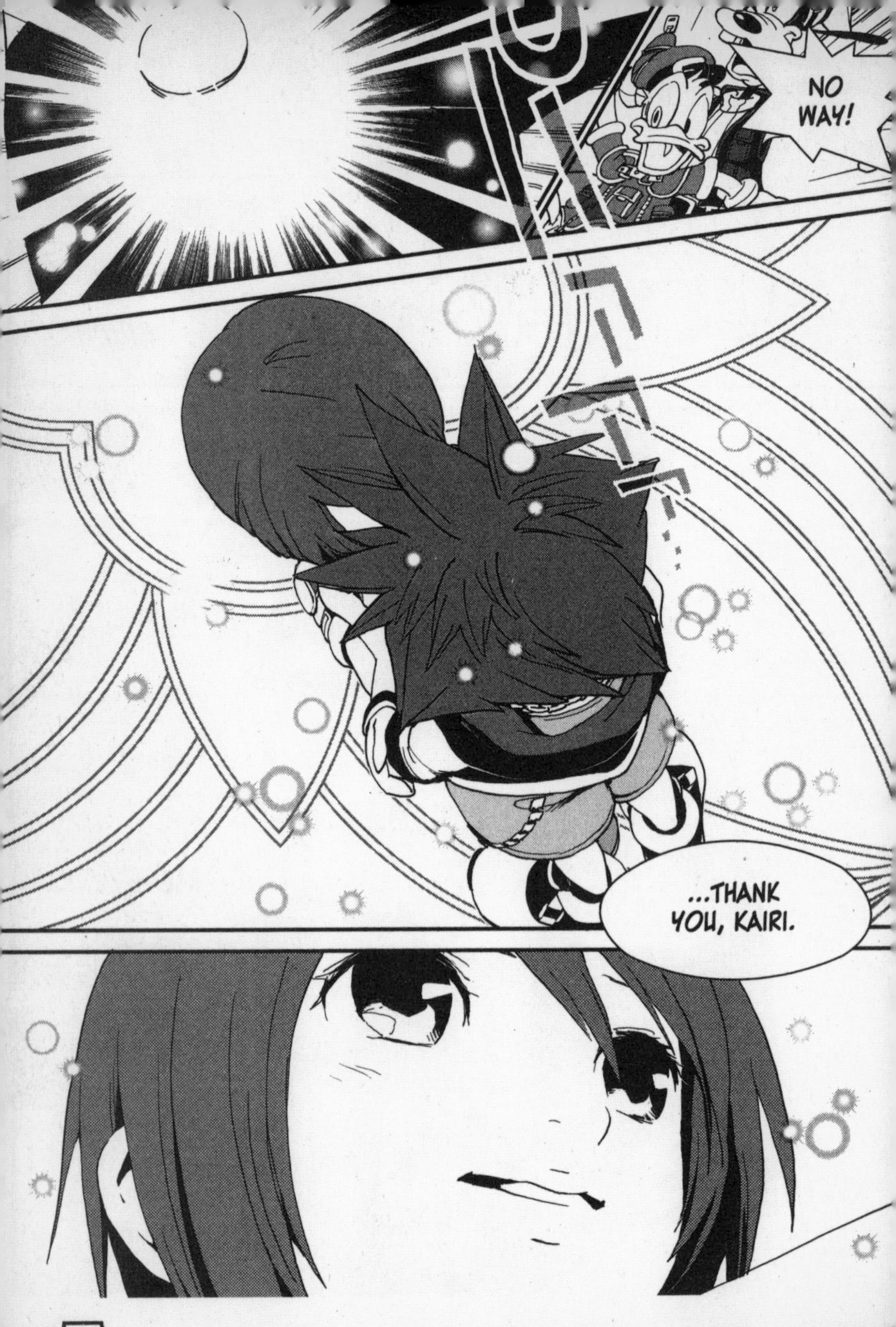
NO WAY!
...THANK YOU, KAIRI.

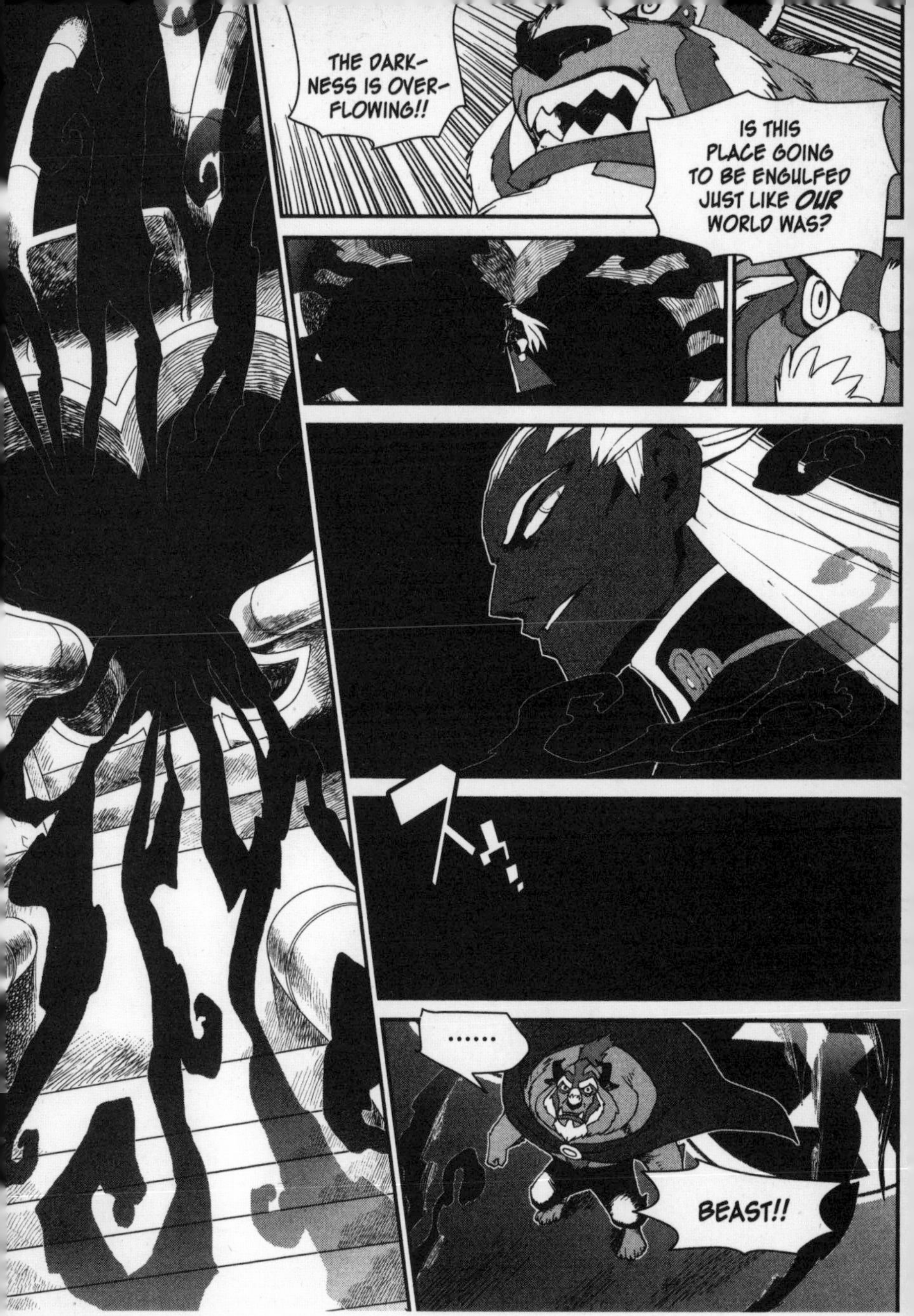
THE DARK-NESS IS OVER-FLOWING!!
IS THIS PLACE GOING TO BE ENGULFED JUST LIKE *OUR* WORLD WAS?
......
BEAST!!

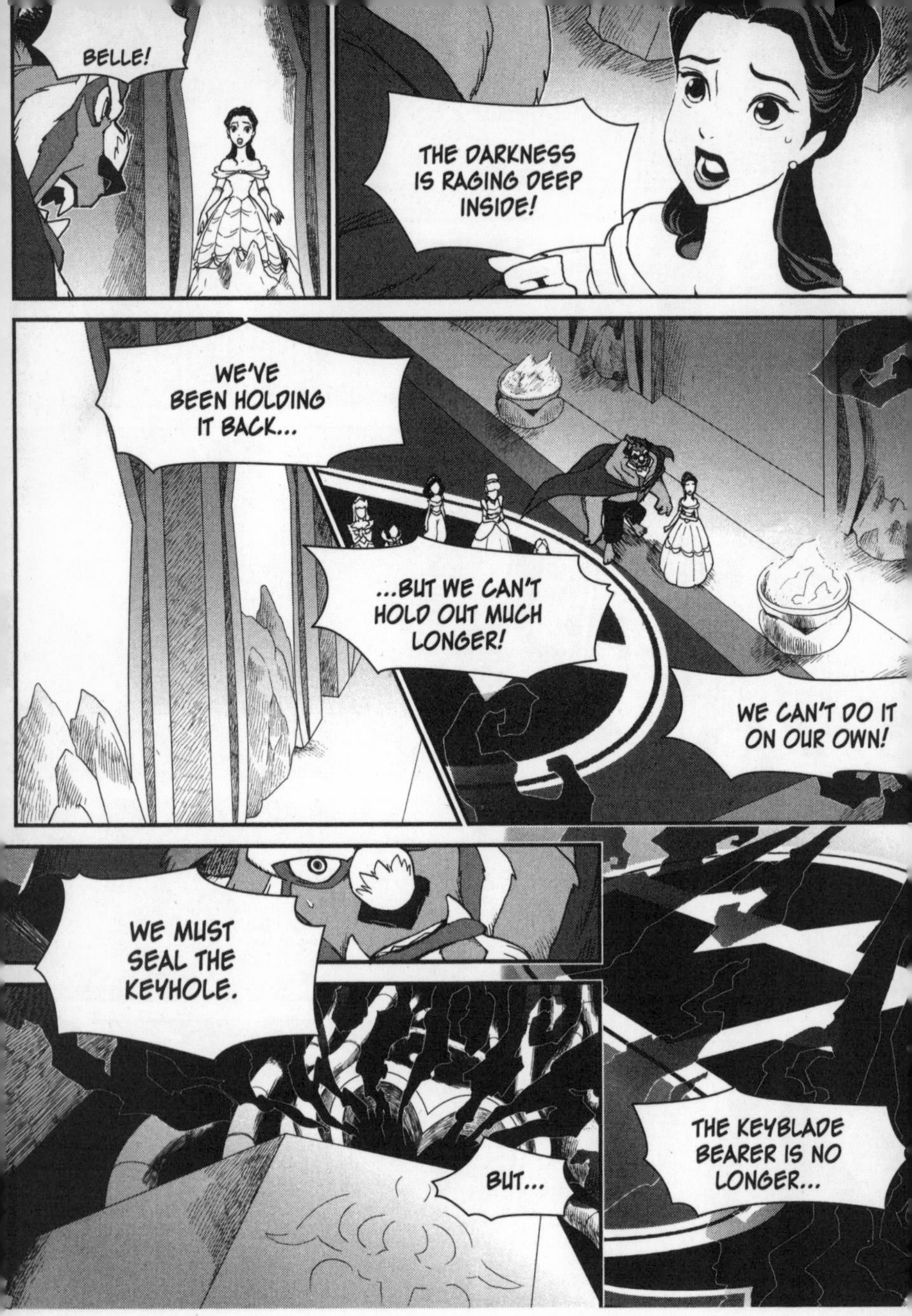
BELLE!
THE DARKNESS IS RAGING DEEP INSIDE!
WE'VE BEEN HOLDING IT BACK...
...BUT WE CAN'T HOLD OUT MUCH LONGER!
WE CAN'T DO IT ON OUR OWN!
WE MUST SEAL THE KEYHOLE.
BUT...
THE KEYBLADE BEARER IS NO LONGER...

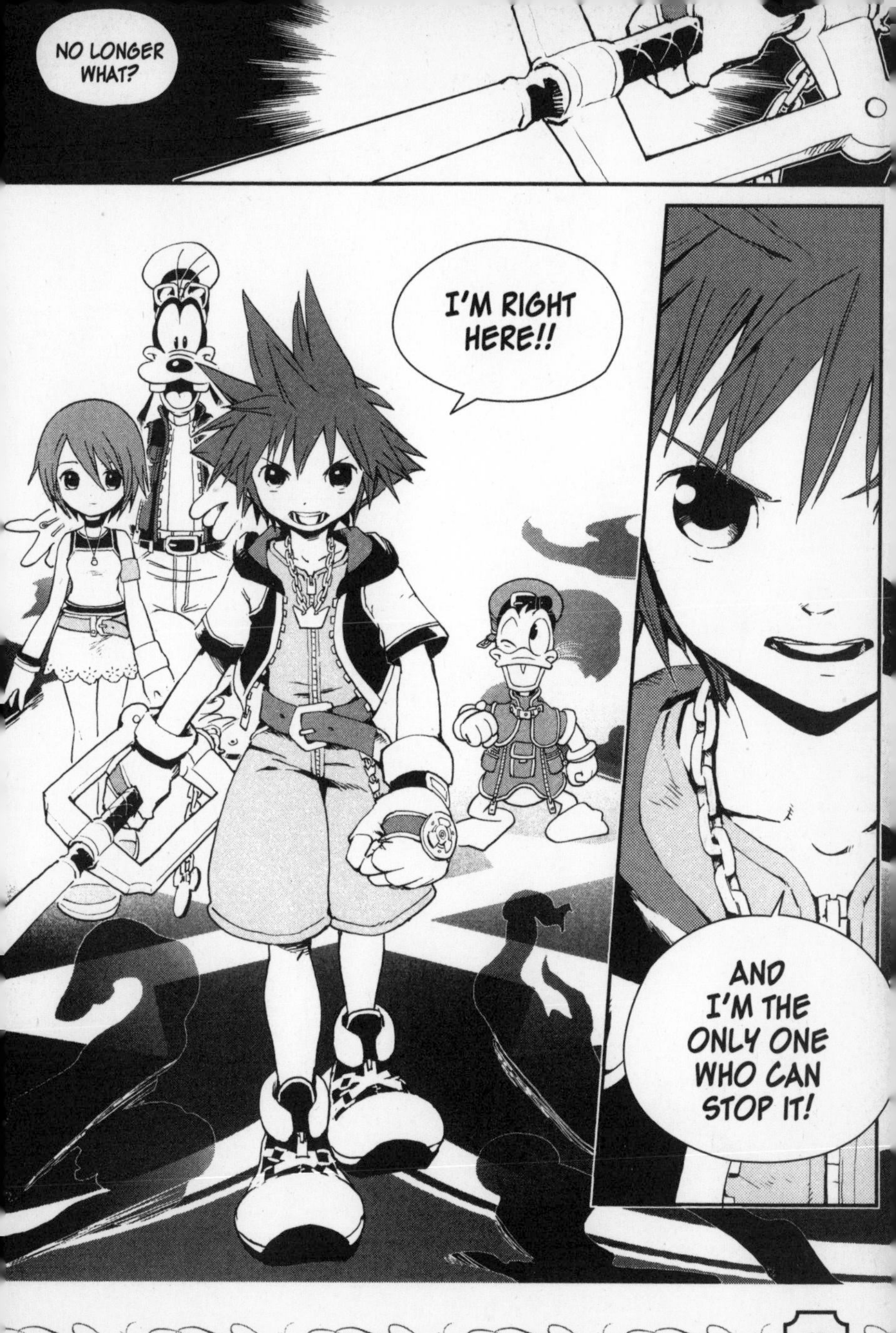
NO LONGER WHAT?
I'M RIGHT HERE!!
AND I'M THE ONLY ONE WHO CAN STOP IT!

Episode 40

I Won't Say Goodbye

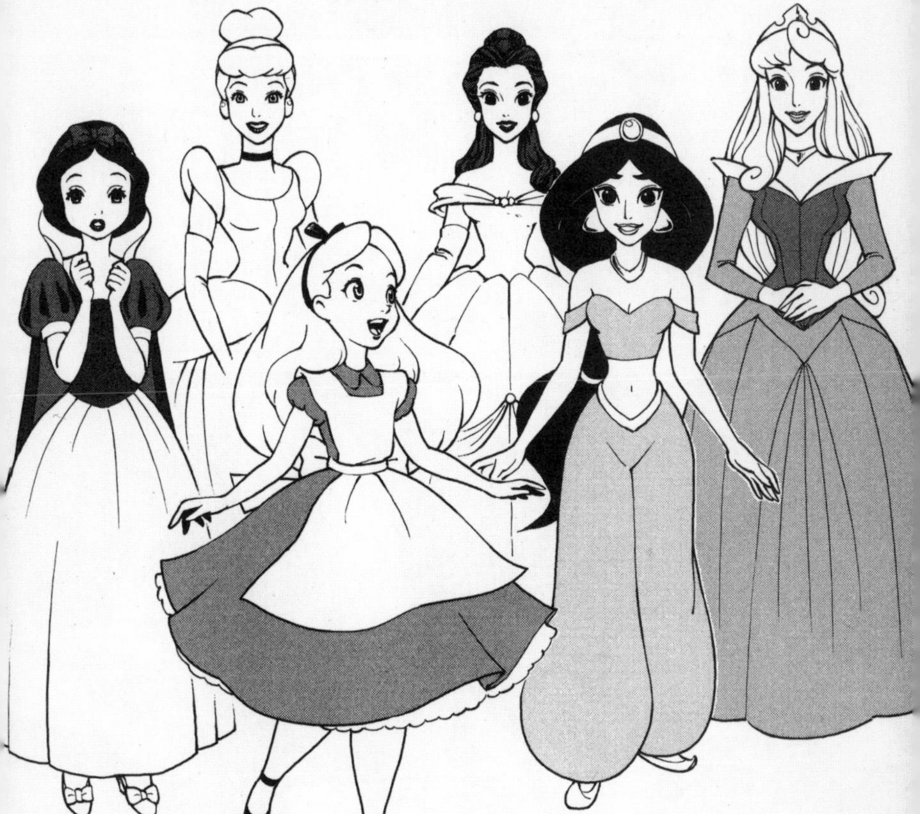

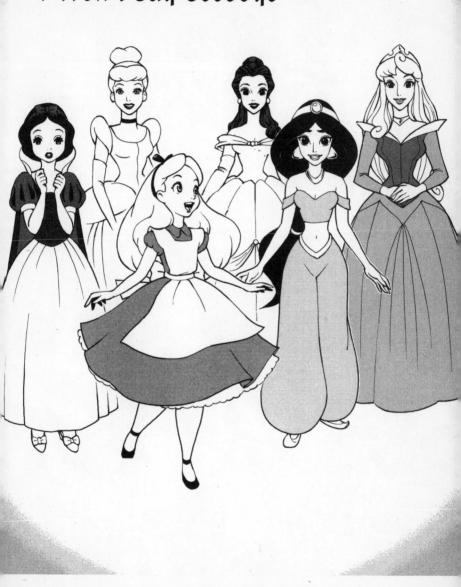

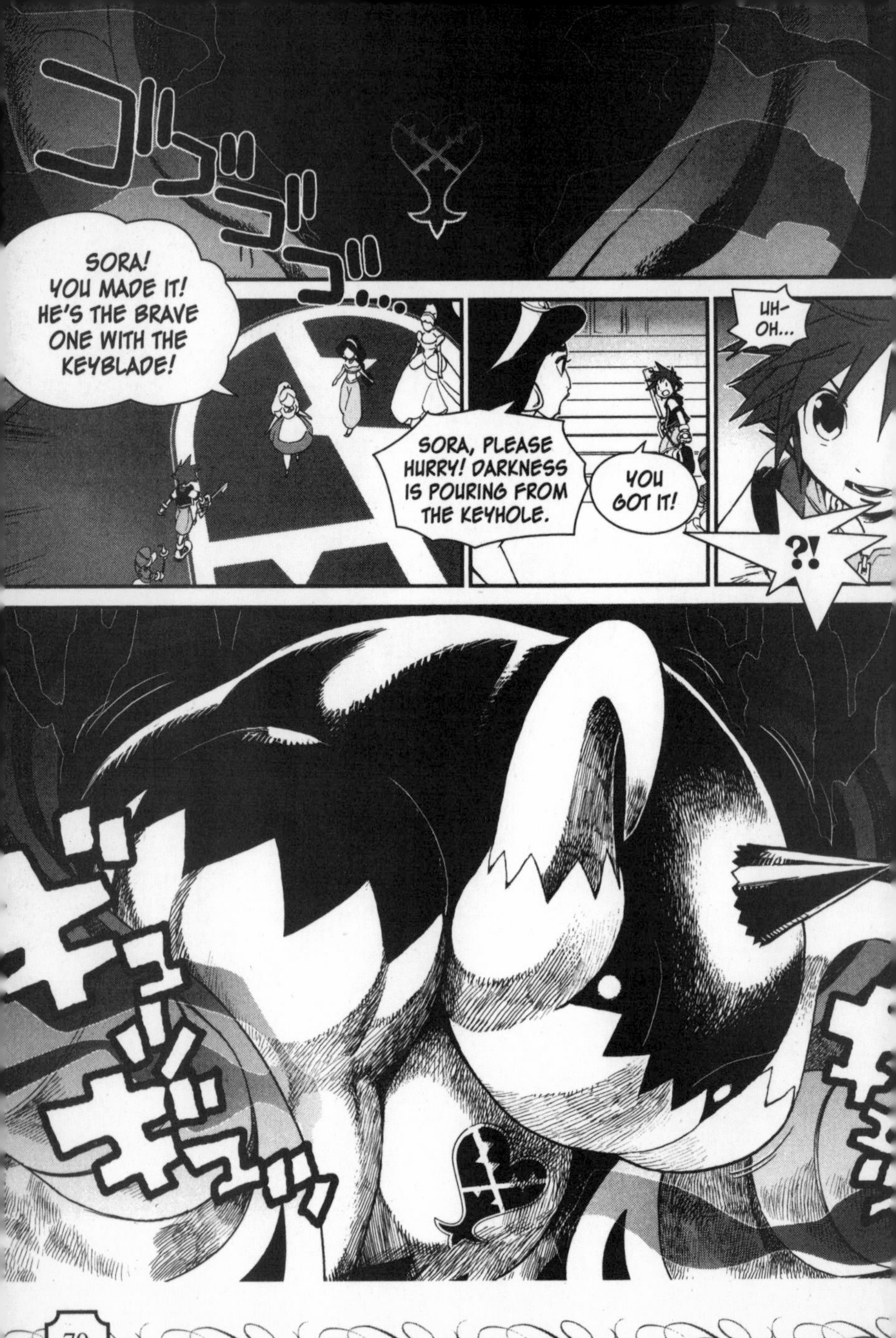
SORA! YOU MADE IT! HE'S THE BRAVE ONE WITH THE KEYBLADE!
SORA, PLEASE HURRY! DARKNESS IS POURING FROM THE KEYHOLE.
YOU GOT IT!
UH-OH...
?!

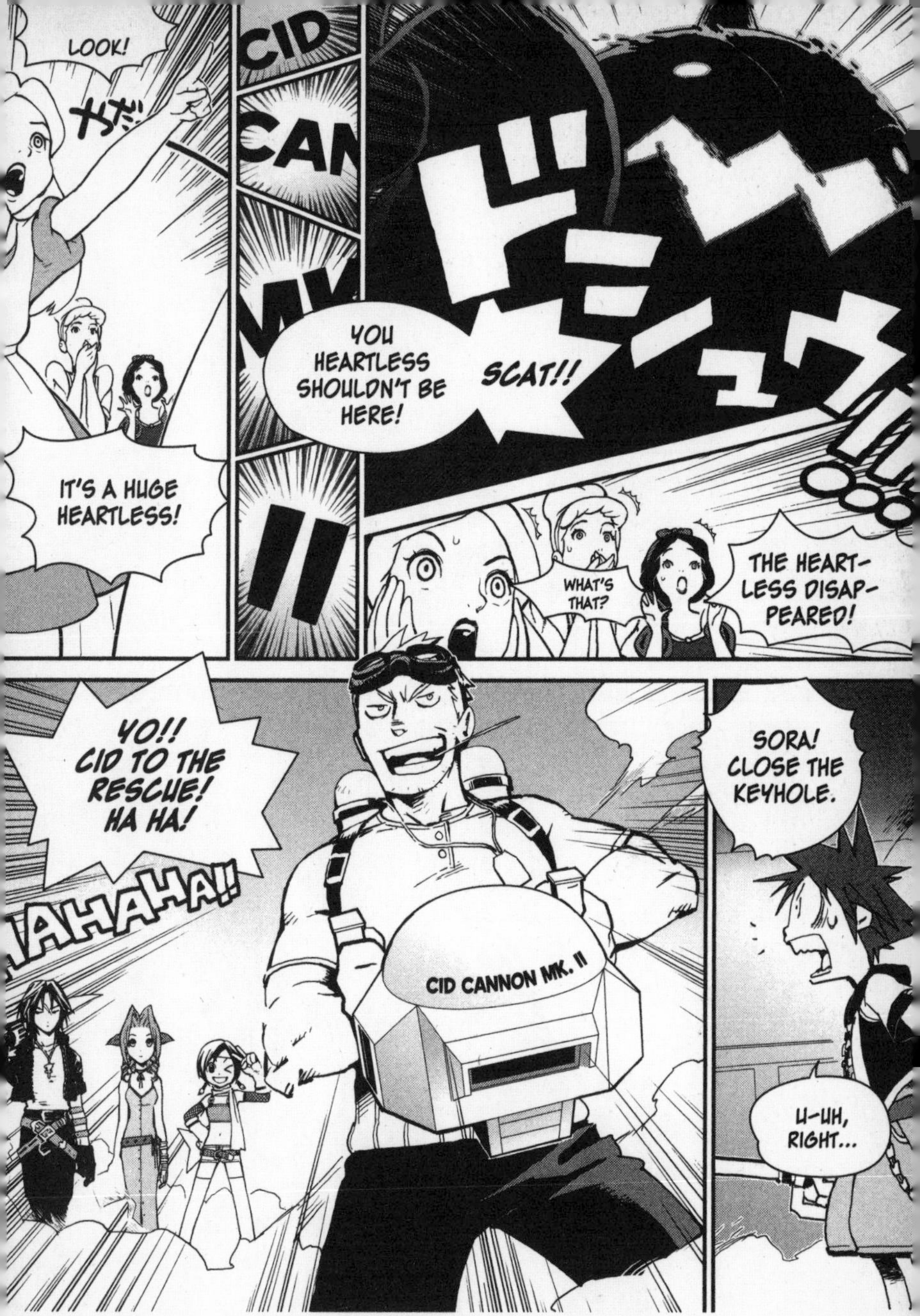
LOOK!
IT'S A HUGE HEARTLESS!
CID
CAN
MK
II
YOU HEARTLESS SHOULDN'T BE HERE!
SCAT!!
WHAT'S THAT?
THE HEART-LESS DISAP-PEARED!
YO!! CID TO THE RESCUE! HA HA!
AHAHAHA!!
CID CANNON MK. II
SORA! CLOSE THE KEYHOLE.
U-UH, RIGHT...

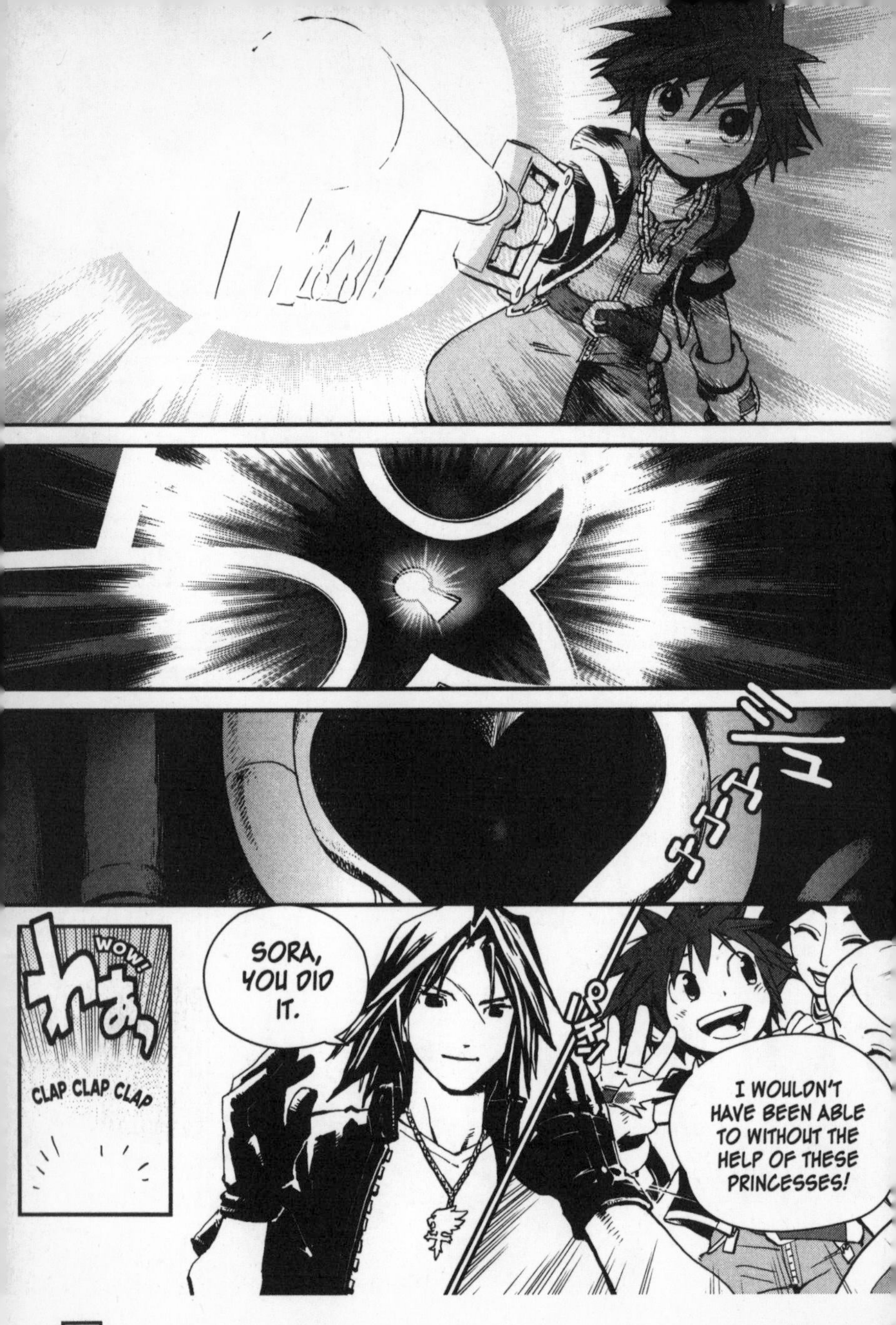
FLASH!
わぁっ
WOW!
CLAP CLAP CLAP
SORA, YOU DID IT.
I WOULDN'T HAVE BEEN ABLE TO WITHOUT THE HELP OF THESE PRINCESSES!

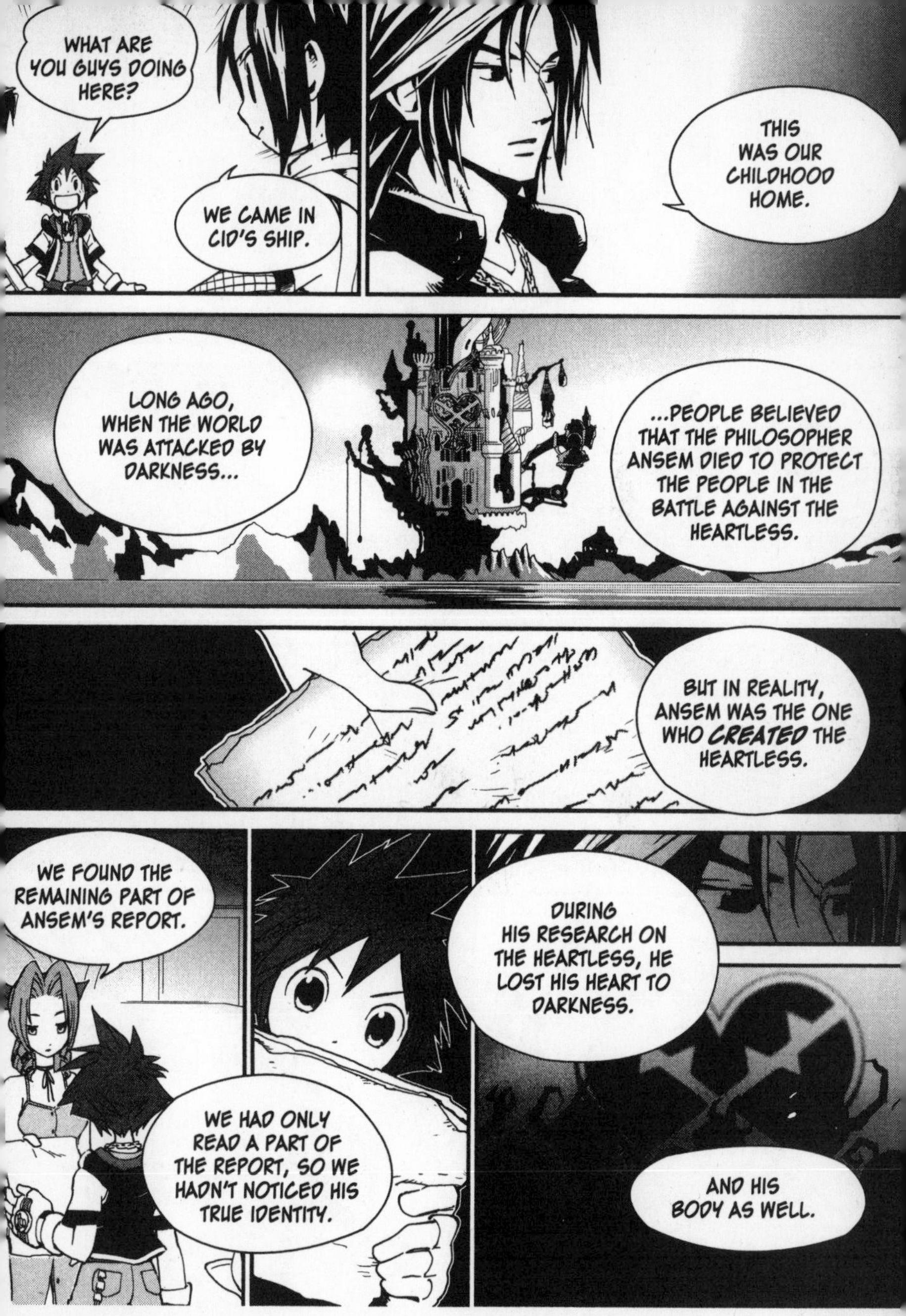
WHAT ARE YOU GUYS DOING HERE?
WE CAME IN CID'S SHIP.
THIS WAS OUR CHILDHOOD HOME.
LONG AGO, WHEN THE WORLD WAS ATTACKED BY DARKNESS...
...PEOPLE BELIEVED THAT THE PHILOSOPHER ANSEM DIED TO PROTECT THE PEOPLE IN THE BATTLE AGAINST THE HEARTLESS.
BUT IN REALITY, ANSEM WAS THE ONE WHO CREATED THE HEARTLESS.
WE FOUND THE REMAINING PART OF ANSEM'S REPORT.
WE HAD ONLY READ A PART OF THE REPORT, SO WE HADN'T NOTICED HIS TRUE IDENTITY.
DURING HIS RESEARCH ON THE HEARTLESS, HE LOST HIS HEART TO DARKNESS.
AND HIS BODY AS WELL.

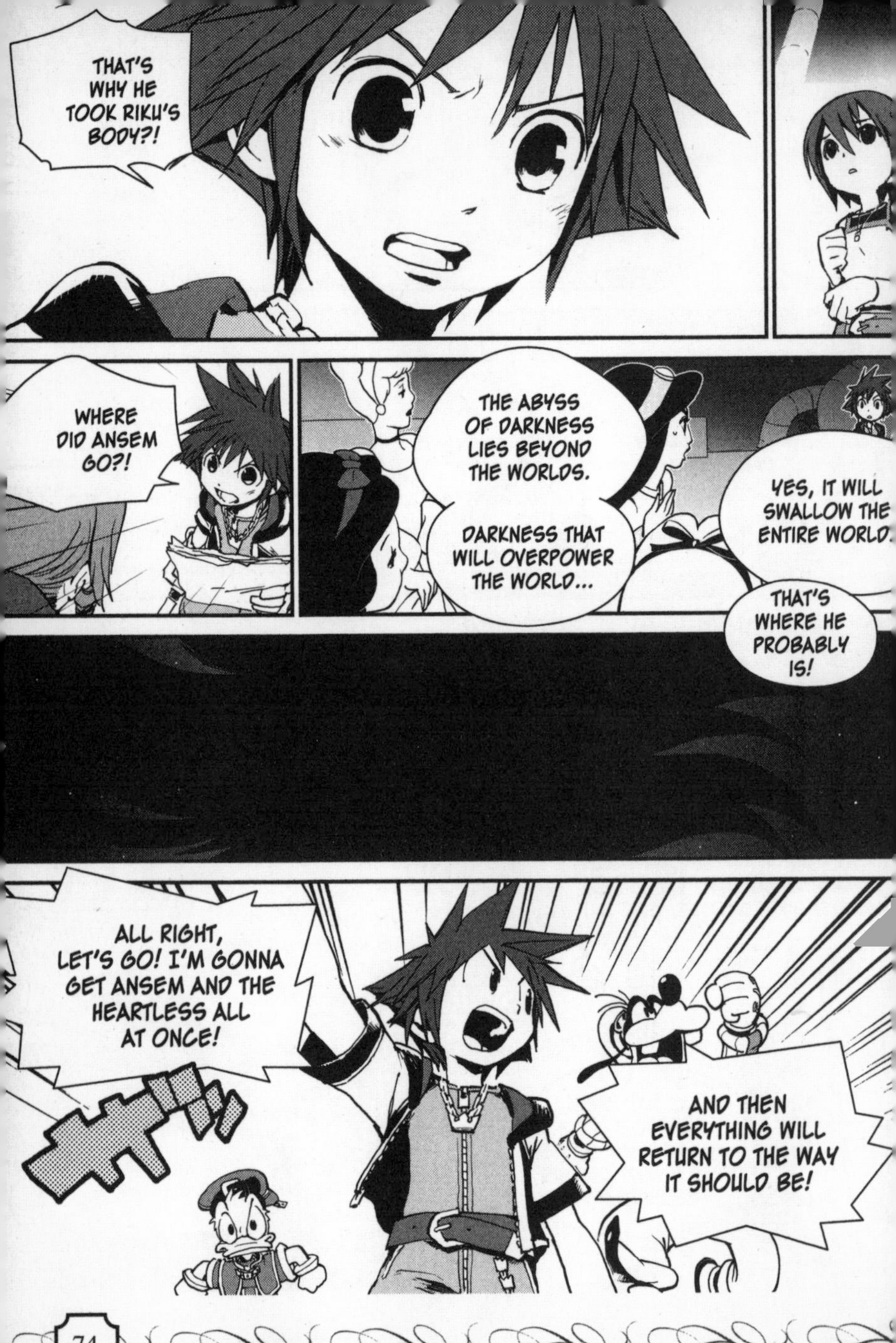
THAT'S WHY HE TOOK RIKU'S BODY?!
WHERE DID ANSEM GO?!
THE ABYSS OF DARKNESS LIES BEYOND THE WORLDS.
DARKNESS THAT WILL OVERPOWER THE WORLD...
YES, IT WILL SWALLOW THE ENTIRE WORLD.
THAT'S WHERE HE PROBABLY IS!
ALL RIGHT, LET'S GO! I'M GONNA GET ANSEM AND THE HEARTLESS ALL AT ONCE!
AND THEN EVERYTHING WILL RETURN TO THE WAY IT SHOULD BE!

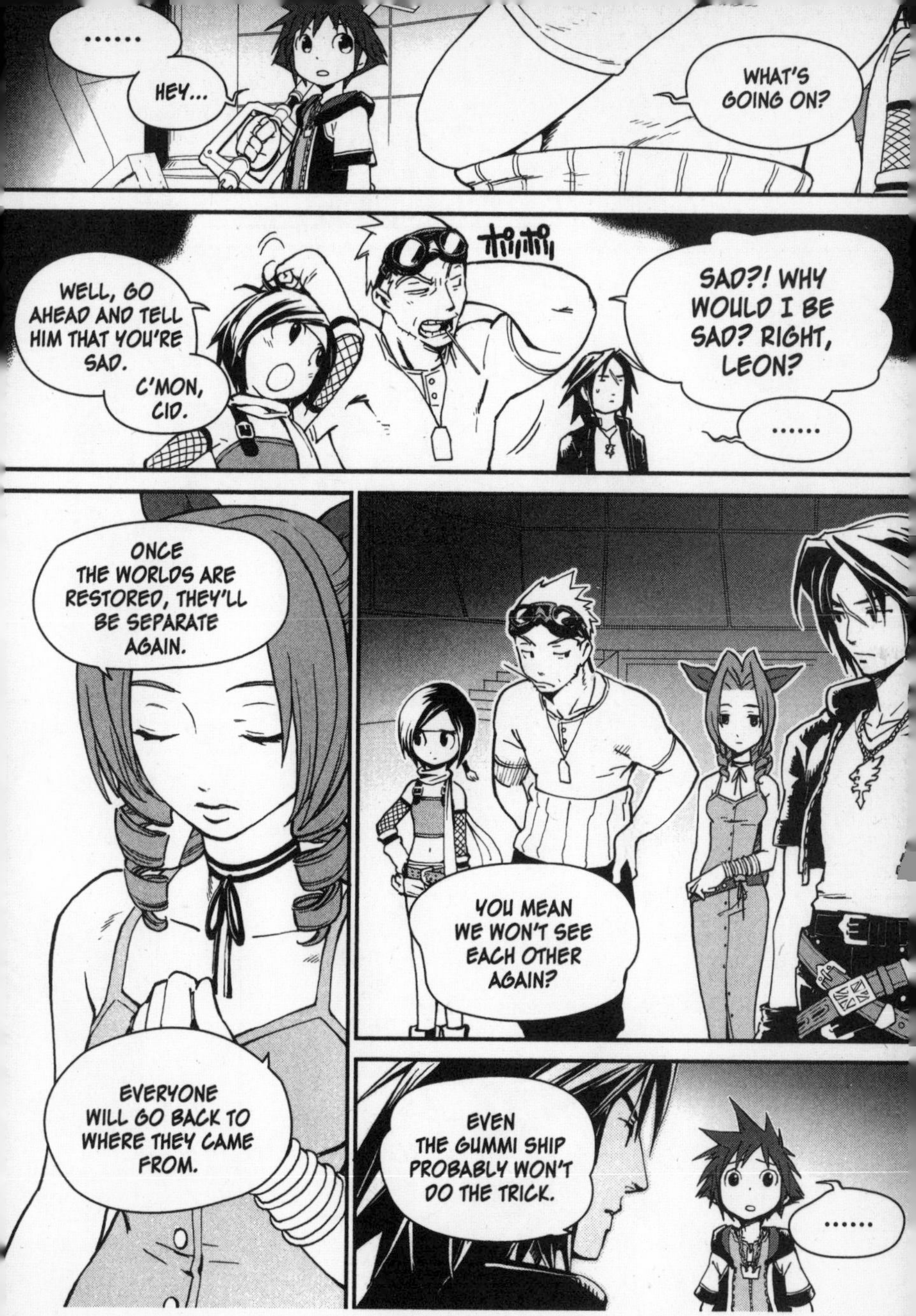
......
HEY...
WHAT'S GOING ON?
WELL, GO AHEAD AND TELL HIM THAT YOU'RE SAD.
C'MON, CID.
SAD?! WHY WOULD I BE SAD? RIGHT, LEON?
......
ONCE THE WORLDS ARE RESTORED, THEY'LL BE SEPARATE AGAIN.
EVERYONE WILL GO BACK TO WHERE THEY CAME FROM.
YOU MEAN WE WON'T SEE EACH OTHER AGAIN?
EVEN THE GUMMI SHIP PROBABLY WON'T DO THE TRICK.
......

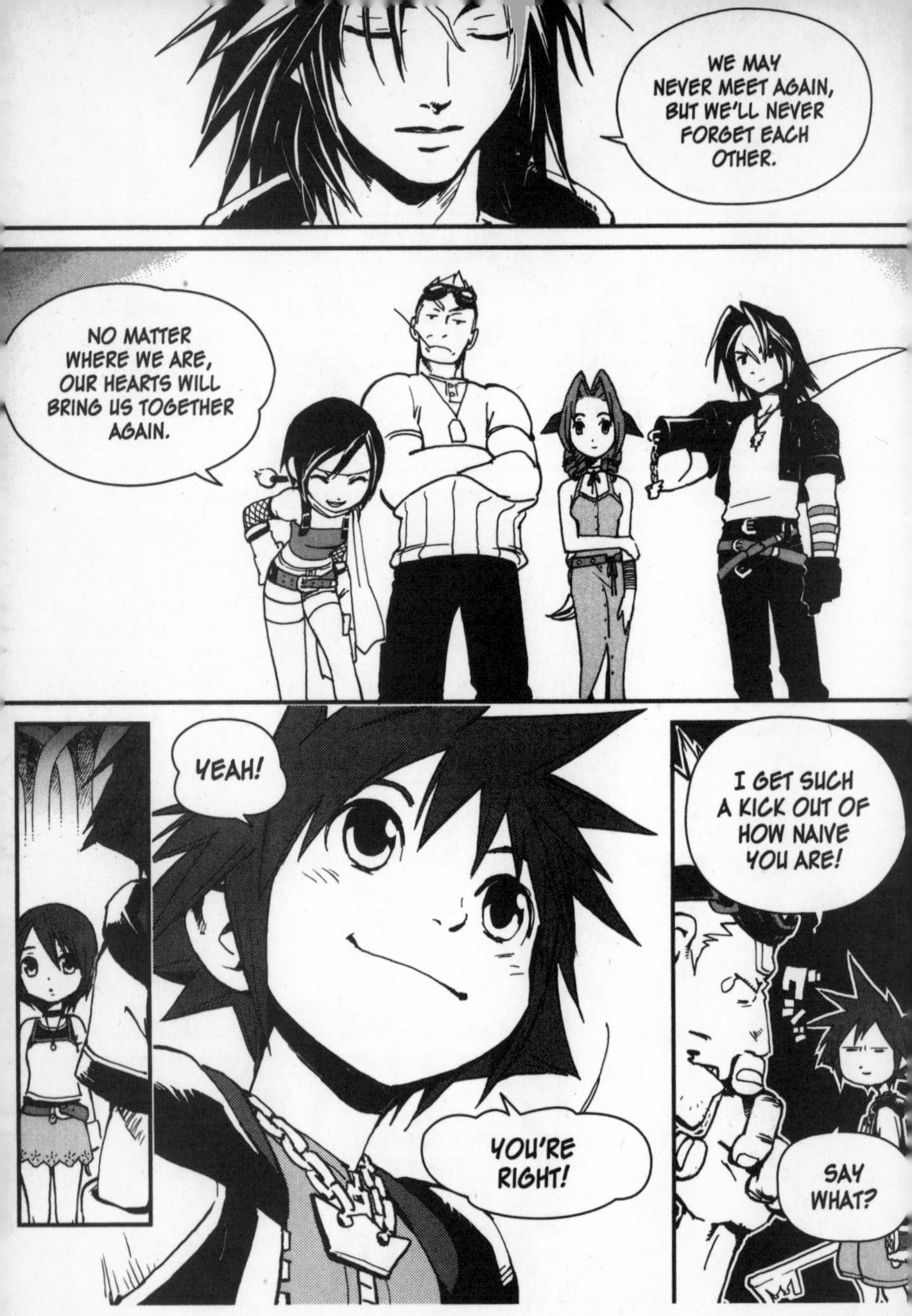
WE MAY NEVER MEET AGAIN, BUT WE'LL NEVER FORGET EACH OTHER.
NO MATTER WHERE WE ARE, OUR HEARTS WILL BRING US TOGETHER AGAIN.
YEAH!
YOU'RE RIGHT!
I GET SUCH A KICK OUT OF HOW NAIVE YOU ARE!
SAY WHAT?

OKAY, I'M GOING.

TAKE CARE, EVERYONE.

I'M NOT SAYING GOODBYE.

HEY, KAIRI-- YOU CAN'T COME!

NOOO!!!

WHY NOT?

BECAUSE IT'S WAY TOO DANGEROUS!

WE MADE IT THIS FAR BY STICKING TOGETHER! IF YOU'RE BY MY SIDE, I'LL BE SAFE.

COME ON, SORA! YOU CAN'T GO ALONE.

HEE HEE!

WIPE THOSE SILLY GRINS OFF YOUR FACES!!

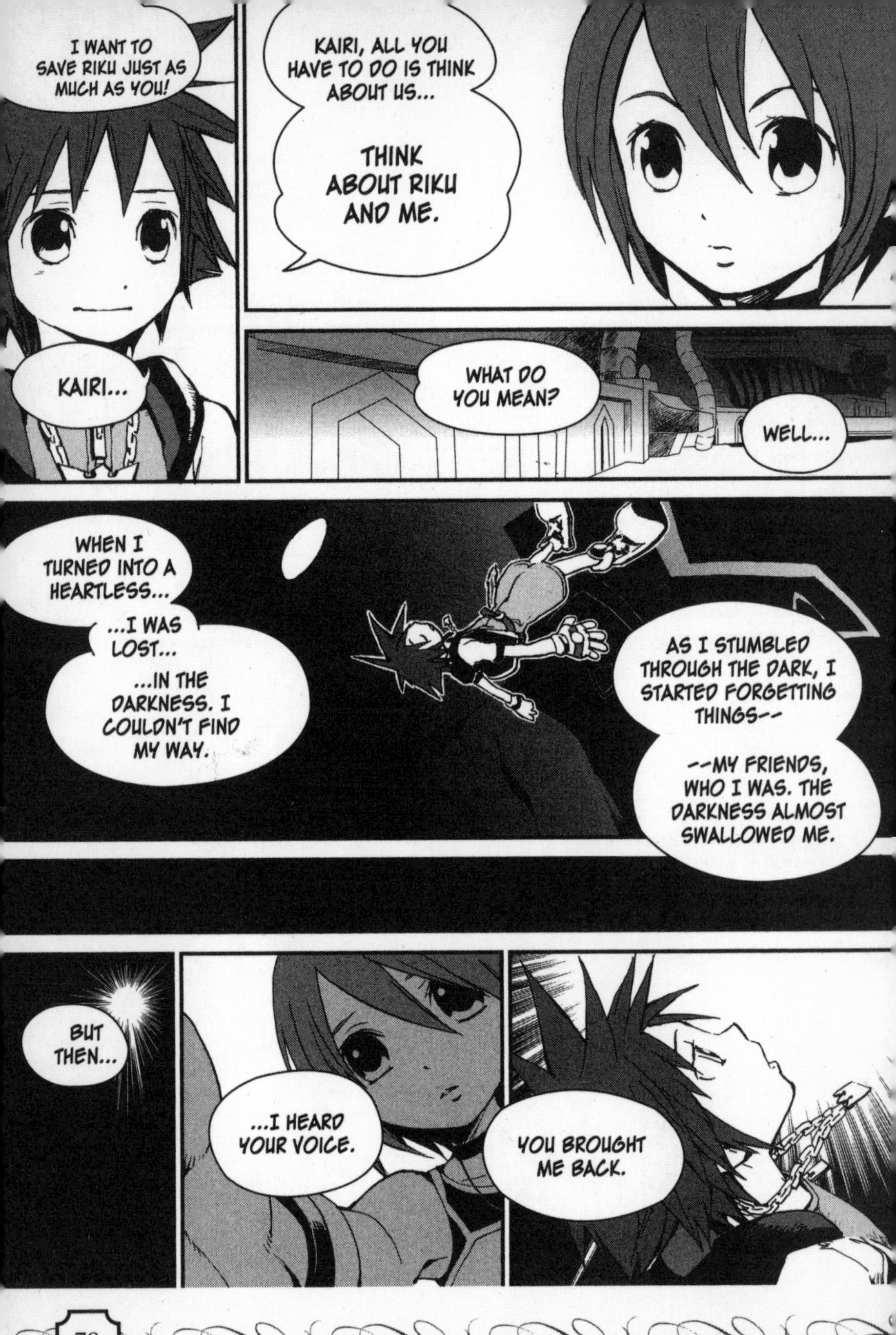
I WANT TO SAVE RIKU JUST AS MUCH AS YOU!
KAIRI, ALL YOU HAVE TO DO IS THINK ABOUT US...
THINK ABOUT RIKU AND ME.
KAIRI...
WHAT DO YOU MEAN?
WELL...
WHEN I TURNED INTO A HEARTLESS...
...I WAS LOST...
...IN THE DARKNESS. I COULDN'T FIND MY WAY.
AS I STUMBLED THROUGH THE DARK, I STARTED FORGETTING THINGS--
--MY FRIENDS, WHO I WAS. THE DARKNESS ALMOST SWALLOWED ME.
BUT THEN...
...I HEARD YOUR VOICE.
YOU BROUGHT ME BACK.

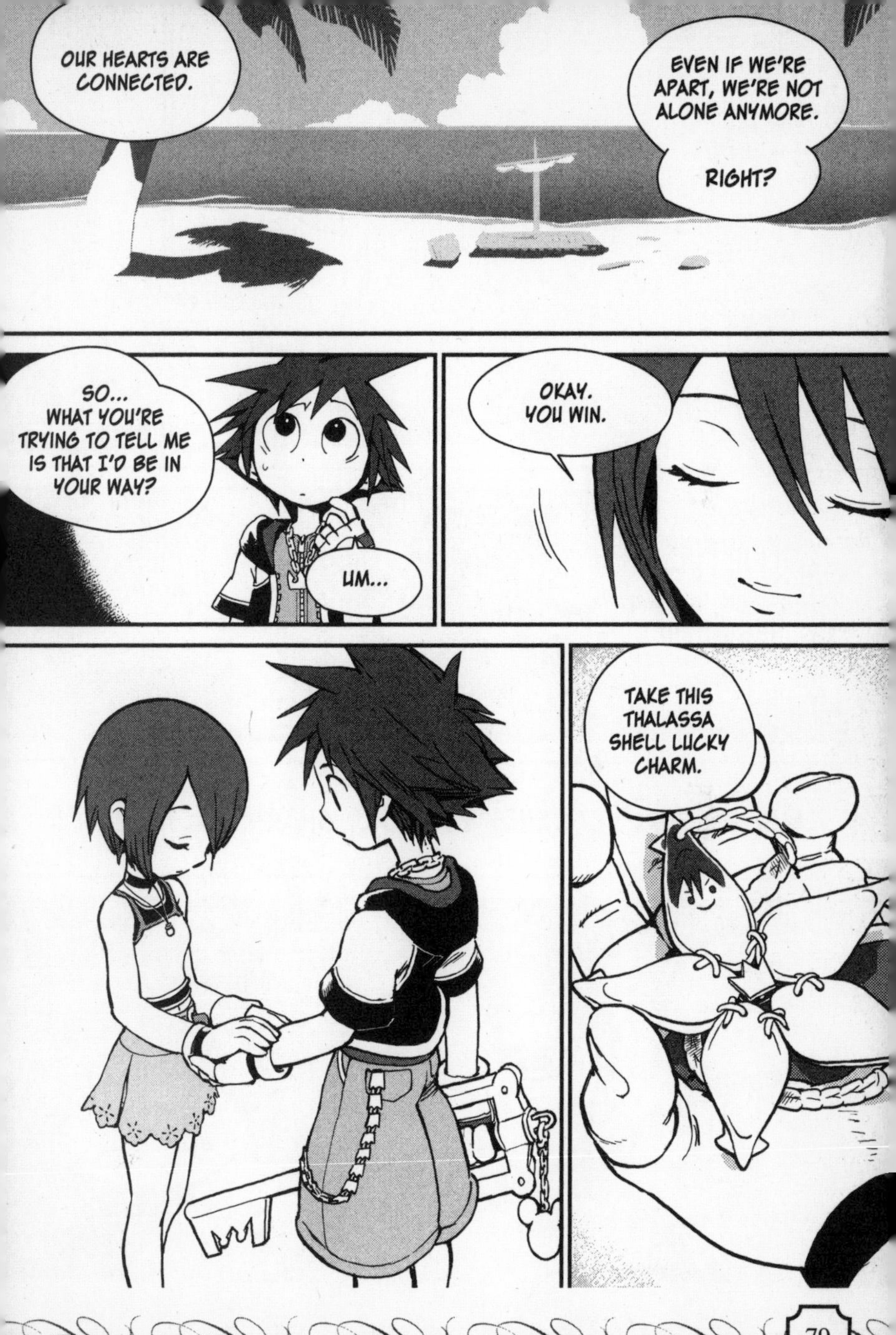
OUR HEARTS ARE CONNECTED.
EVEN IF WE'RE APART, WE'RE NOT ALONE ANYMORE.
RIGHT?
SO... WHAT YOU'RE TRYING TO TELL ME IS THAT I'D BE IN YOUR WAY?
UM...
OKAY. YOU WIN.
TAKE THIS THALASSA SHELL LUCKY CHARM.

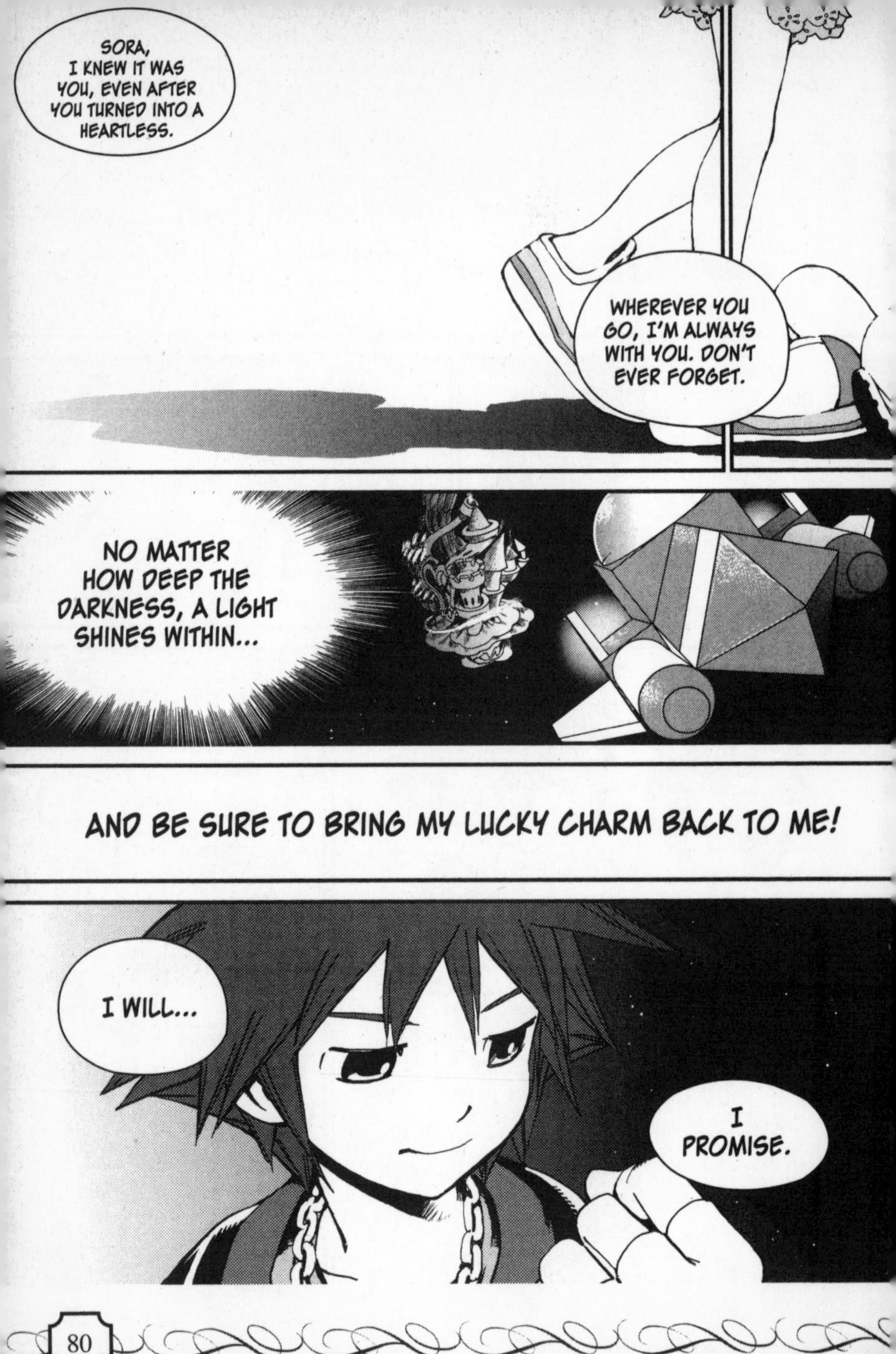
SORA, I KNEW IT WAS YOU, EVEN AFTER YOU TURNED INTO A HEARTLESS.
WHEREVER YOU GO, I'M ALWAYS WITH YOU. DON'T EVER FORGET.
NO MATTER HOW DEEP THE DARKNESS, A LIGHT SHINES WITHIN...
AND BE SURE TO BRING MY LUCKY CHARM BACK TO ME!
I WILL...
I PROMISE.

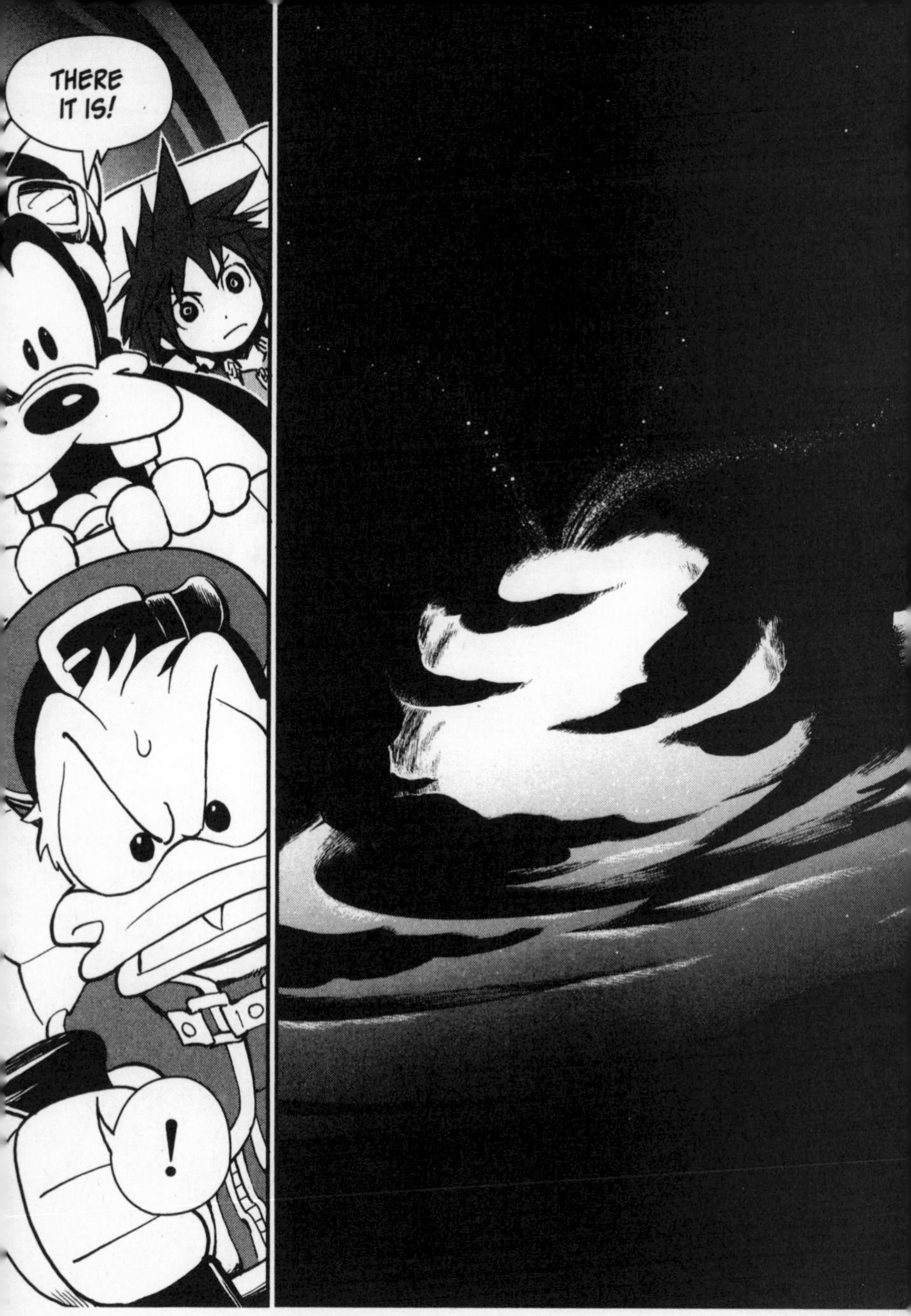
THERE IT IS!
!

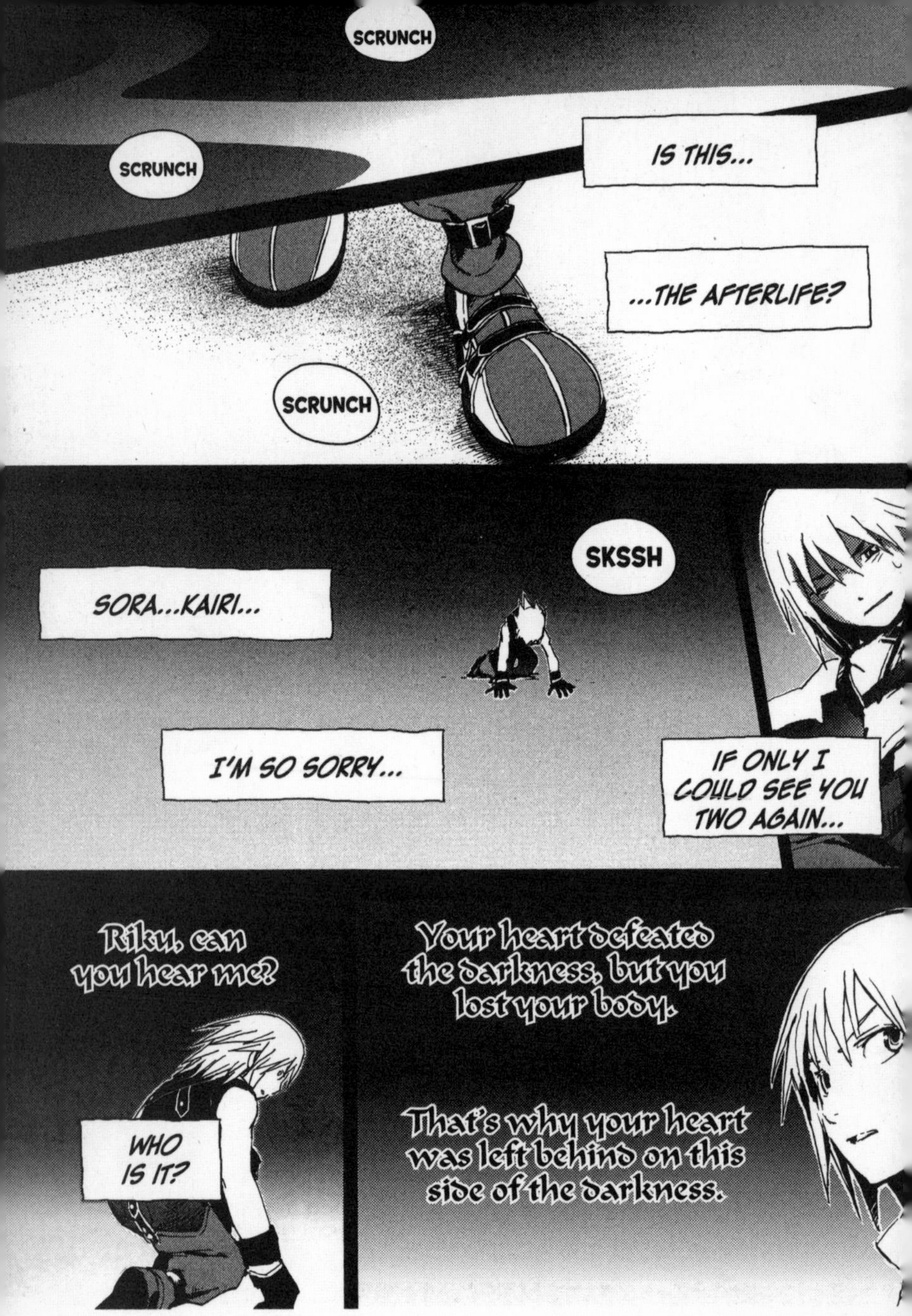
SCRUNCH
SCRUNCH
IS THIS...
...THE AFTERLIFE?
SCRUNCH
SORA...KAIRI...
SKSSH
I'M SO SORRY...
IF ONLY I COULD SEE YOU TWO AGAIN...
Riku, can you hear me?
WHO IS IT?
Your heart defeated the darkness, but you lost your body.
That's why your heart was left behind on this side of the darkness.

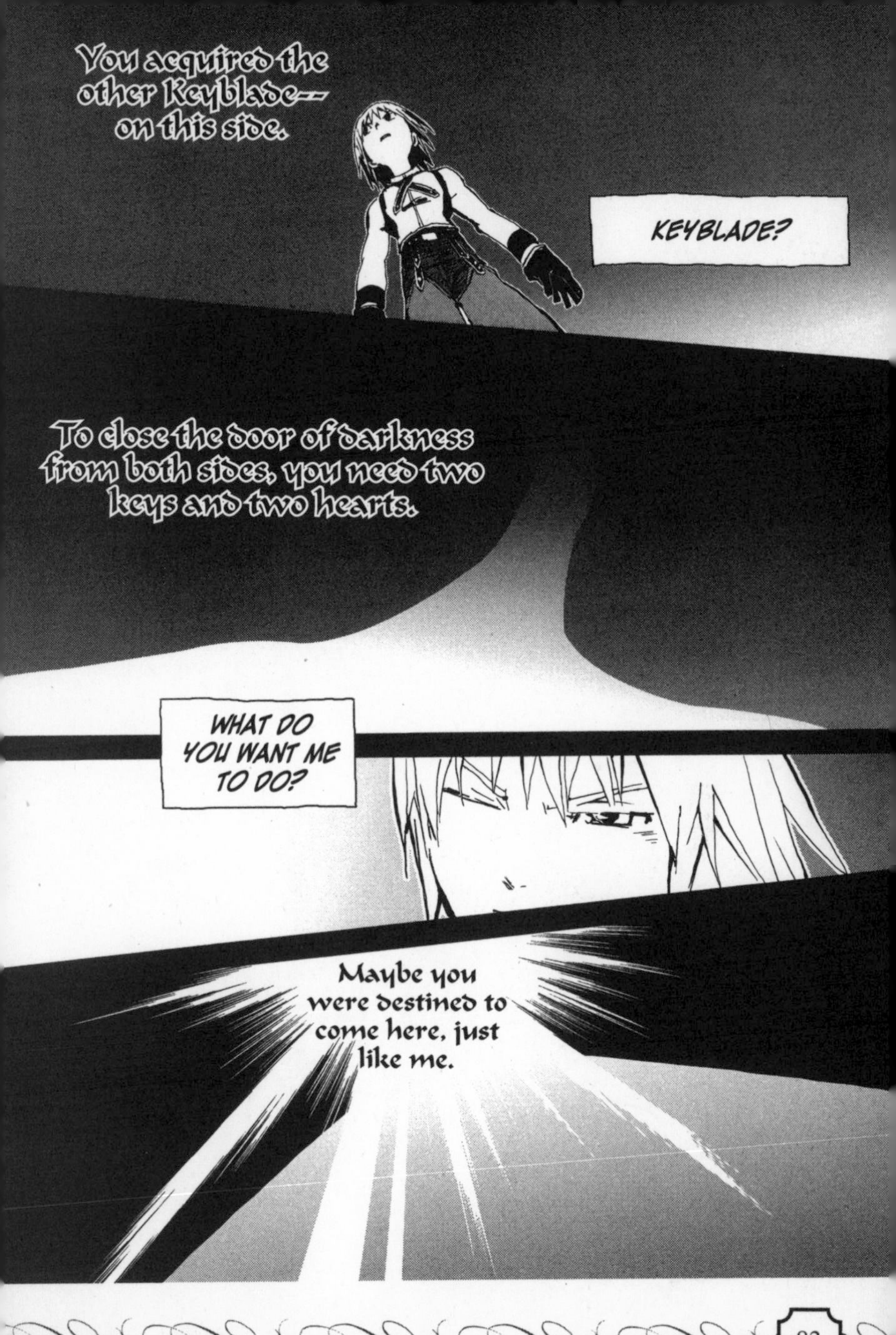
You acquired the other Keyblade--on this side.
KEYBLADE?
To close the door of darkness from both sides, you need two keys and two hearts.
WHAT DO YOU WANT ME TO DO?
Maybe you were destined to come here, just like me.

Episode 41

Infinite Darkness

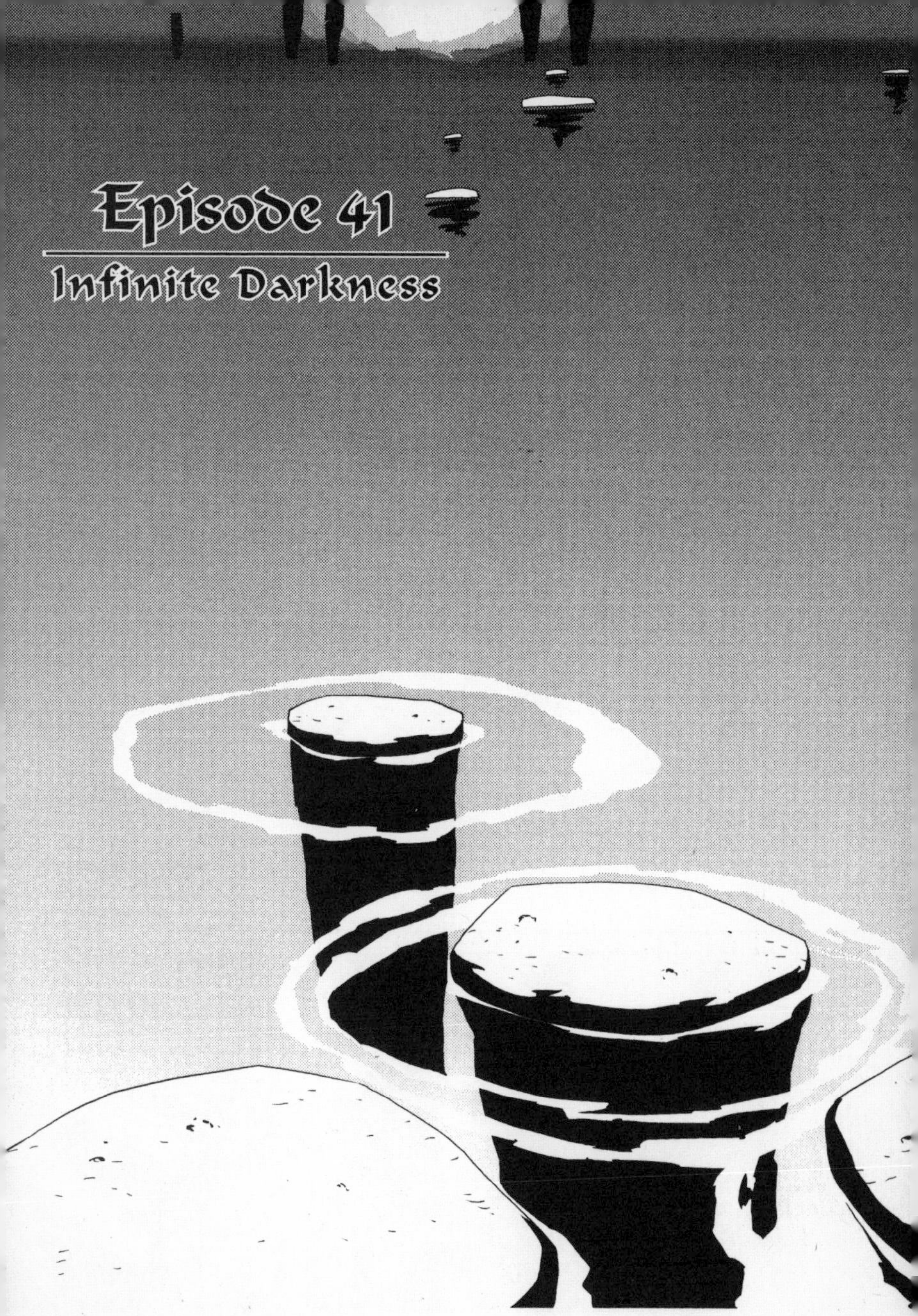

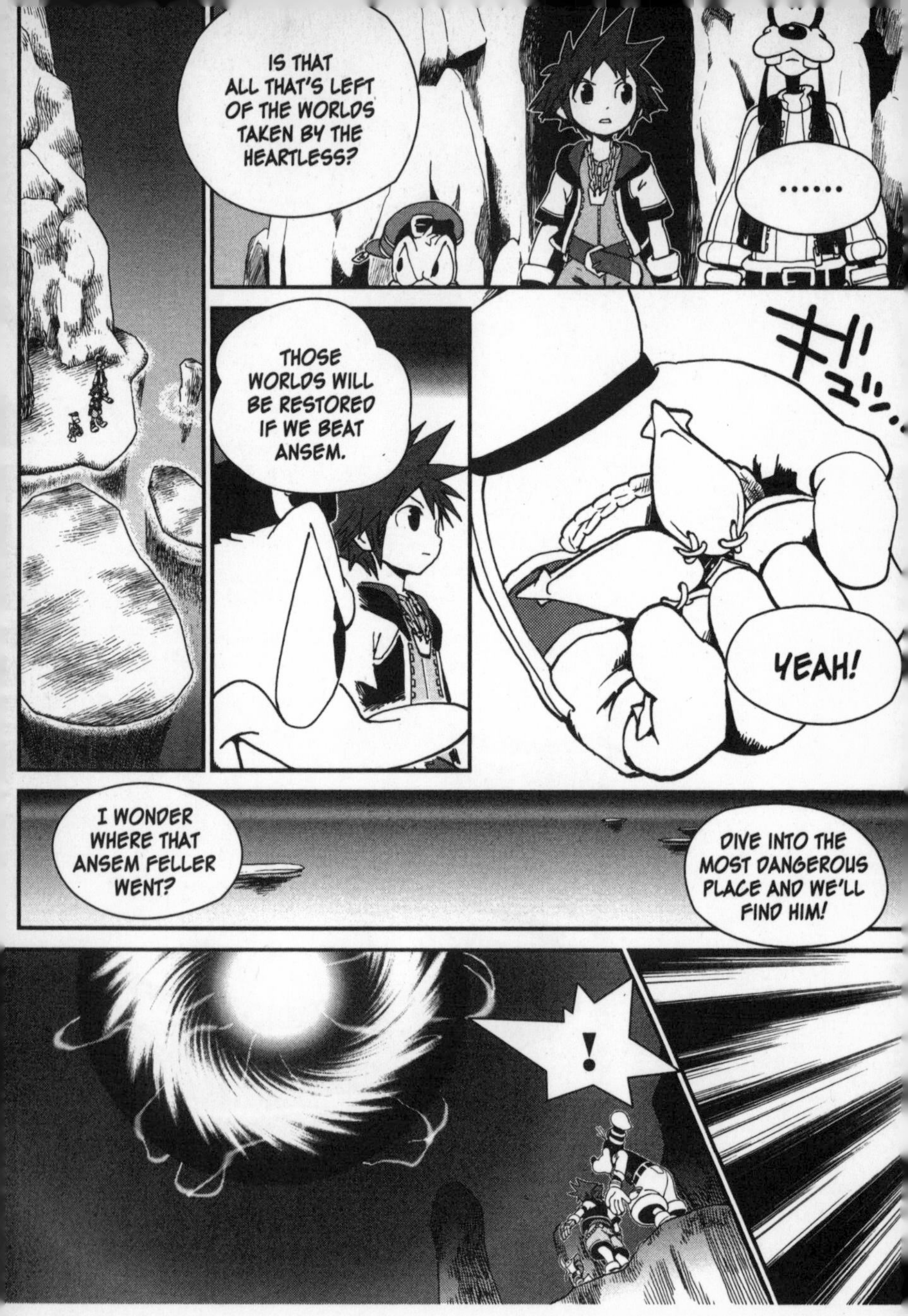
IS THAT ALL THAT'S LEFT OF THE WORLDS TAKEN BY THE HEARTLESS?
....
THOSE WORLDS WILL BE RESTORED IF WE BEAT ANSEM.
ギュッ...
YEAH!
I WONDER WHERE THAT ANSEM FELLER WENT?
DIVE INTO THE MOST DANGEROUS PLACE AND WE'LL FIND HIM!
!

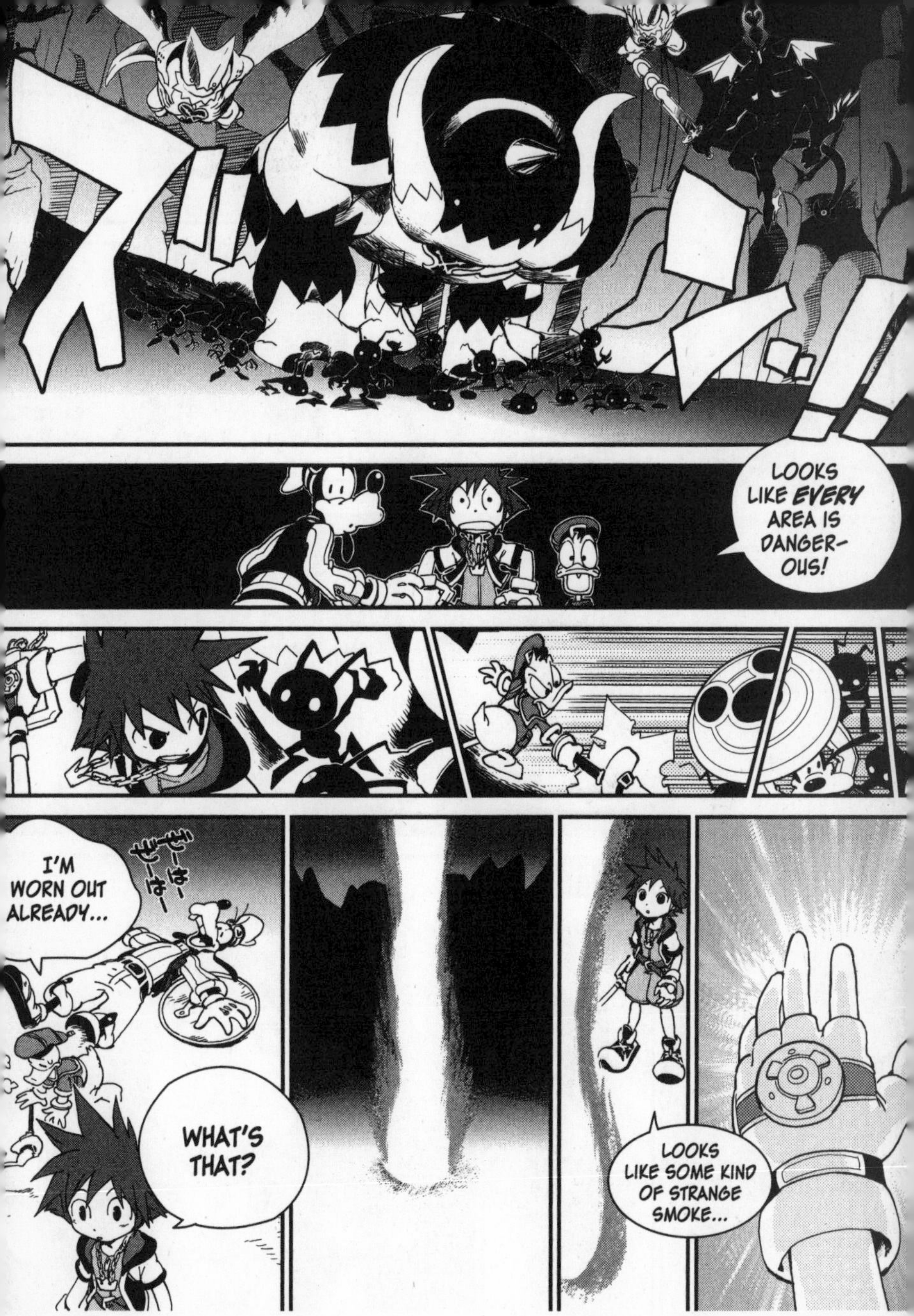
LOOKS LIKE *EVERY* AREA IS DANGER-OUS!
I'M WORN OUT ALREADY...
ぜーはー
ぜーはー
WHAT'S THAT?
LOOKS LIKE SOME KIND OF STRANGE SMOKE...

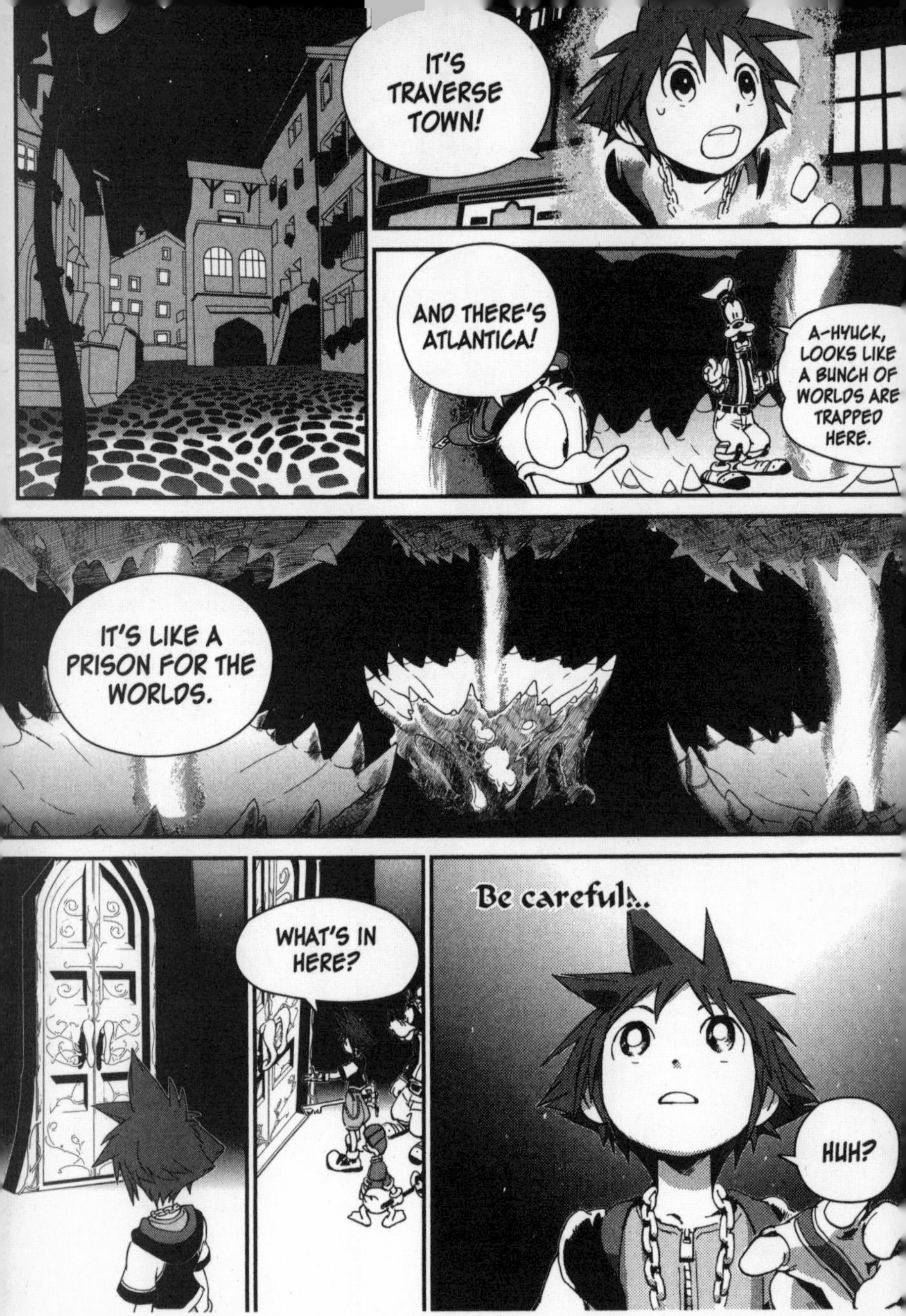
IT'S TRAVERSE TOWN!
AND THERE'S ATLANTICA!
A-HYUCK, LOOKS LIKE A BUNCH OF WORLDS ARE TRAPPED HERE.
IT'S LIKE A PRISON FOR THE WORLDS.
WHAT'S IN HERE?
Be careful!...
HUH?

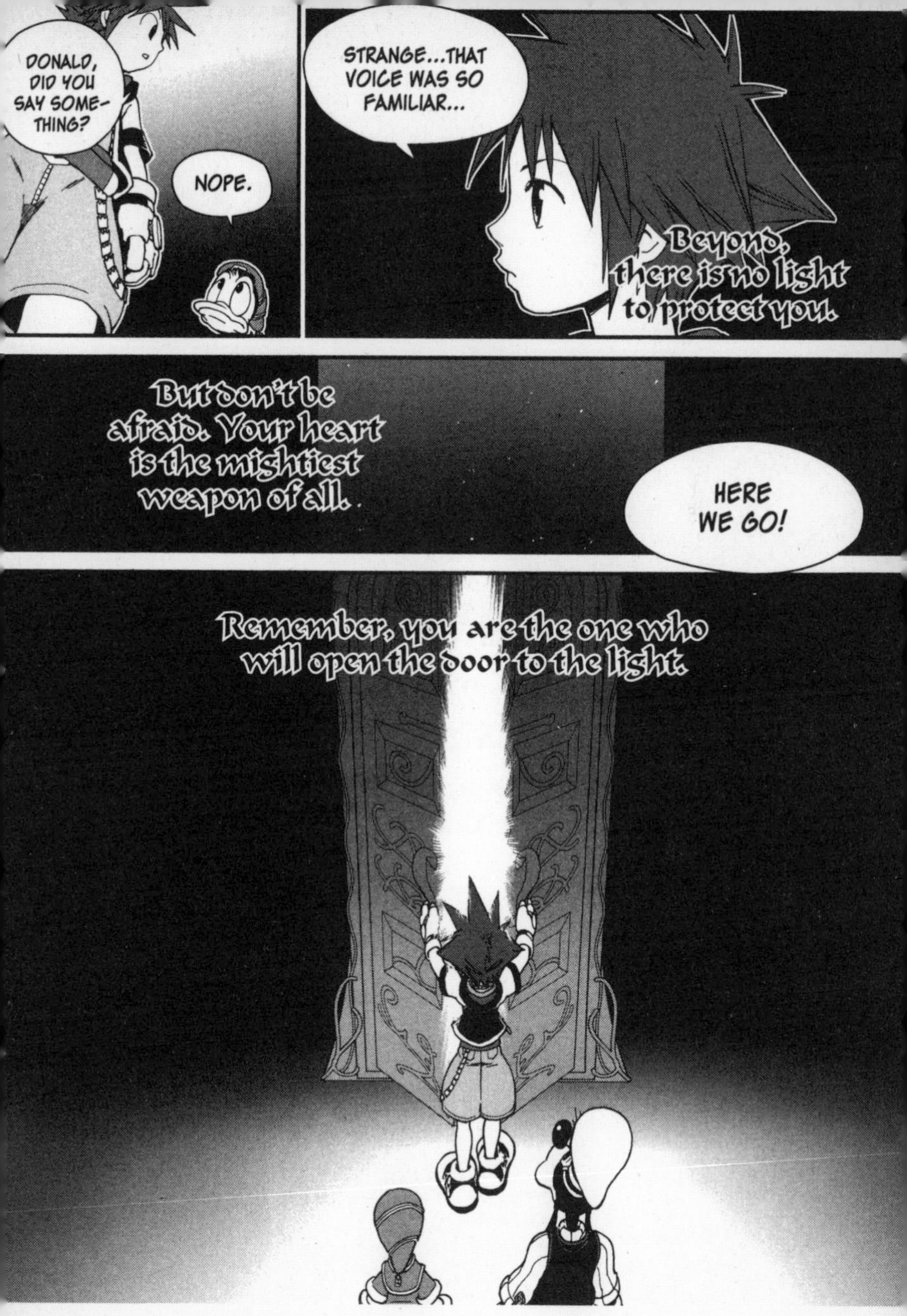
DONALD, DID YOU SAY SOME-THING?
NOPE.
STRANGE...THAT VOICE WAS SO FAMILIAR...
Beyond, there is no light to protect you.
But don't be afraid. Your heart is the mightiest weapon of all.
HERE WE GO!
Remember, you are the one who will open the door to the light.

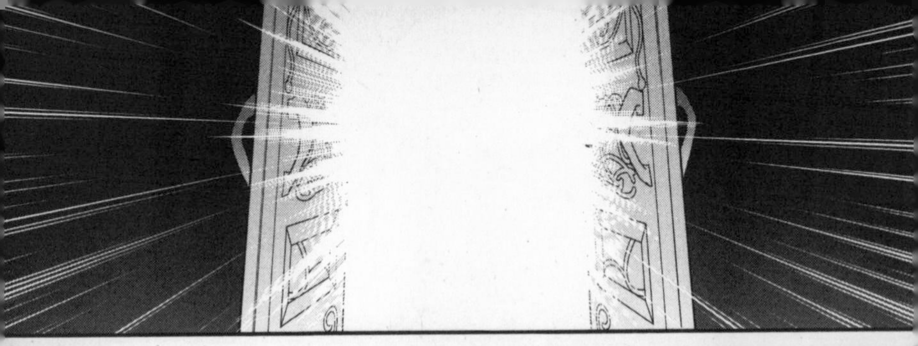

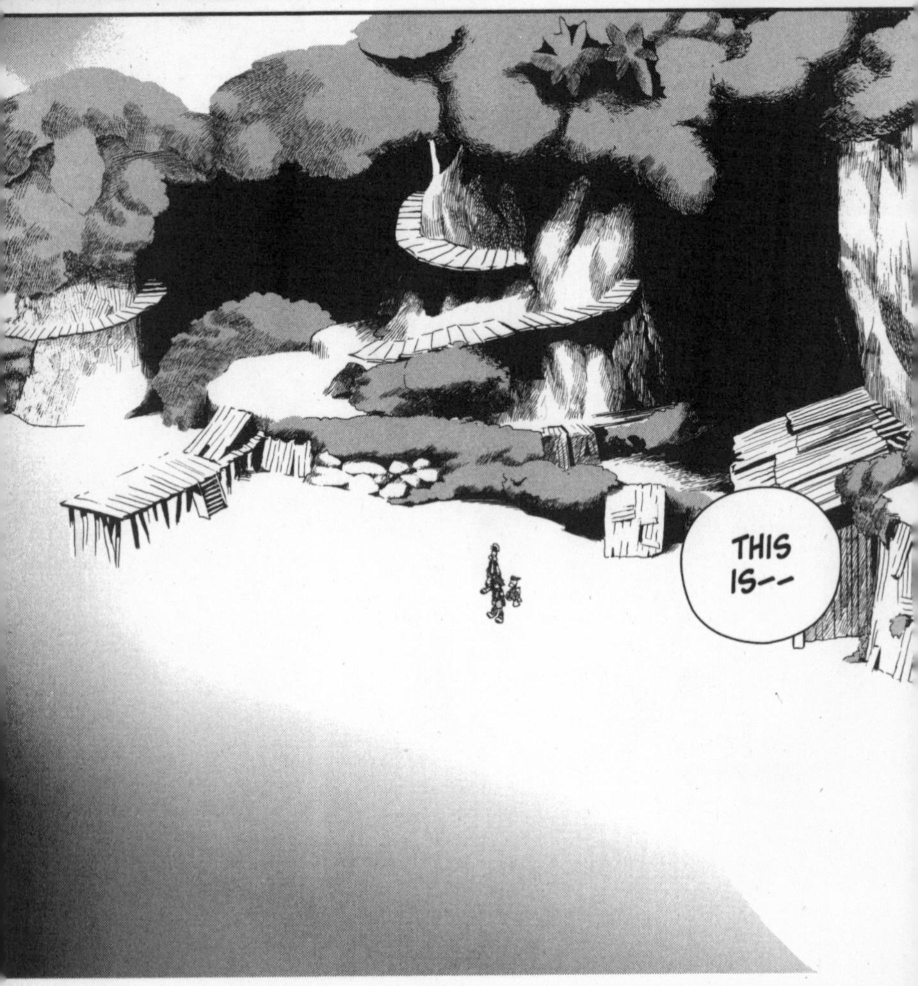
THIS IS--

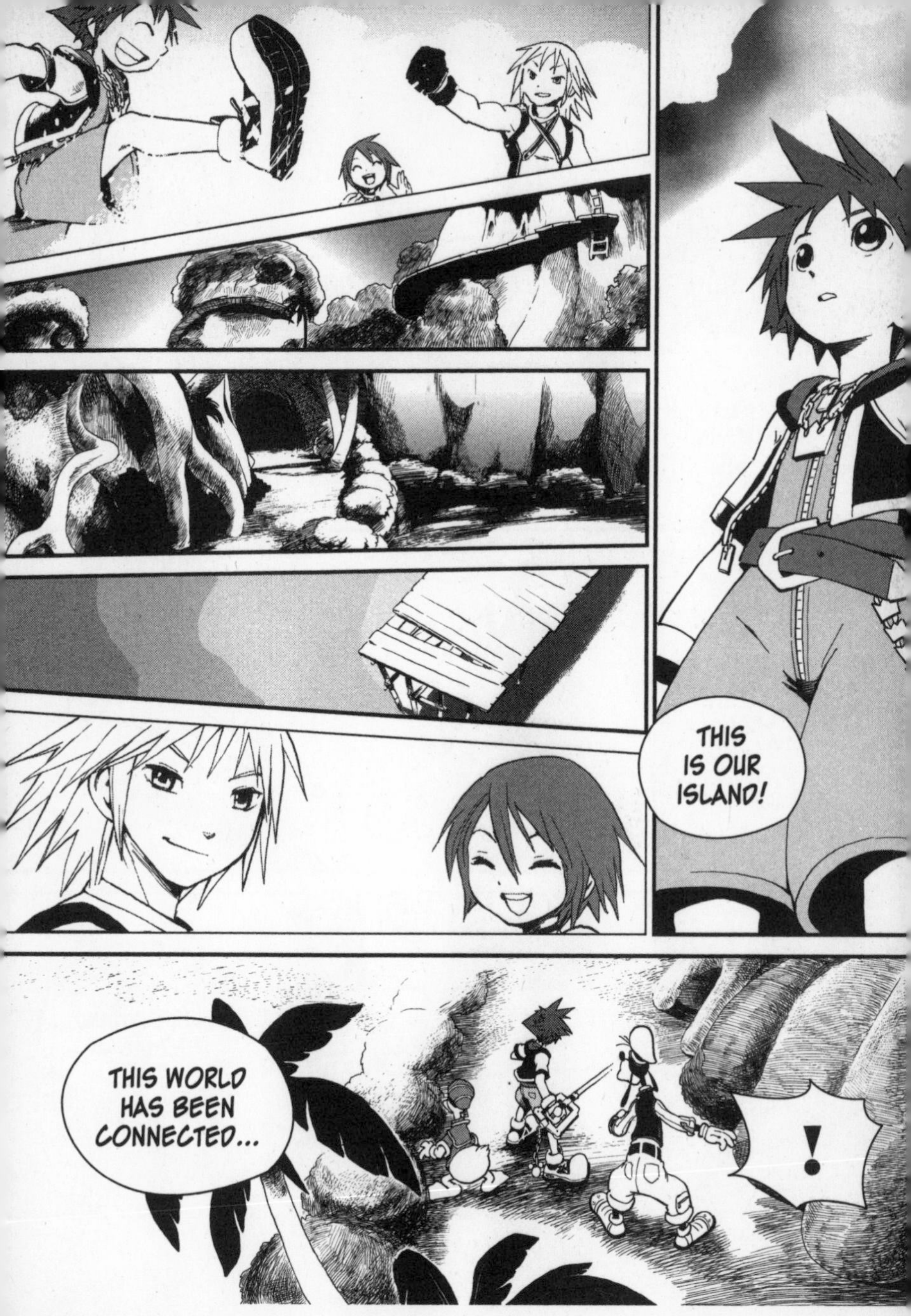
THIS IS OUR ISLAND!
THIS WORLD HAS BEEN CONNECTED...
!

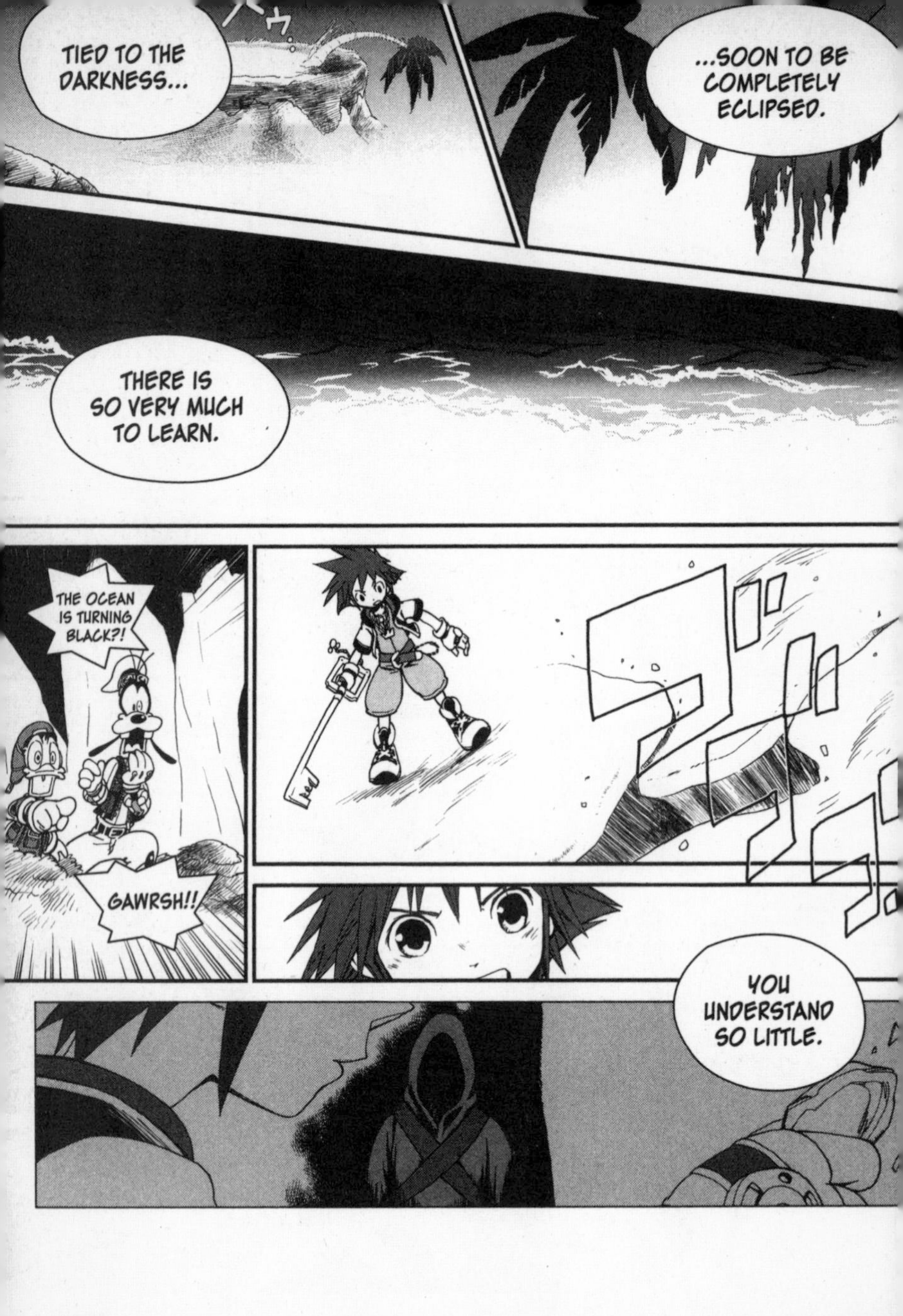
TIED TO THE DARKNESS...
...SOON TO BE COMPLETELY ECLIPSED.
THERE IS SO VERY MUCH TO LEARN.
THE OCEAN IS TURNING BLACK?!
GAWRSH!!
YOU UNDERSTAND SO LITTLE.

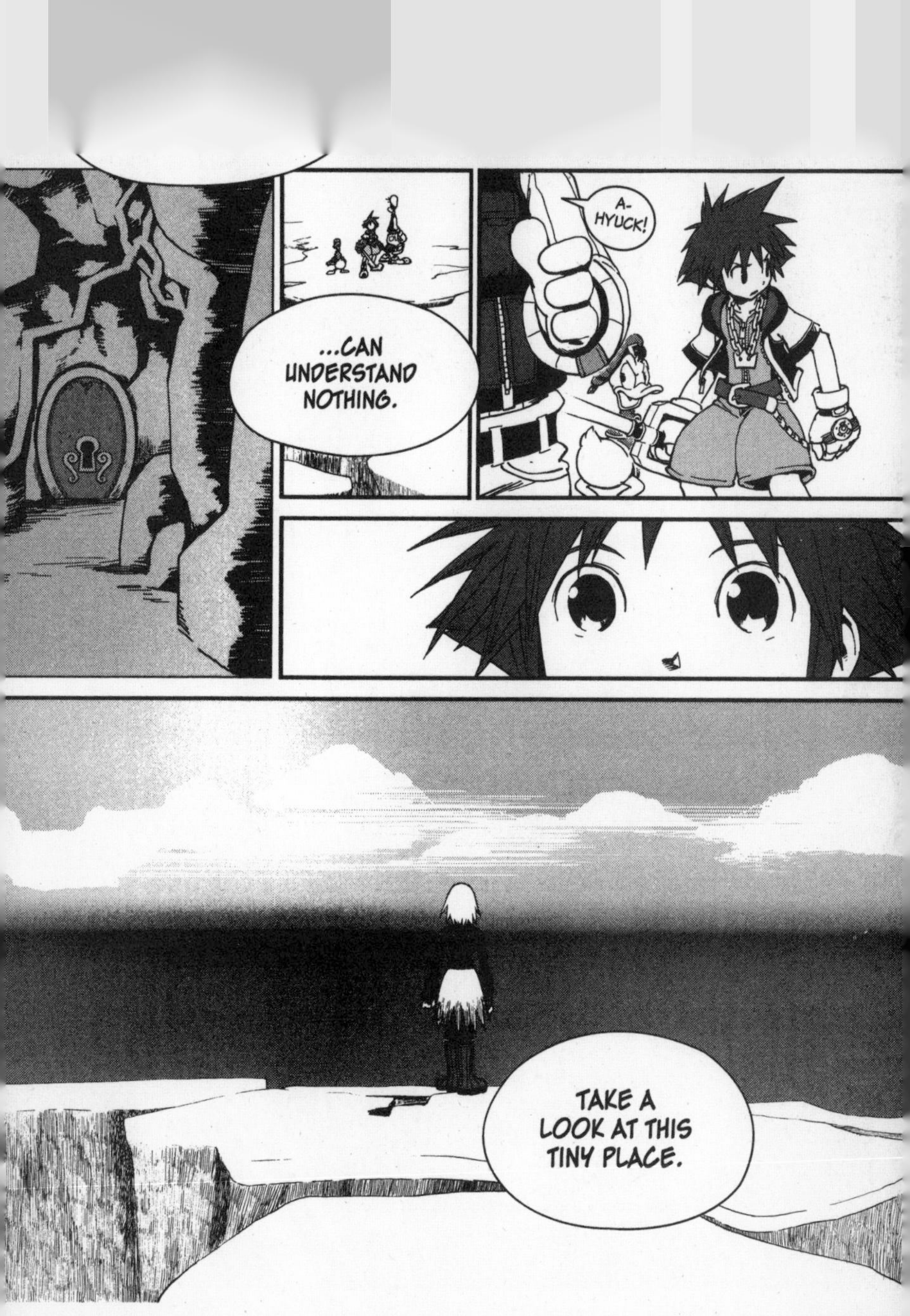
...CAN UNDERSTAND NOTHING.
A-HYUCK!
TAKE A LOOK AT THIS TINY PLACE.

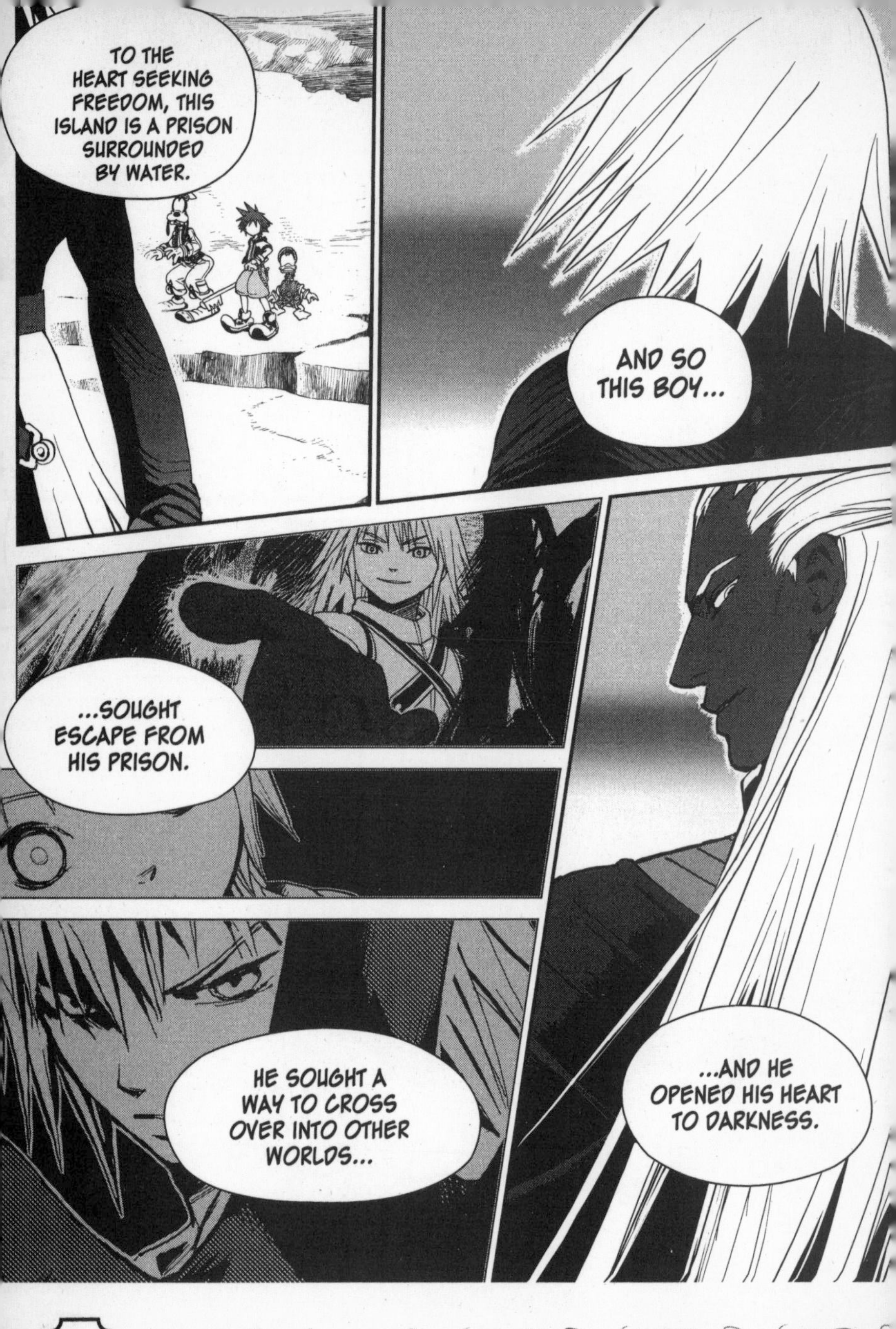
TO THE HEART SEEKING FREEDOM, THIS ISLAND IS A PRISON SURROUNDED BY WATER.
AND SO THIS BOY...
...SOUGHT ESCAPE FROM HIS PRISON.
HE SOUGHT A WAY TO CROSS OVER INTO OTHER WORLDS...
...AND HE OPENED HIS HEART TO DARKNESS.

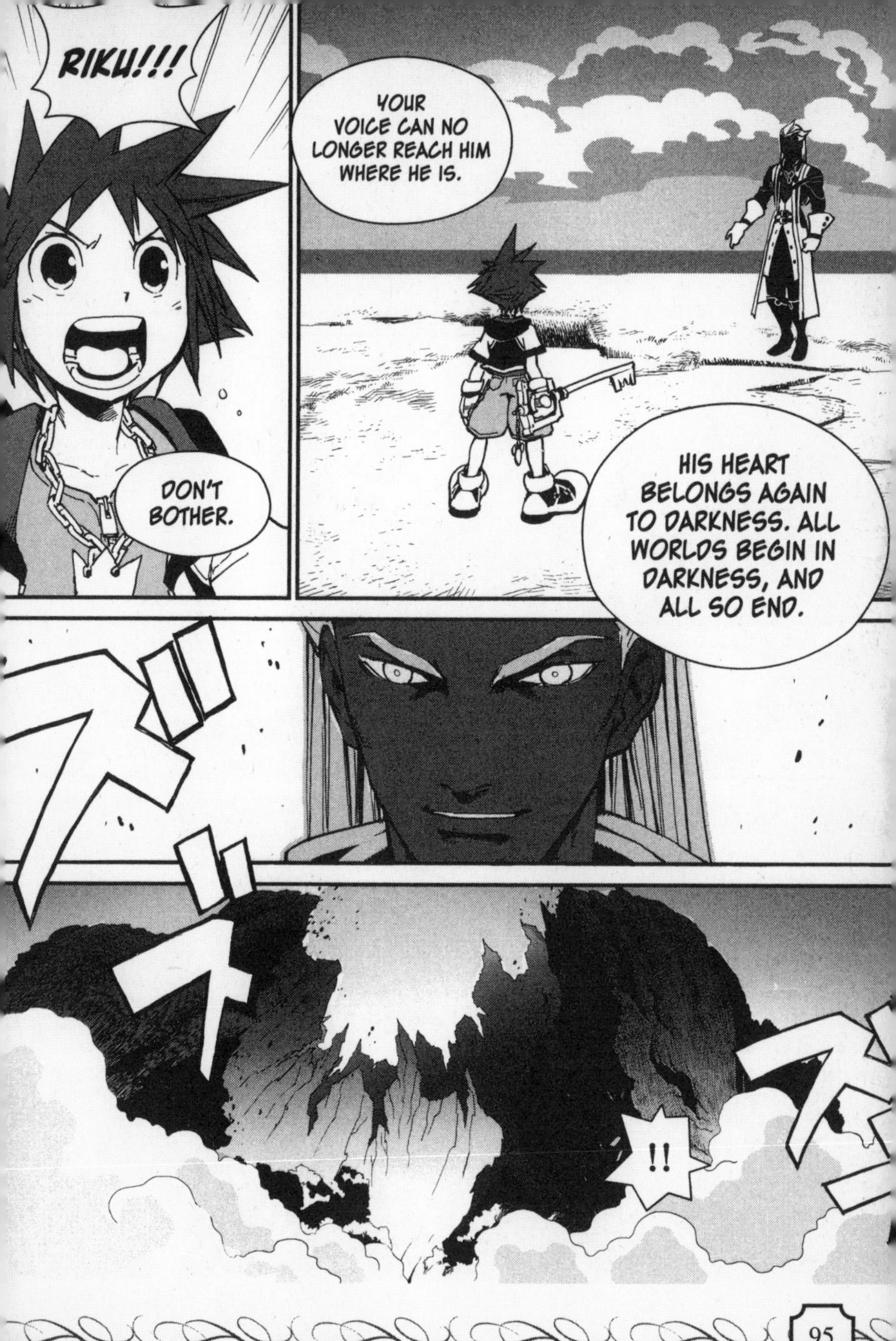
RIKU!!!
DON'T BOTHER.
YOUR VOICE CAN NO LONGER REACH HIM WHERE HE IS.
HIS HEART BELONGS AGAIN TO DARKNESS. ALL WORLDS BEGIN IN DARKNESS, AND ALL SO END.
!!

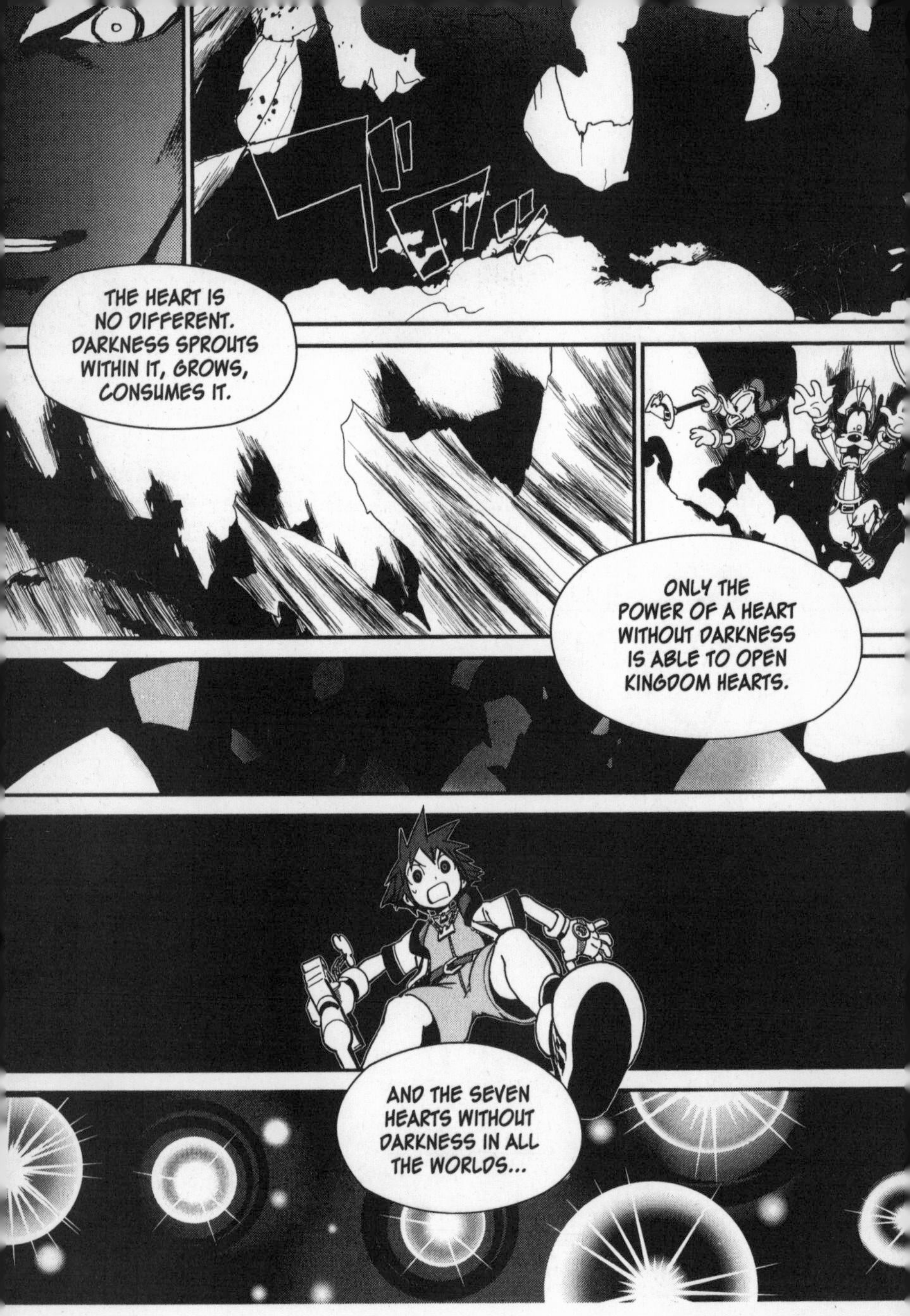
THE HEART IS NO DIFFERENT. DARKNESS SPROUTS WITHIN IT, GROWS, CONSUMES IT.
ONLY THE POWER OF A HEART WITHOUT DARKNESS IS ABLE TO OPEN KINGDOM HEARTS.
AND THE SEVEN HEARTS WITHOUT DARKNESS IN ALL THE WORLDS...

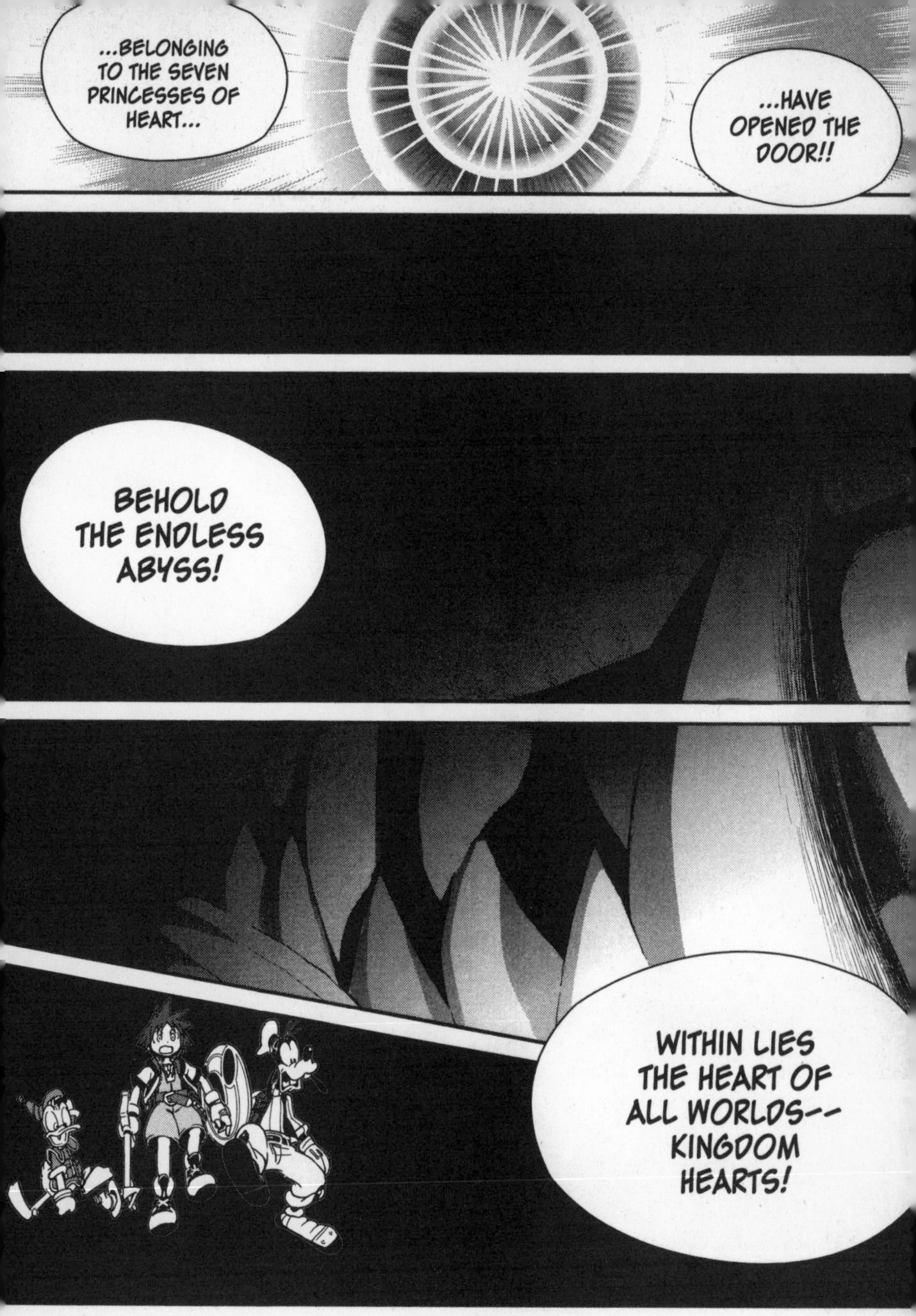
...BELONGING TO THE SEVEN PRINCESSES OF HEART...
...HAVE OPENED THE DOOR!!
BEHOLD THE ENDLESS ABYSS!
WITHIN LIES THE HEART OF ALL WORLDS--KINGDOM HEARTS!

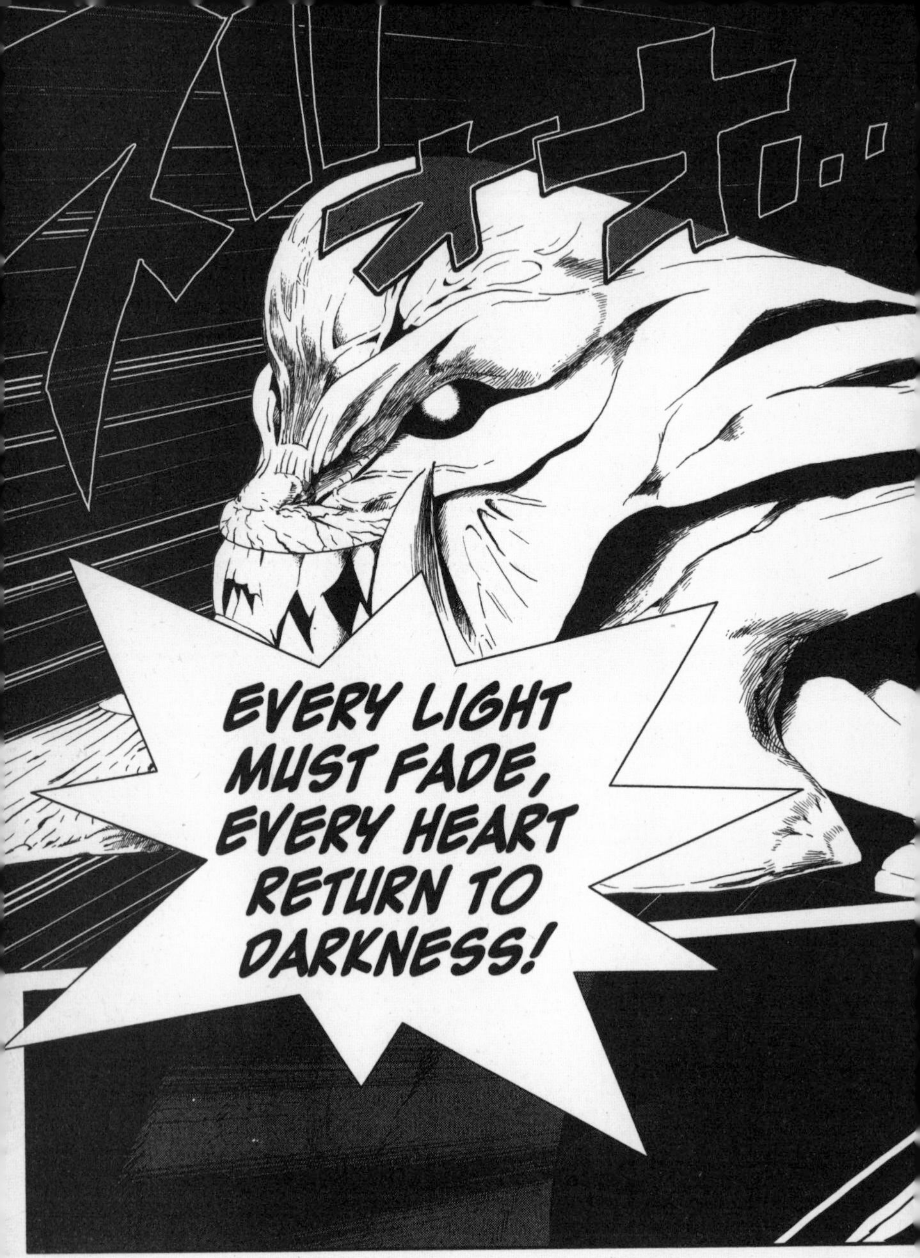
EVERY LIGHT MUST FADE, EVERY HEART RETURN TO DARKNESS!

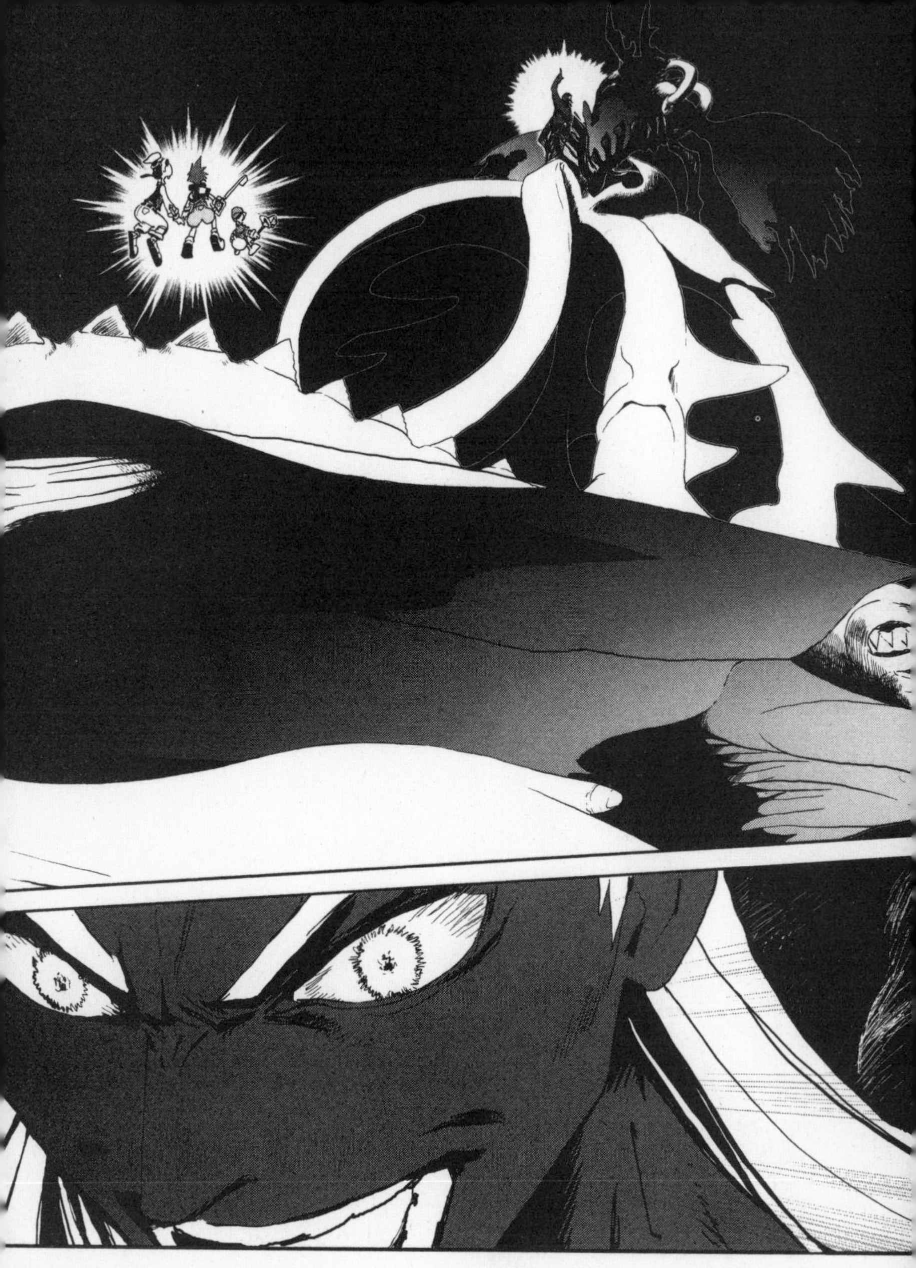

Episode 42

Behind the Door

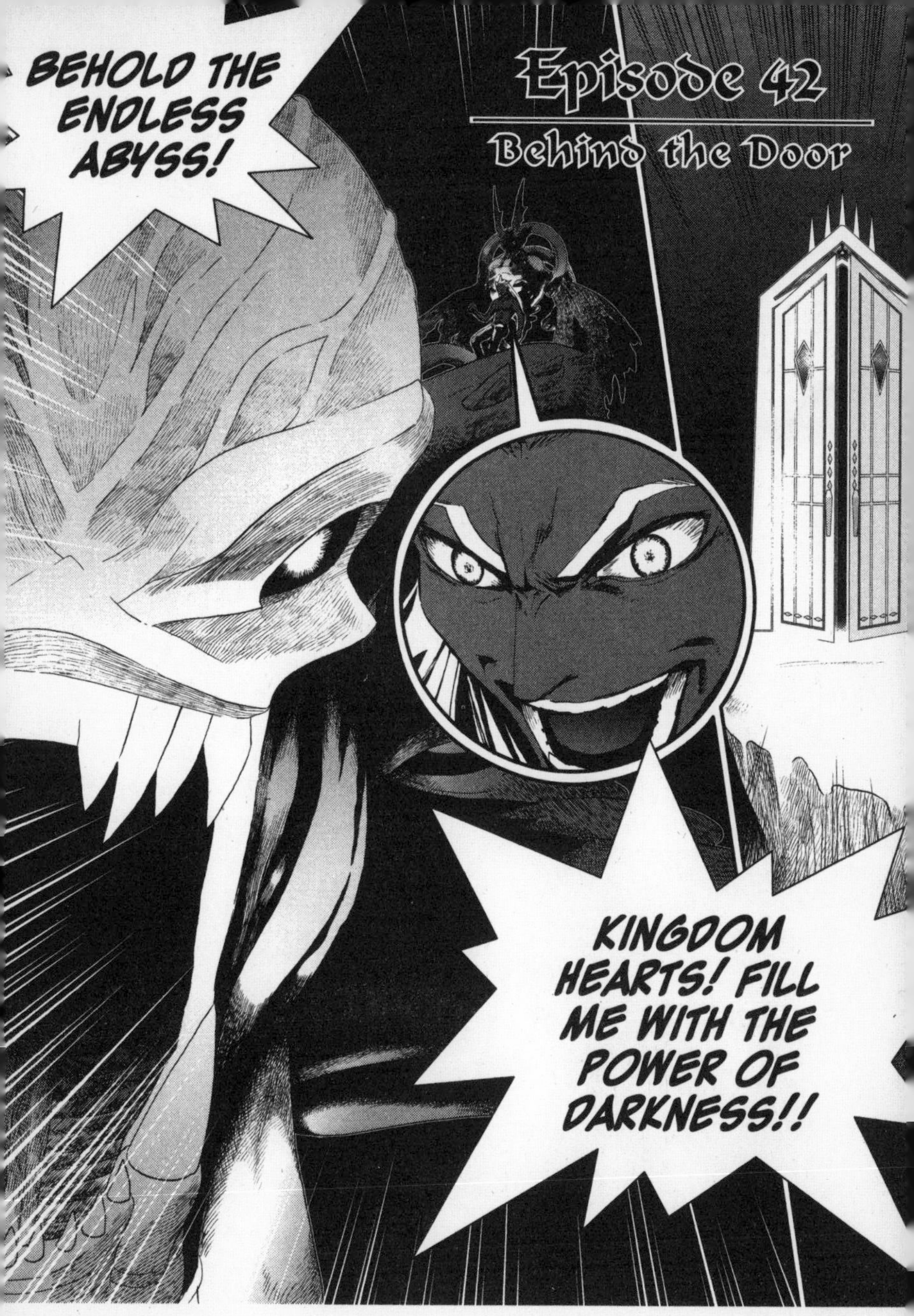
BEHOLD THE ENDLESS ABYSS!
KINGDOM HEARTS! FILL ME WITH THE POWER OF DARKNESS!!

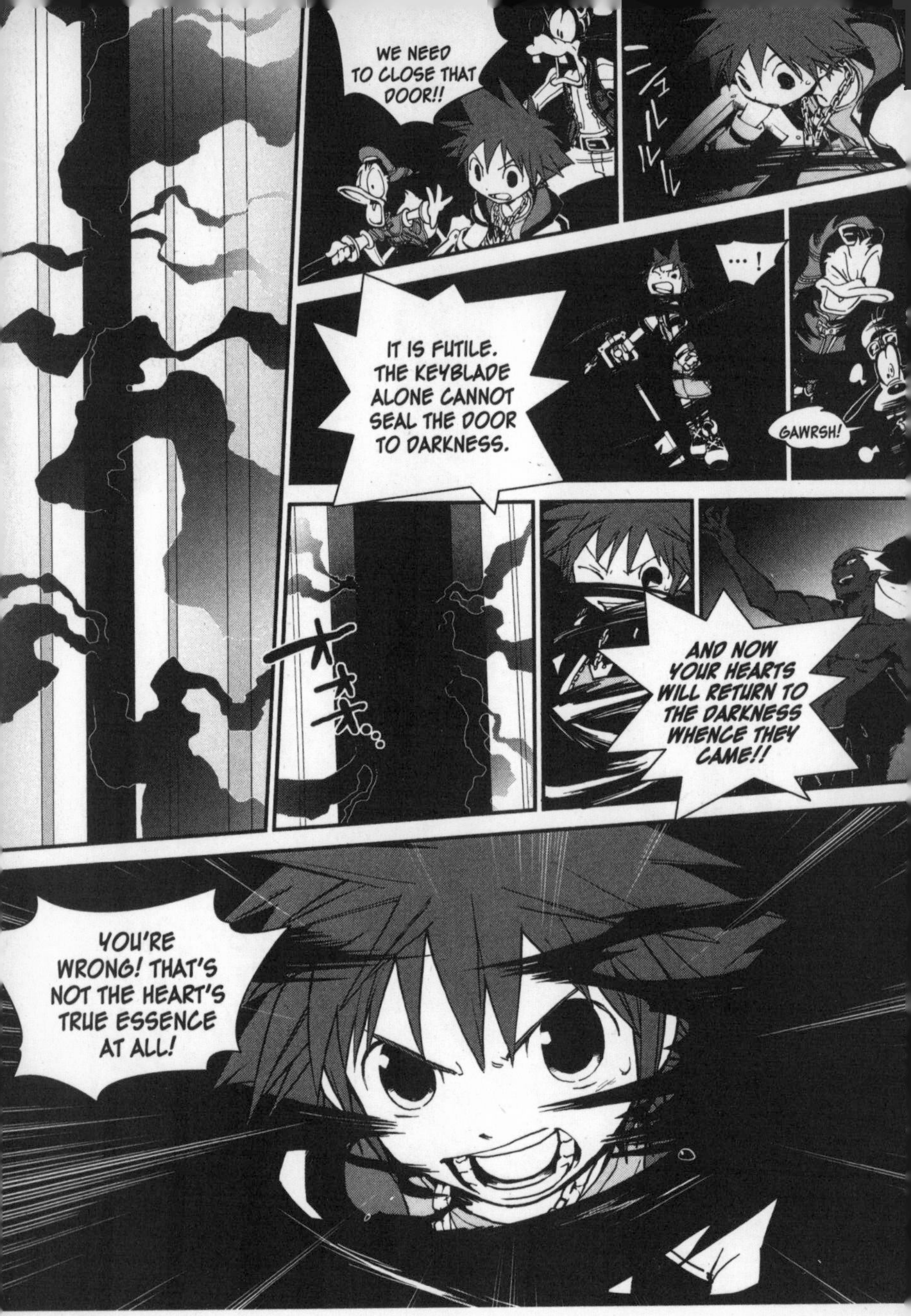
WE NEED TO CLOSE THAT DOOR!!
IT IS FUTILE. THE KEYBLADE ALONE CANNOT SEAL THE DOOR TO DARKNESS.
...!
GAWRSH!
AND NOW YOUR HEARTS WILL RETURN TO THE DARKNESS WHENCE THEY CAME!!
YOU'RE WRONG! THAT'S NOT THE HEART'S TRUE ESSENCE AT ALL!

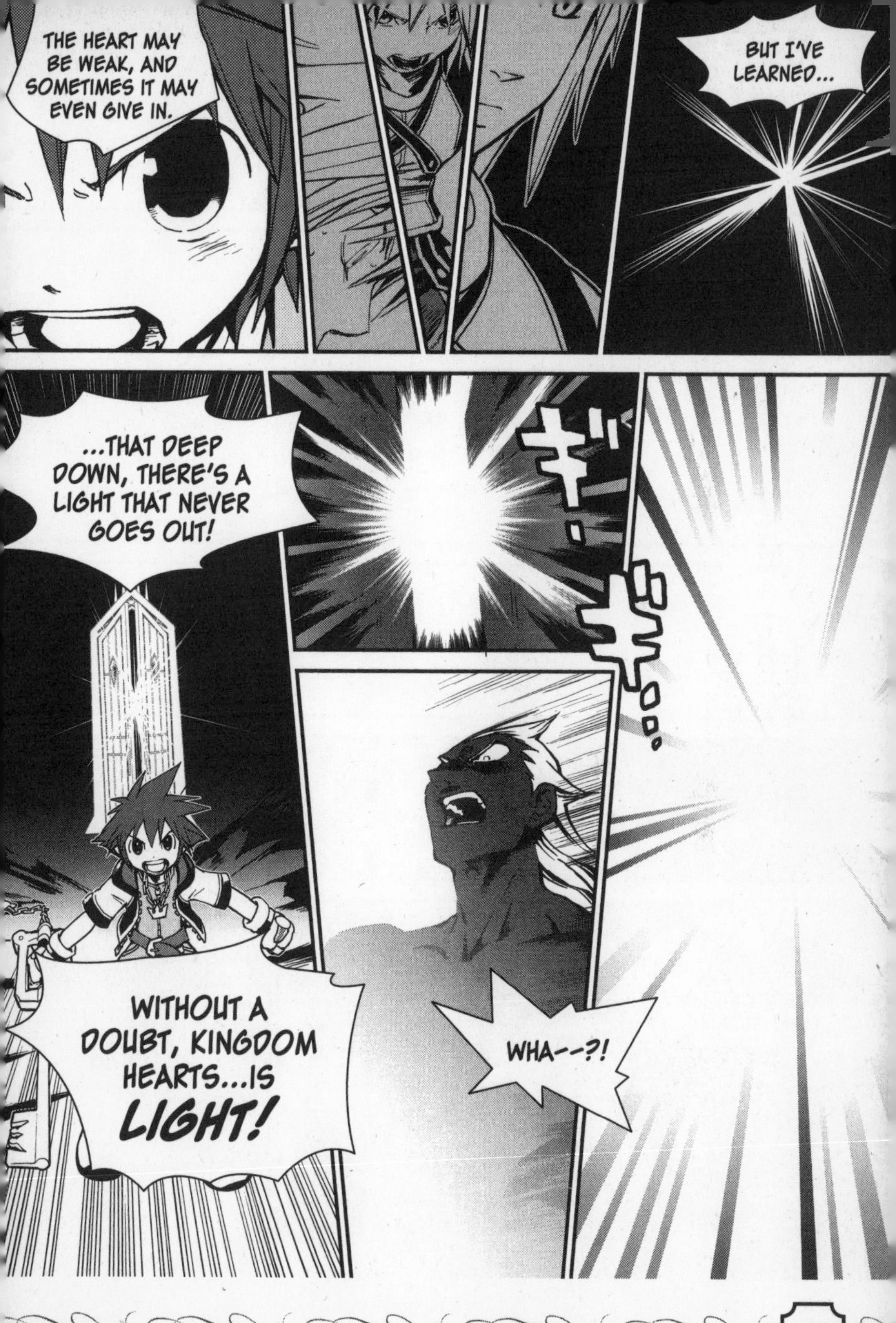

THE HEART MAY BE WEAK, AND SOMETIMES IT MAY EVEN GIVE IN.
BUT I'VE LEARNED...
...THAT DEEP DOWN, THERE'S A LIGHT THAT NEVER GOES OUT!
ギギ…
ギ…
WITHOUT A DOUBT, KINGDOM HEARTS...IS LIGHT!
WHA--?!

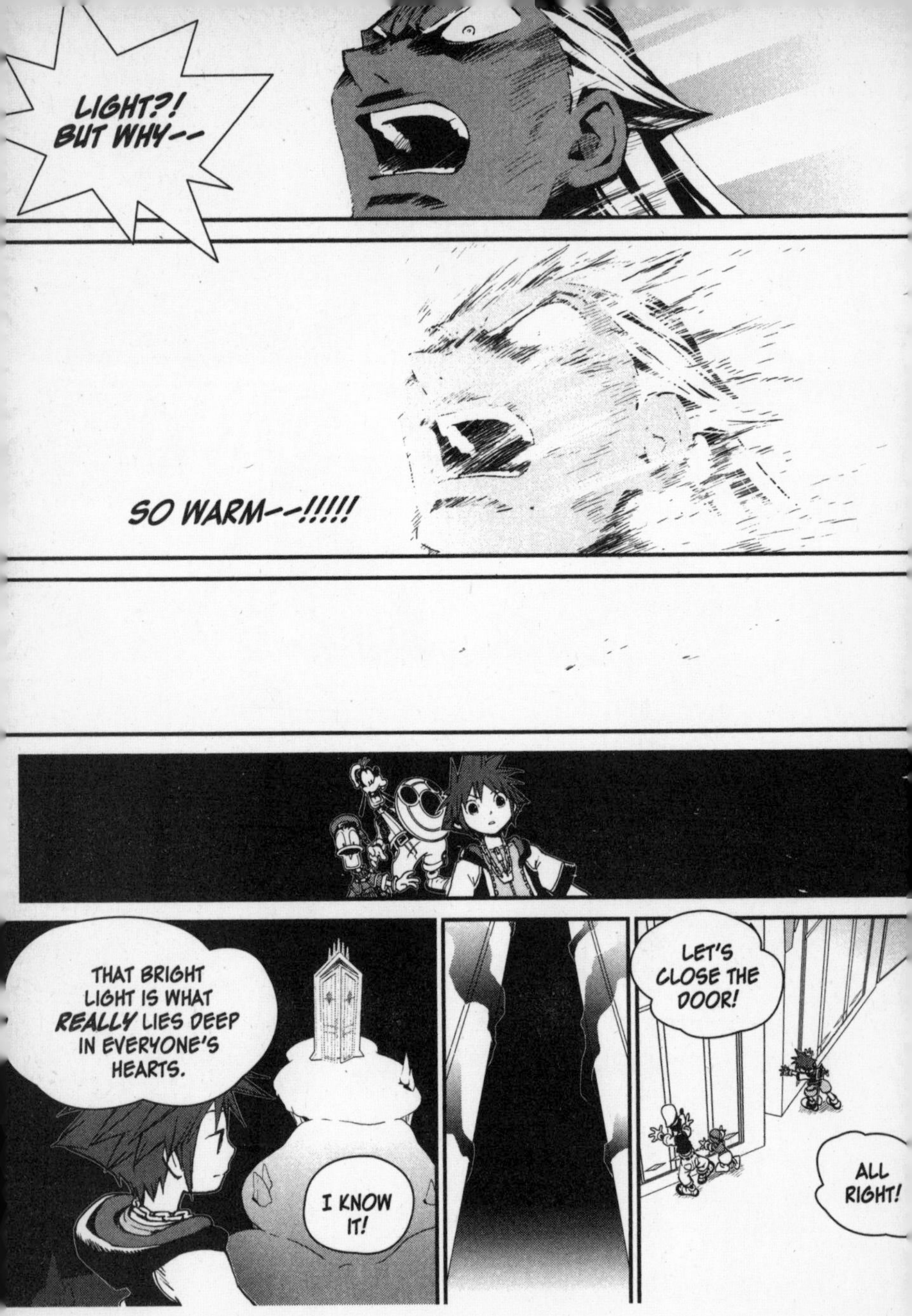
LIGHT?! BUT WHY--
SO WARM--!!!!!
THAT BRIGHT LIGHT IS WHAT *REALLY* LIES DEEP IN EVERYONE'S HEARTS.
I KNOW IT!
LET'S CLOSE THE DOOR!
ALL RIGHT!

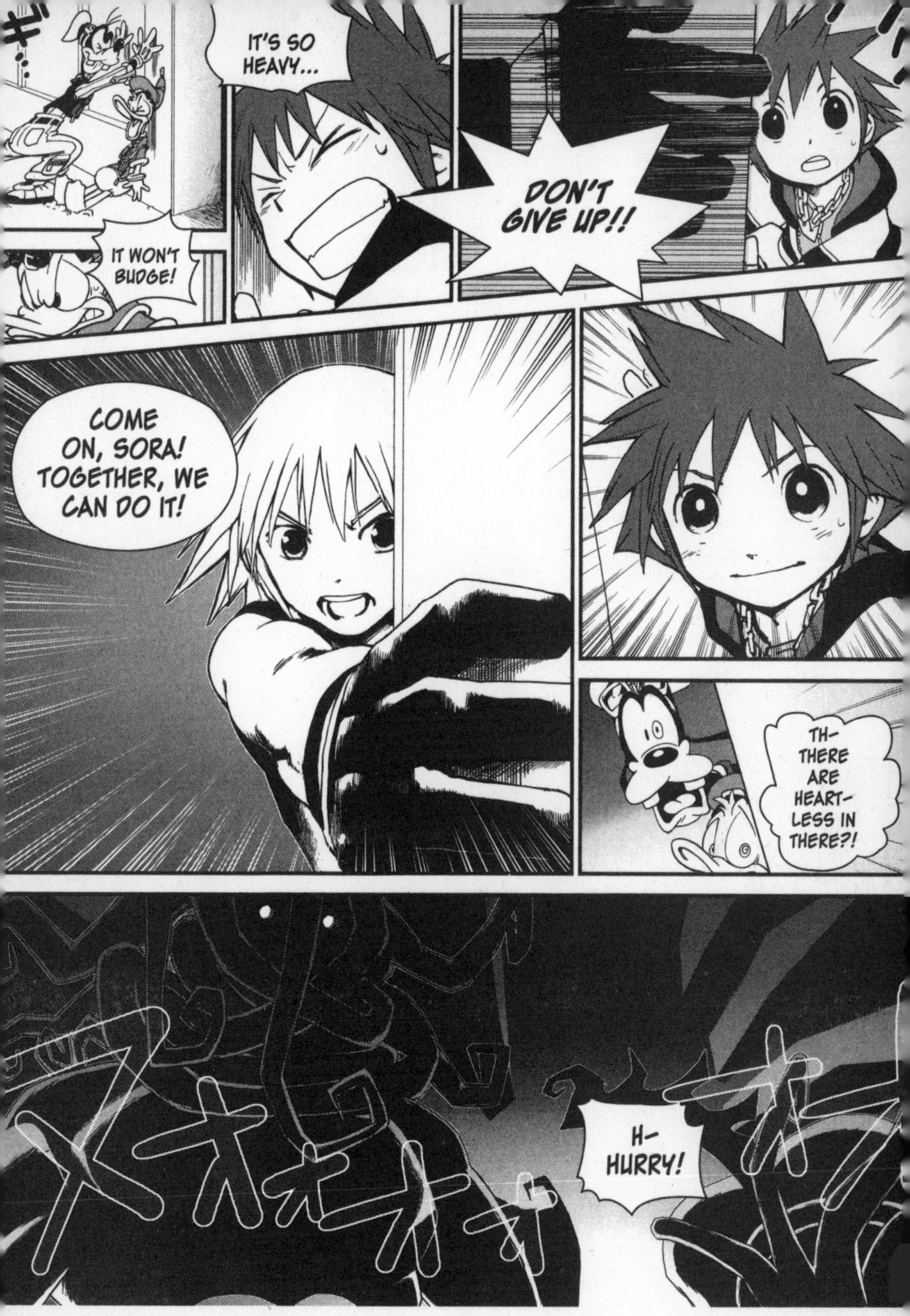
IT WON'T BUDGE!
IT'S SO HEAVY...
DON'T GIVE UP!!
COME ON, SORA! TOGETHER, WE CAN DO IT!
TH-THERE ARE HEART-LESS IN THERE?!
H-HURRY!

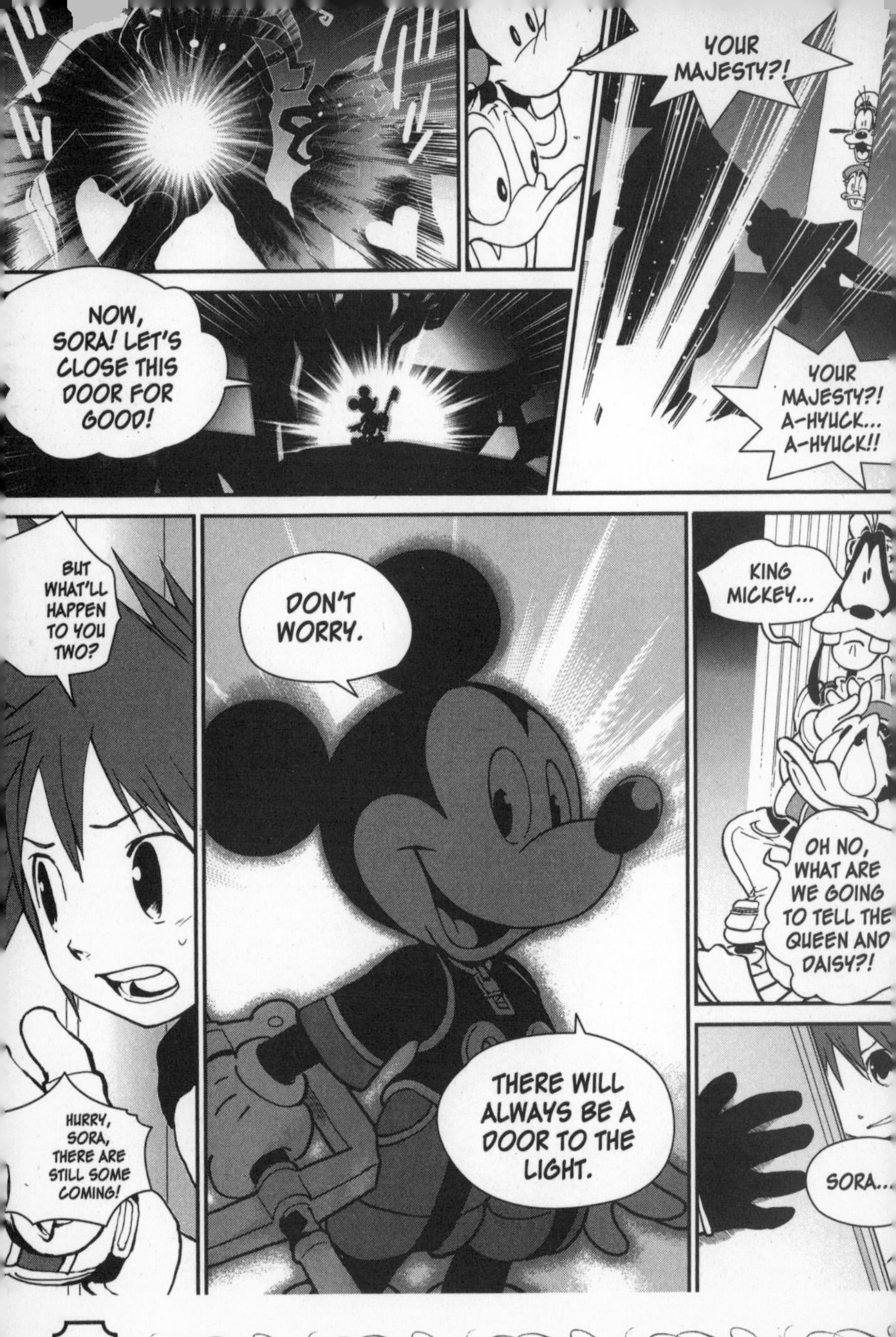
YOUR MAJESTY?!
YOUR MAJESTY?! A-HYUCK... A-HYUCK!!
NOW, SORA! LET'S CLOSE THIS DOOR FOR GOOD!
KING MICKEY...
OH NO, WHAT ARE WE GOING TO TELL THE QUEEN AND DAISY?!
SORA...
DON'T WORRY.
THERE WILL ALWAYS BE A DOOR TO THE LIGHT.
BUT WHAT'LL HAPPEN TO YOU TWO?
HURRY, SORA, THERE ARE STILL SOME COMING!

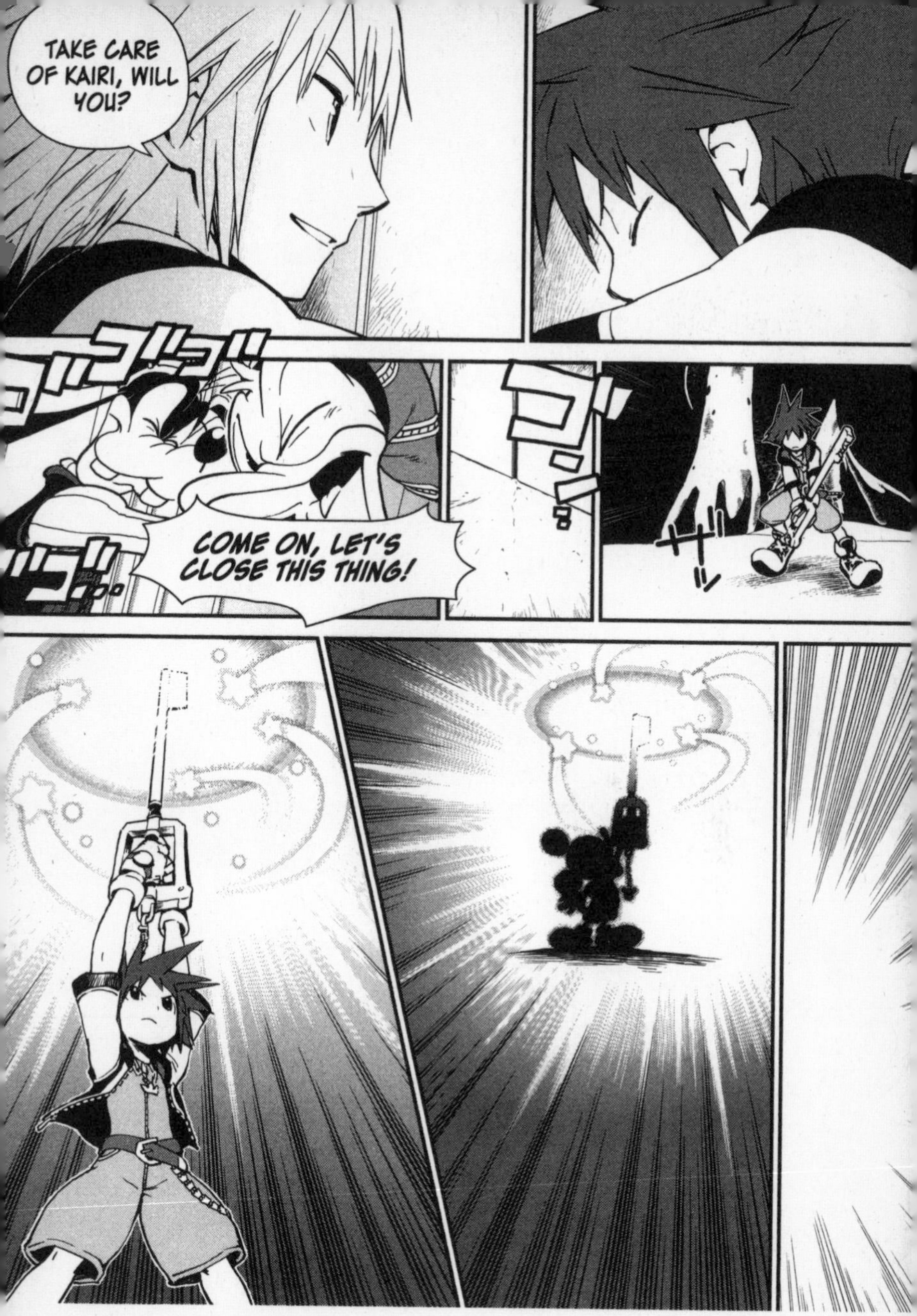
TAKE CARE OF KAIRI, WILL YOU?
COME ON, LET'S CLOSE THIS THING!

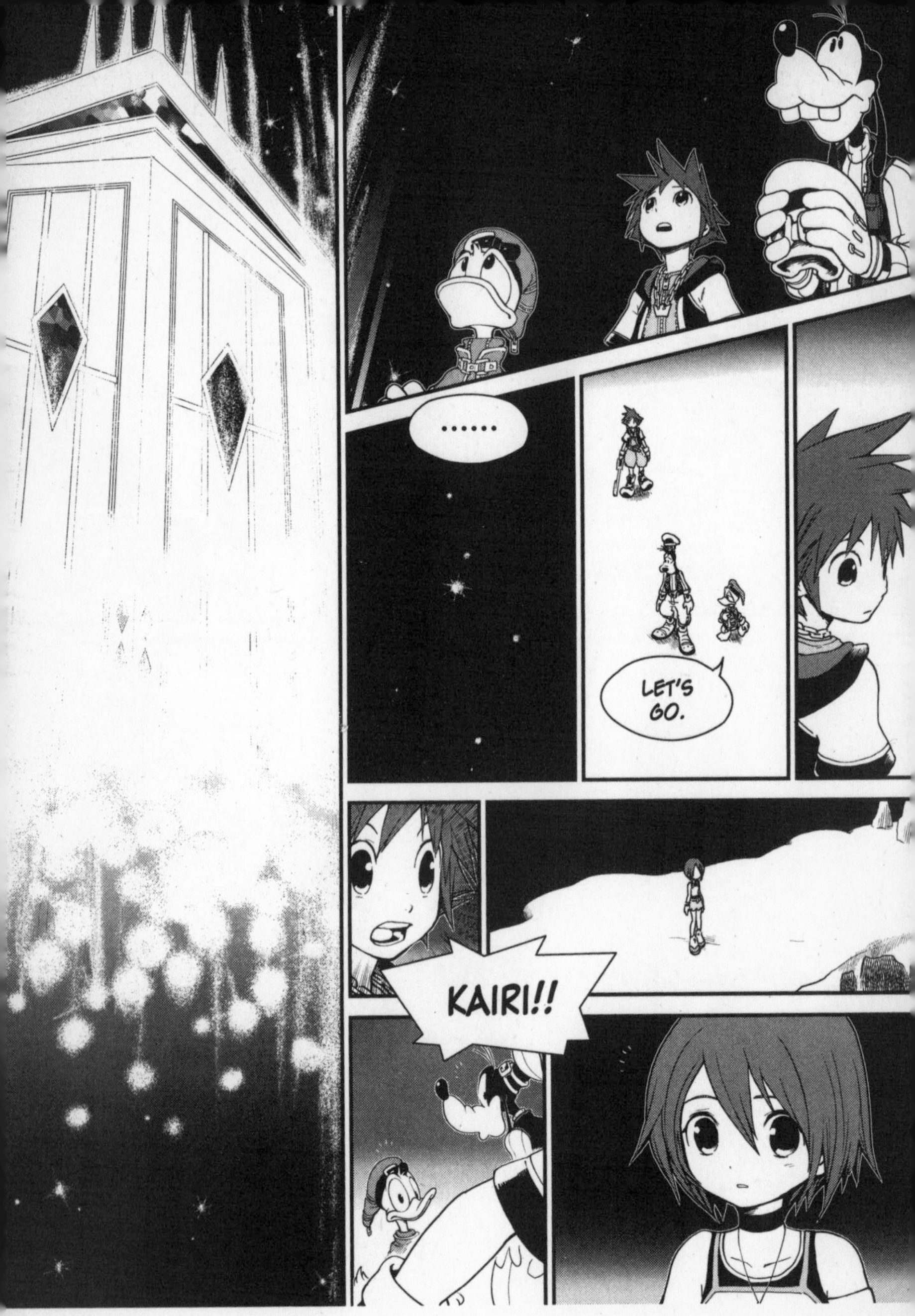

....
LET'S GO.
KAIRI!!

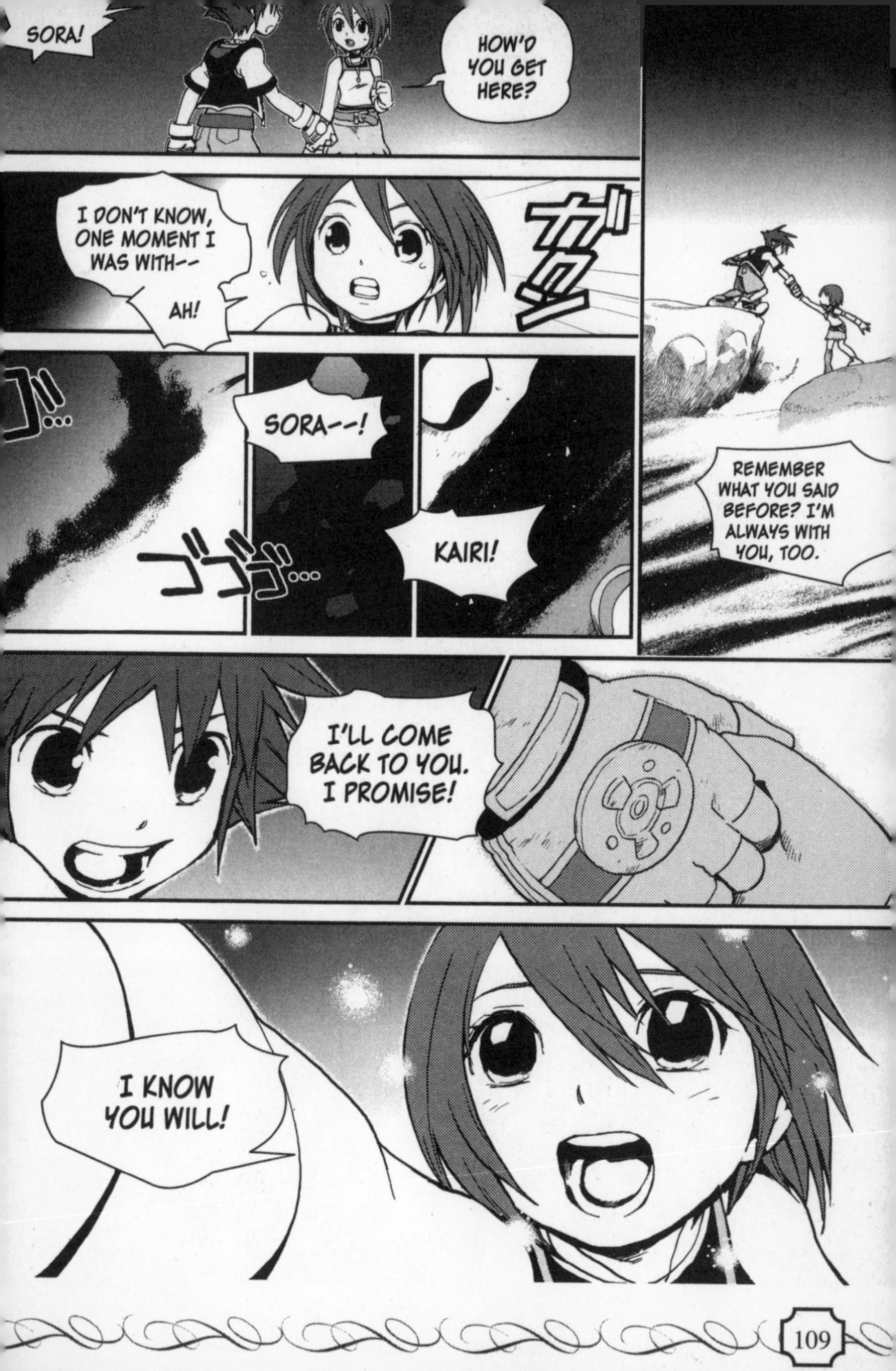
SORA!
HOW'D YOU GET HERE?
I DON'T KNOW, ONE MOMENT I WAS WITH--
AH!
ゴ…
ゴゴゴ…
SORA--!
KAIRI!
REMEMBER WHAT YOU SAID BEFORE? I'M ALWAYS WITH YOU, TOO.
I'LL COME BACK TO YOU. I PROMISE!
I KNOW YOU WILL!

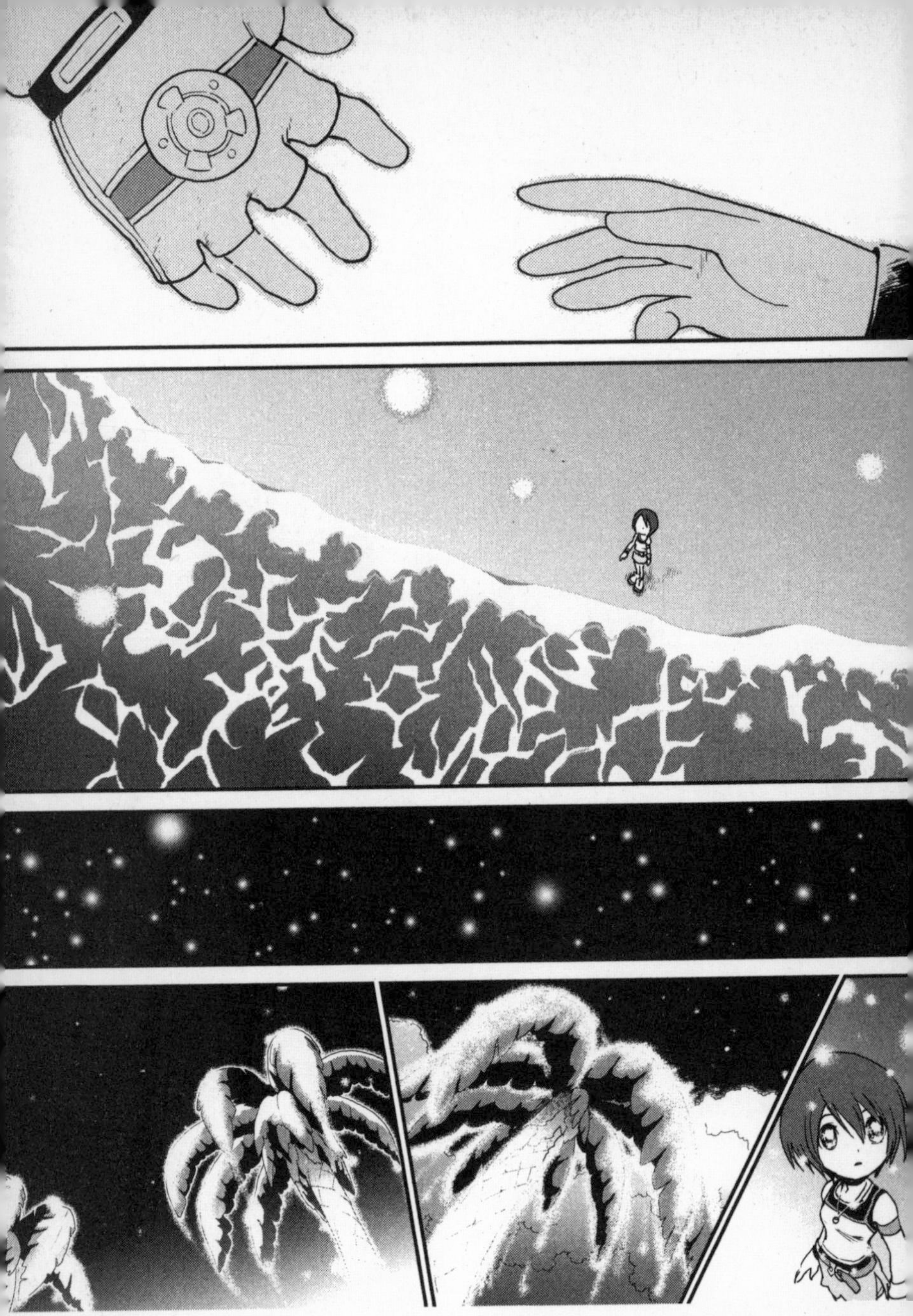

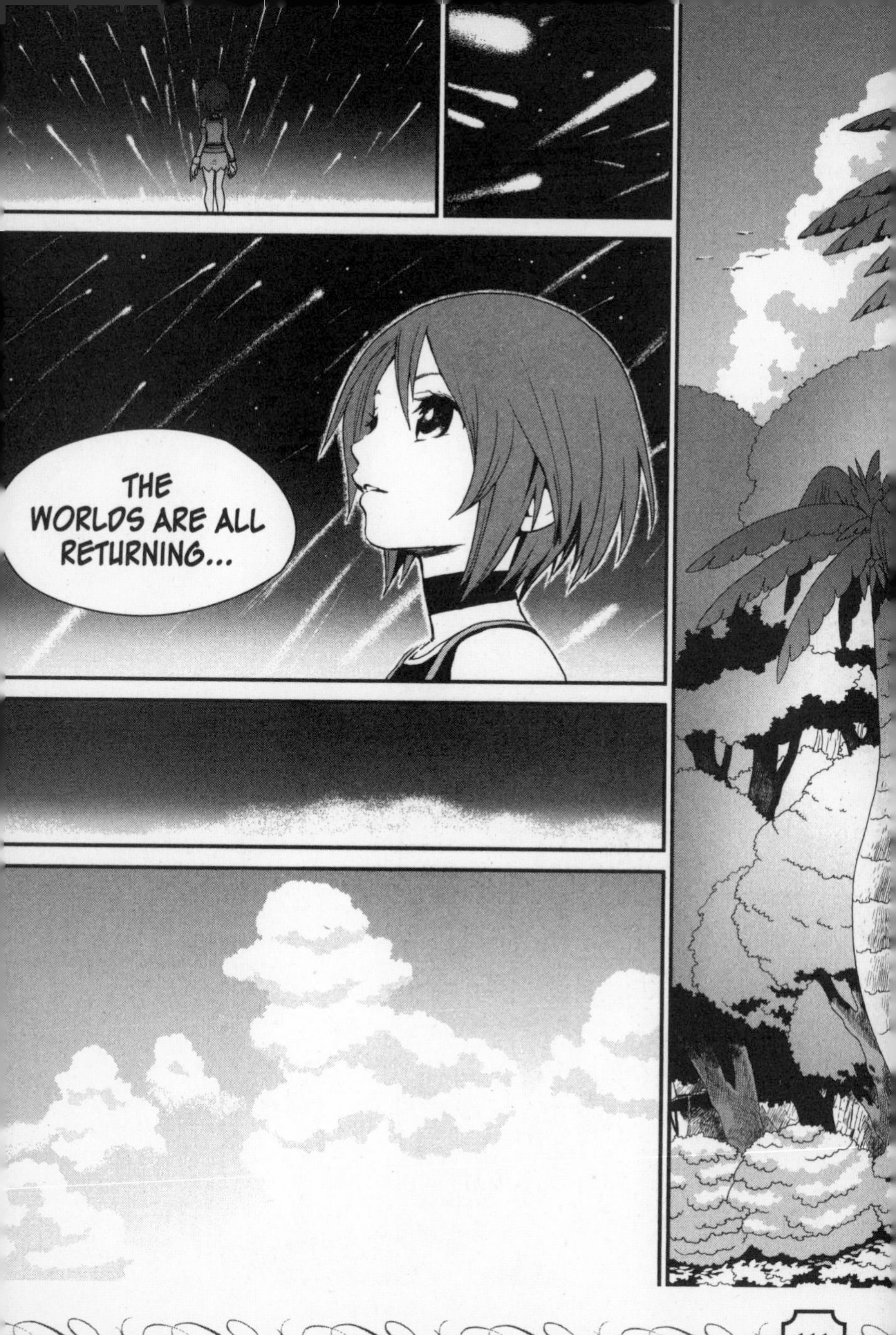
THE WORLDS ARE ALL RETURNING...

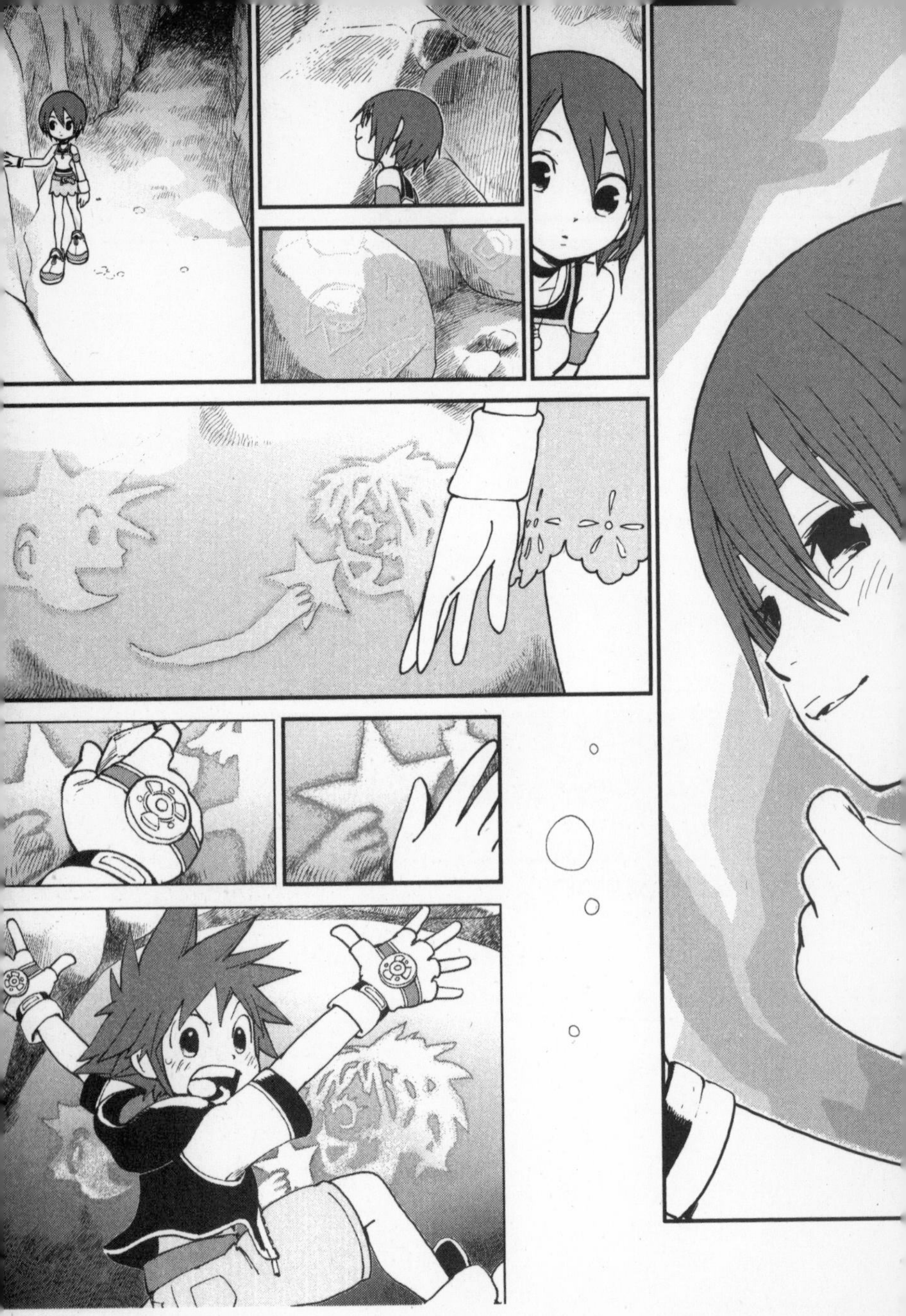

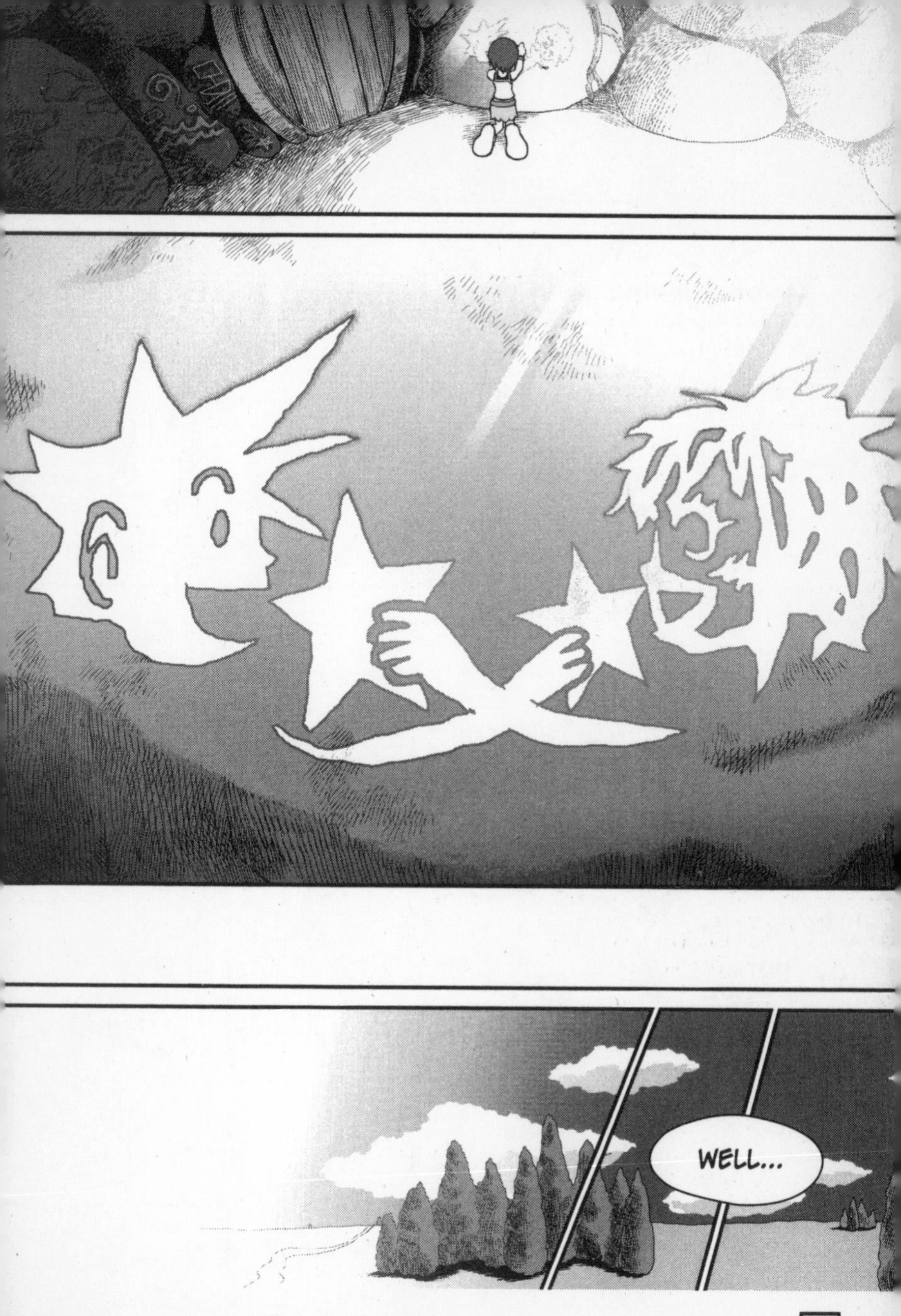
WELL...

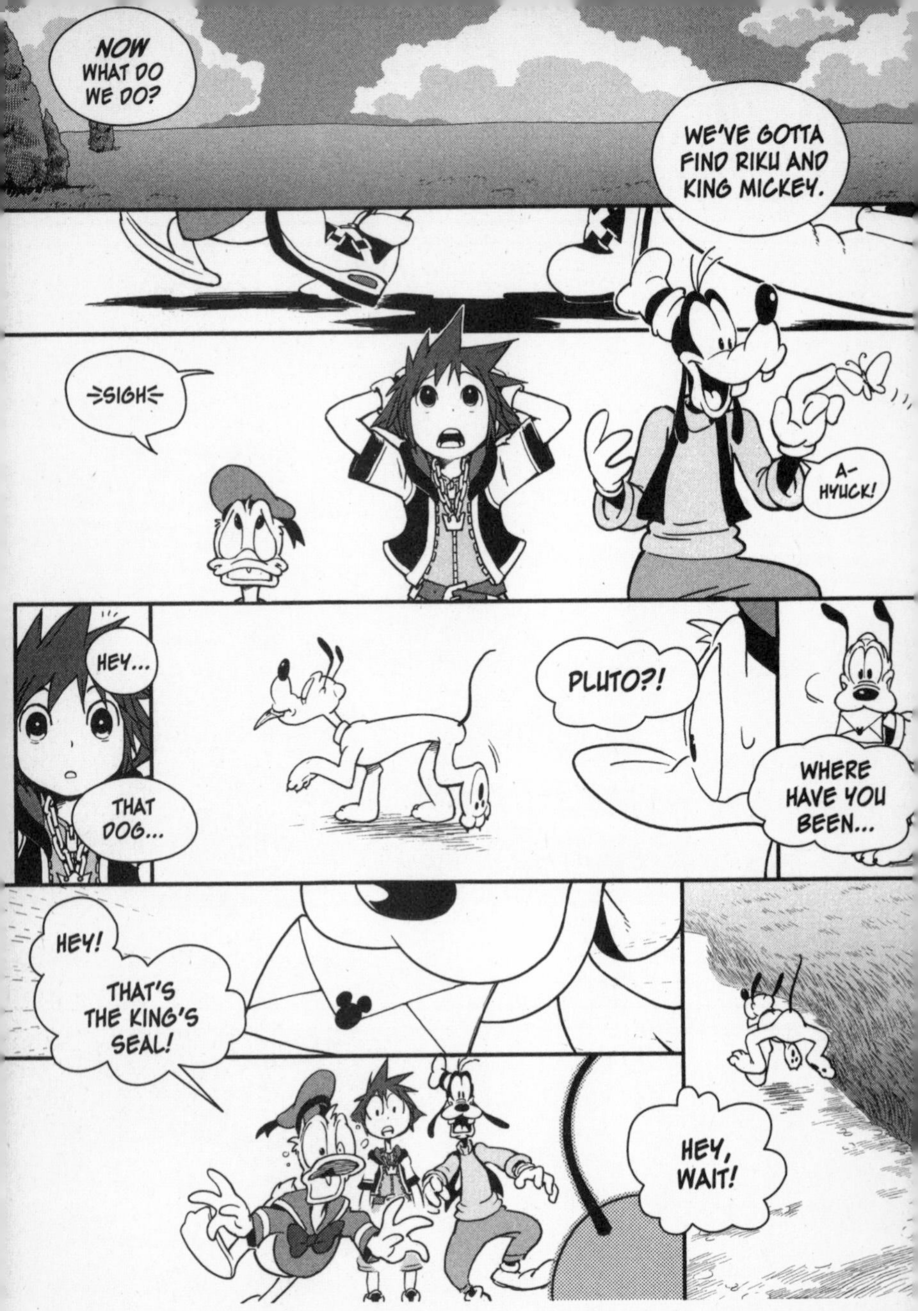
NOW WHAT DO WE DO?
WE'VE GOTTA FIND RIKU AND KING MICKEY.
SIGH
A-HYUCK!
HEY...
THAT DOG...
PLUTO?!
WHERE HAVE YOU BEEN...
HEY!
THAT'S THE KING'S SEAL!
HEY, WAIT!

HEEEY!

Remember, Sora.

You are the one
who will open the
door to the light.

DISNEY · SQUARESOFT

KINGDOM HEARTS

THE END

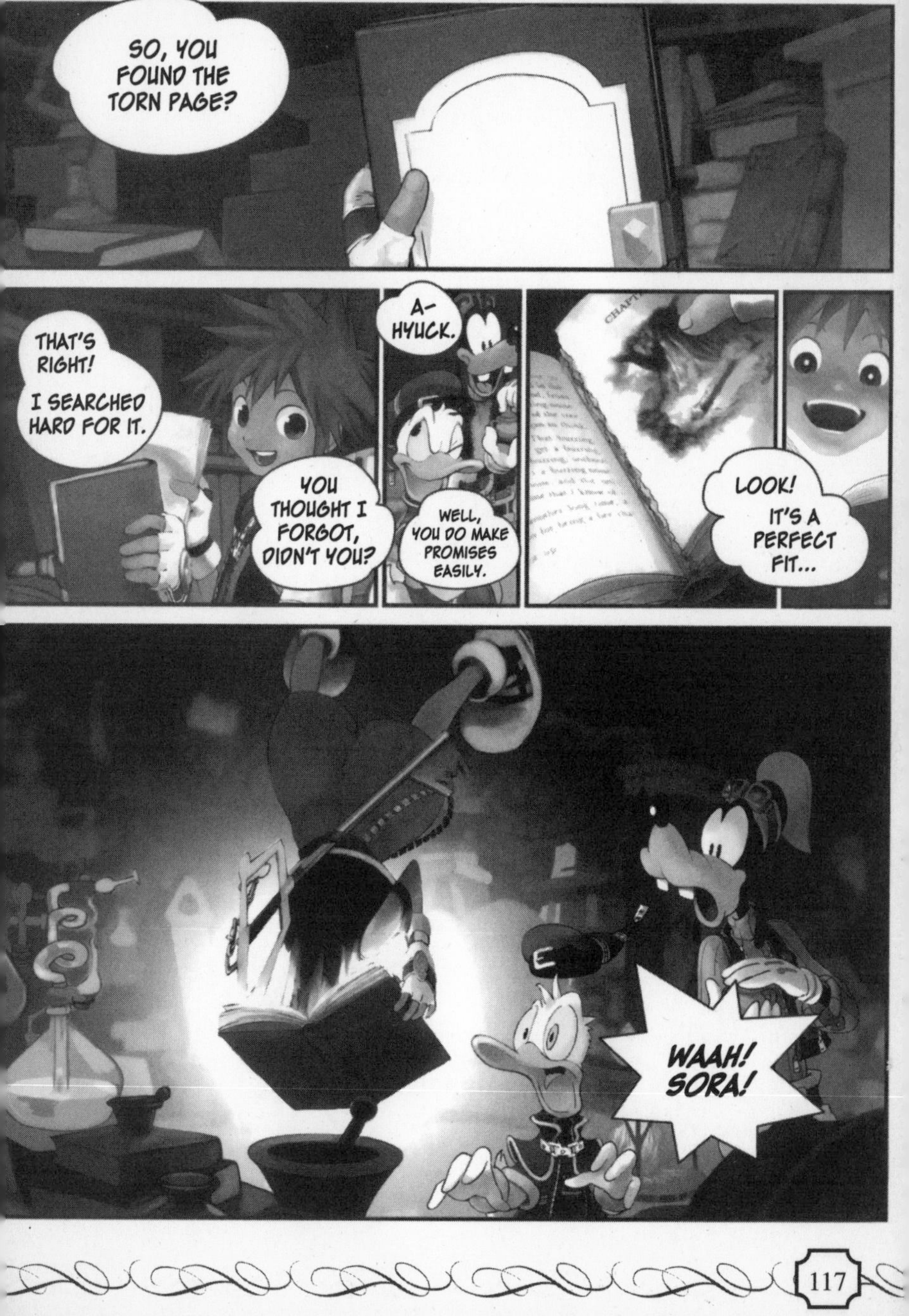
SO, YOU FOUND THE TORN PAGE?
THAT'S RIGHT!
I SEARCHED HARD FOR IT.
YOU THOUGHT I FORGOT, DIDN'T YOU?
A-HYUCK.
WELL, YOU DO MAKE PROMISES EASILY.
LOOK!
IT'S A PERFECT FIT...
WAAH! SORA!

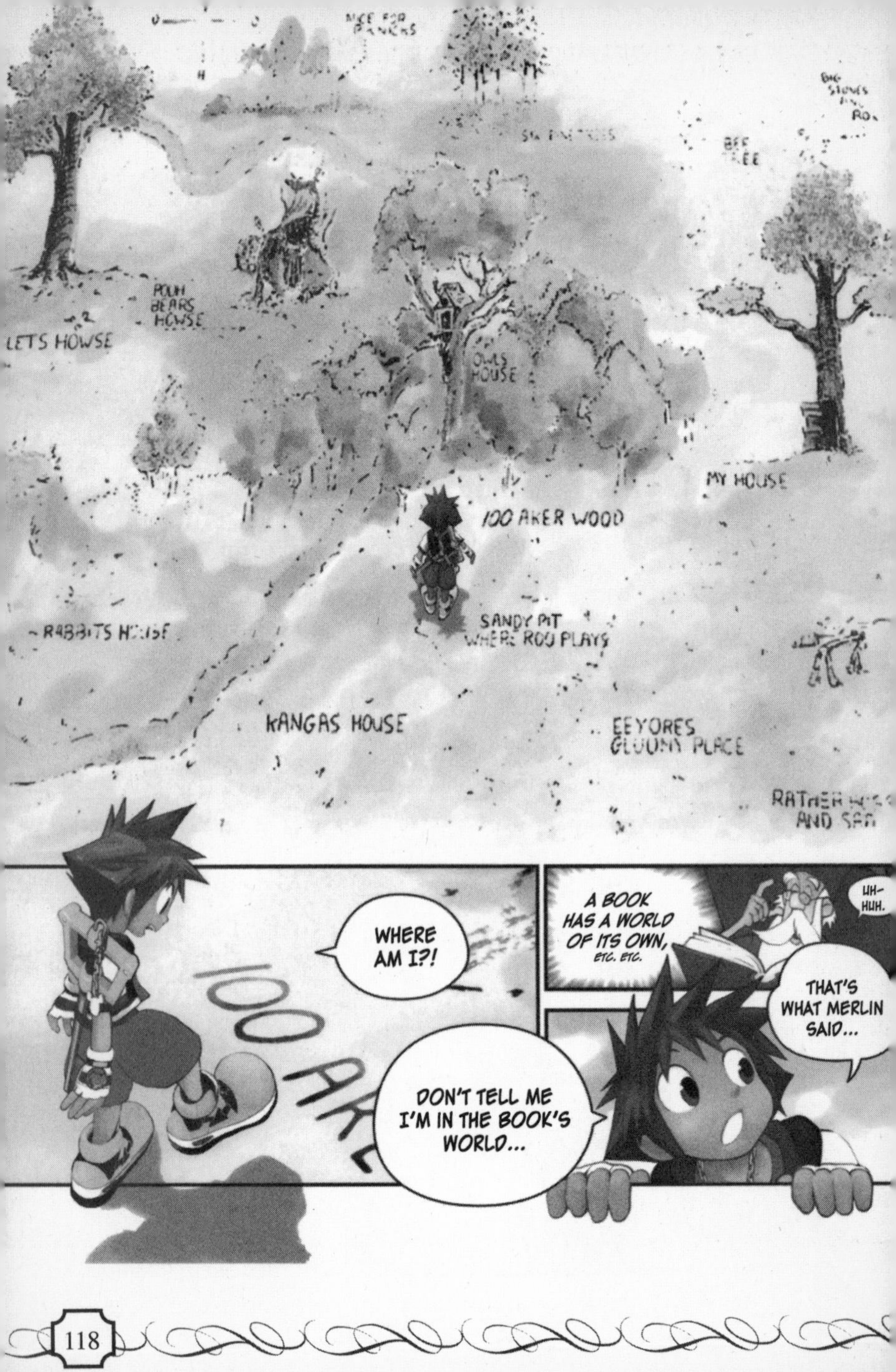
LETS HOWSE
POOH BEARS HOWSE
OWLS HOUSE
MY HOUSE
100 AKER WOOD
SANDY PIT WHERE ROO PLAYS
KANGAS HOUSE
EEYORES GLOOMY PLACE
WHERE AM I?!
100 AKE
A BOOK HAS A WORLD OF ITS OWN, ETC. ETC.
UH-HUH.
THAT'S WHAT MERLIN SAID...
DON'T TELL ME I'M IN THE BOOK'S WORLD...

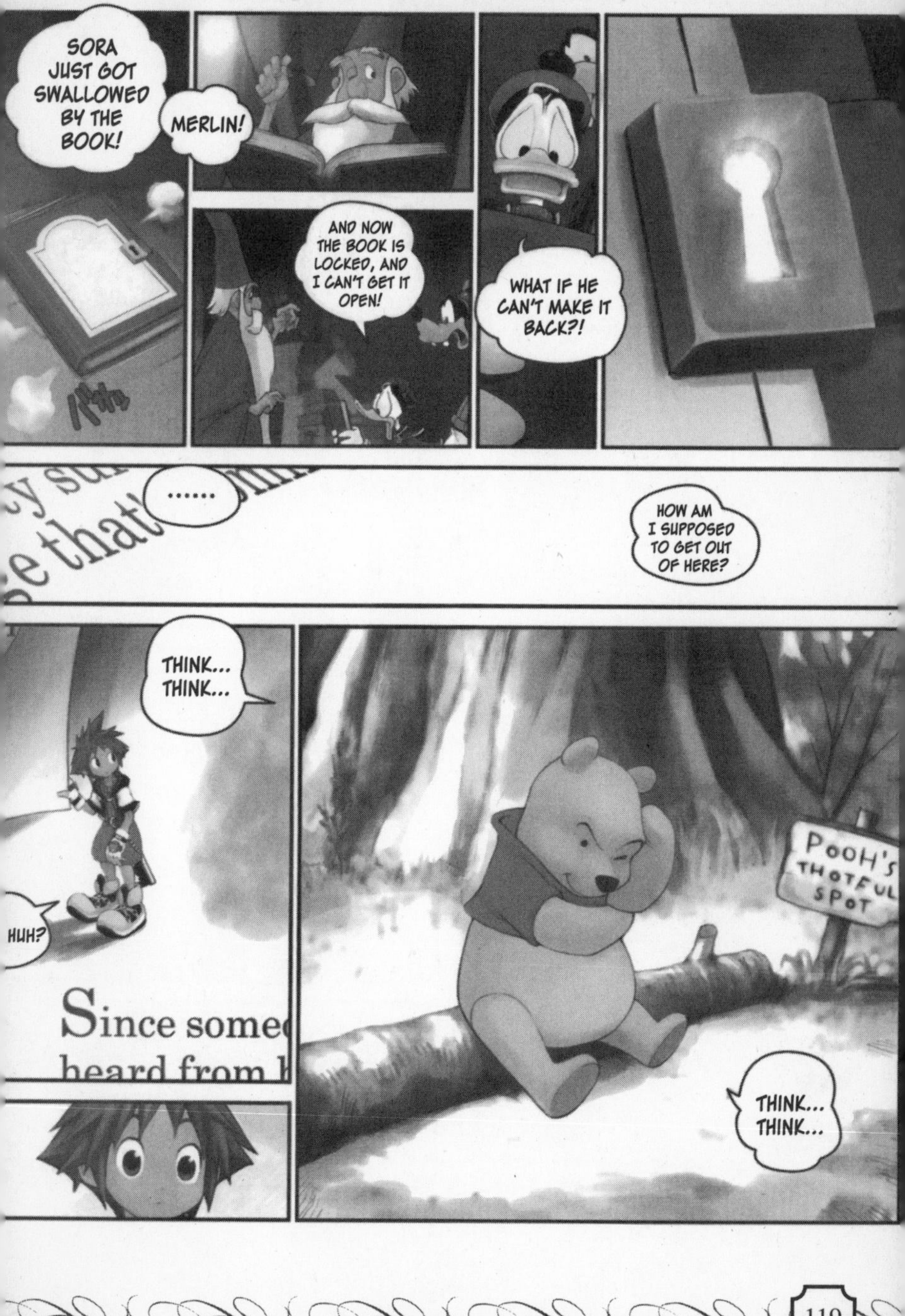
SORA JUST GOT SWALLOWED BY THE BOOK!
MERLIN!
AND NOW THE BOOK IS LOCKED, AND I CAN'T GET IT OPEN!
WHAT IF HE CAN'T MAKE IT BACK?!
......
HOW AM I SUPPOSED TO GET OUT OF HERE?
THINK... THINK...
HUH?
Since some
heard from
POOH'S THOTFUL SPOT
THINK... THINK...

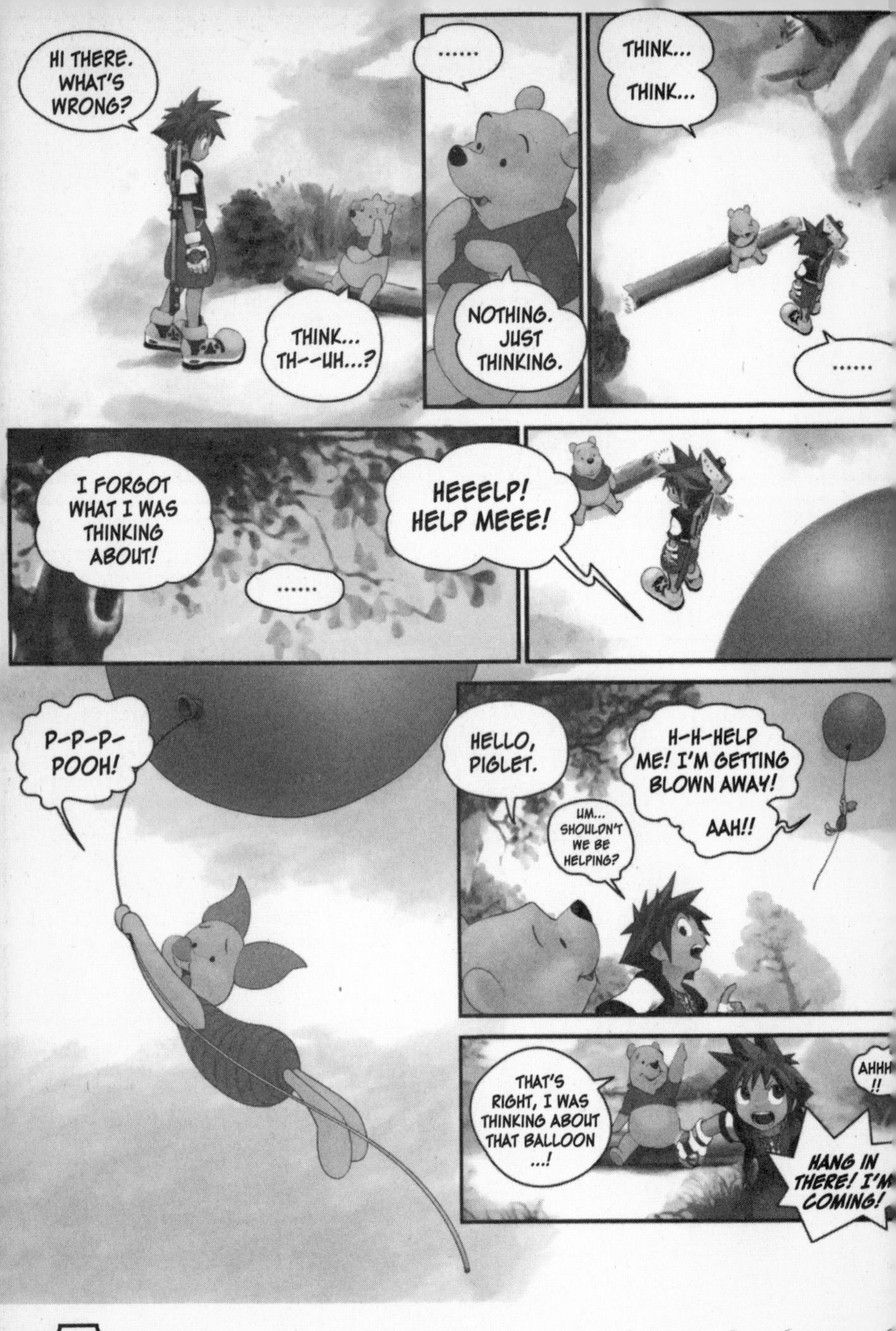
HI THERE. WHAT'S WRONG?
THINK... TH--UH...?
......
NOTHING. JUST THINKING.
THINK...
THINK...
......
I FORGOT WHAT I WAS THINKING ABOUT!
......
HEEEELP! HELP MEEE!
P-P-P-POOH!
HELLO, PIGLET.
H-H-HELP ME! I'M GETTING BLOWN AWAY!
AAH!!
UM... SHOULDN'T WE BE HELPING?
THAT'S RIGHT, I WAS THINKING ABOUT THAT BALLOON ...!
AHHH !!
HANG IN THERE! I'M COMING!

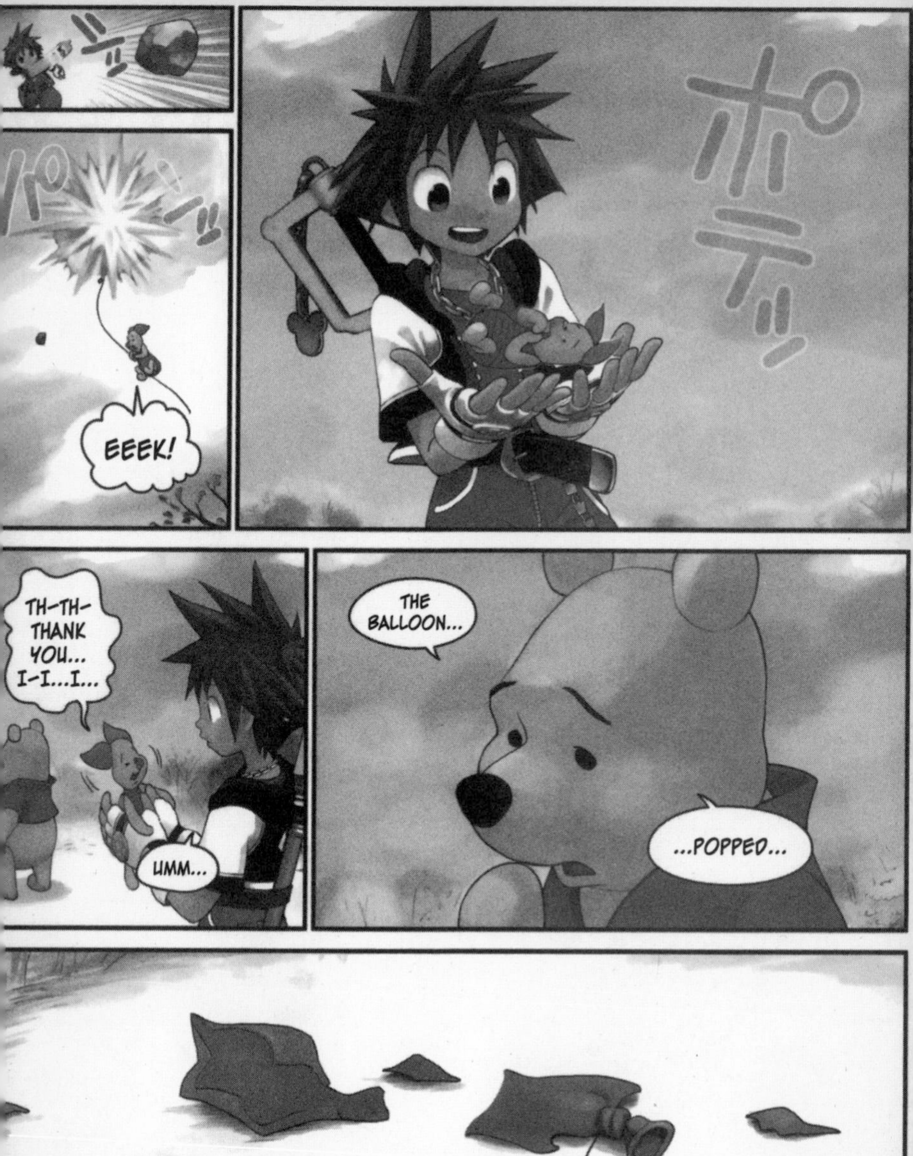
EEEK!
ポテッ
TH-TH-THANK YOU... I-I...I...
UMM...
THE BALLOON...
...POPPED...

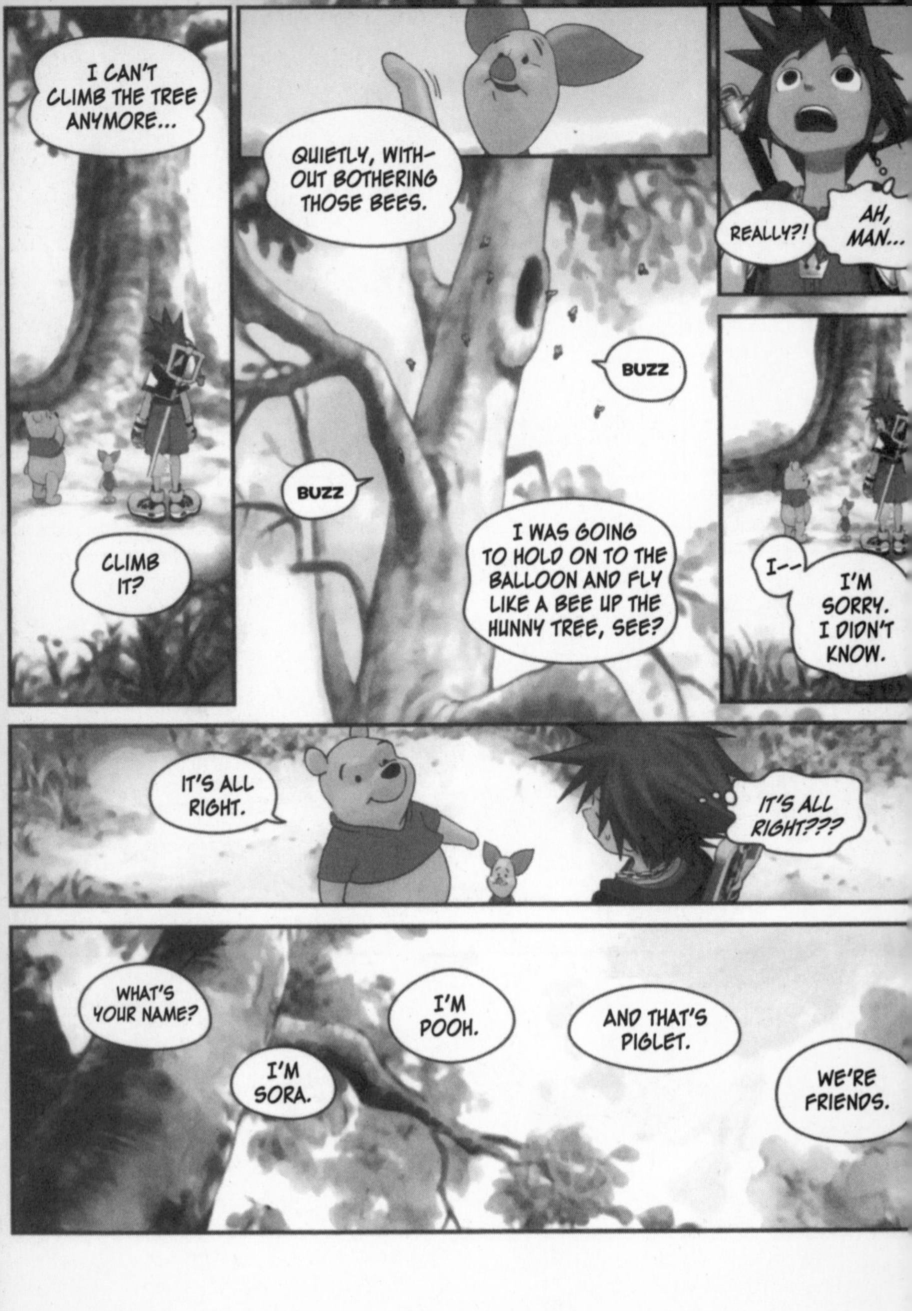
I CAN'T CLIMB THE TREE ANYMORE...
CLIMB IT?
QUIETLY, WITH-OUT BOTHERING THOSE BEES.
BUZZ
BUZZ
I WAS GOING TO HOLD ON TO THE BALLOON AND FLY LIKE A BEE UP THE HUNNY TREE, SEE?
REALLY?!
AH, MAN...
I--
I'M SORRY. I DIDN'T KNOW.
IT'S ALL RIGHT.
IT'S ALL RIGHT???
WHAT'S YOUR NAME?
I'M SORA.
I'M POOH.
AND THAT'S PIGLET.
WE'RE FRIENDS.

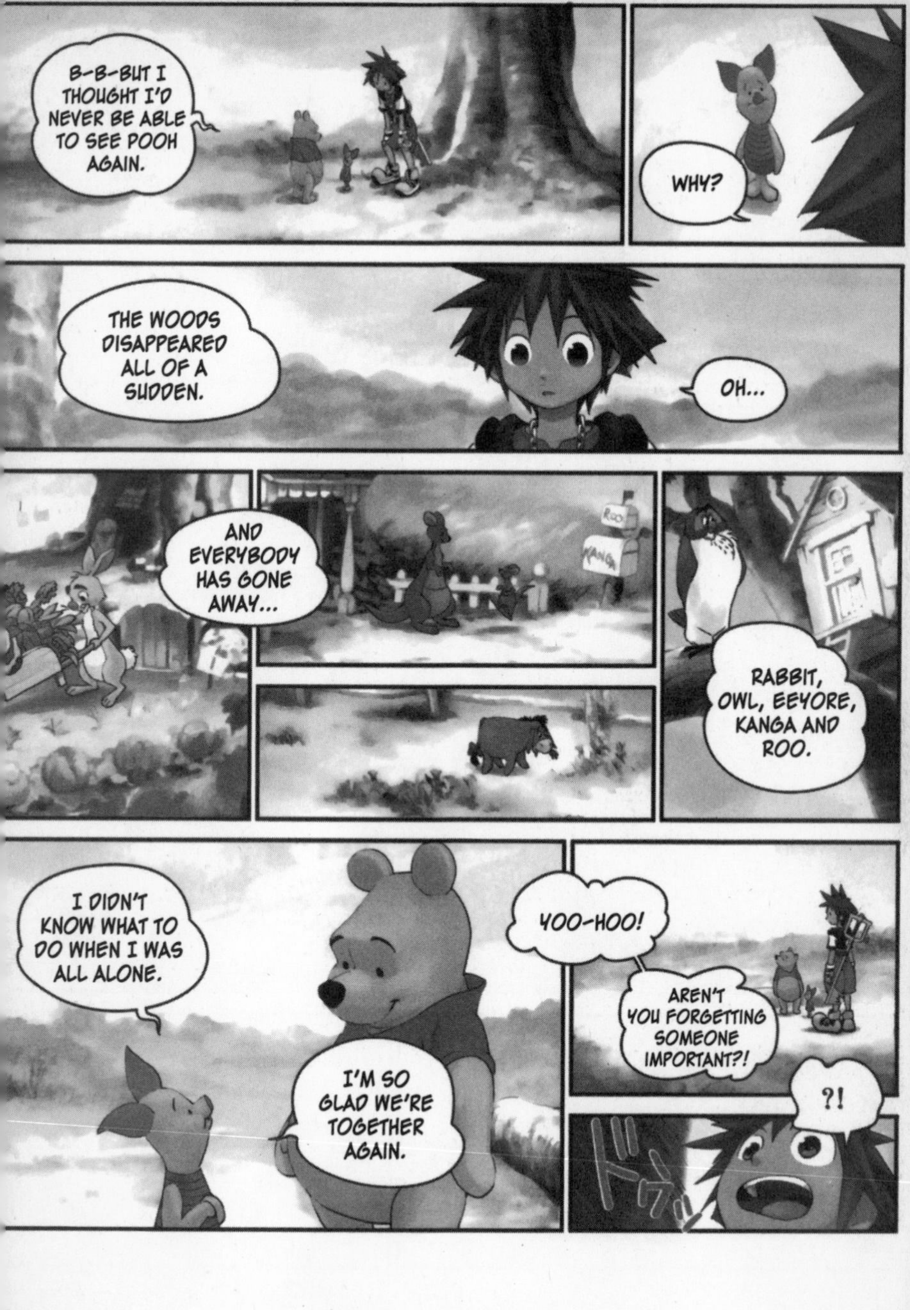
B-B-BUT I THOUGHT I'D NEVER BE ABLE TO SEE POOH AGAIN.
WHY?
THE WOODS DISAPPEARED ALL OF A SUDDEN.
OH...
AND EVERYBODY HAS GONE AWAY...
ROO
KANGA
RABBIT, OWL, EEYORE, KANGA AND ROO.
I DIDN'T KNOW WHAT TO DO WHEN I WAS ALL ALONE.
I'M SO GLAD WE'RE TOGETHER AGAIN.
YOO-HOO!
AREN'T YOU FORGETTING SOMEONE IMPORTANT?!
?!
ドゥ

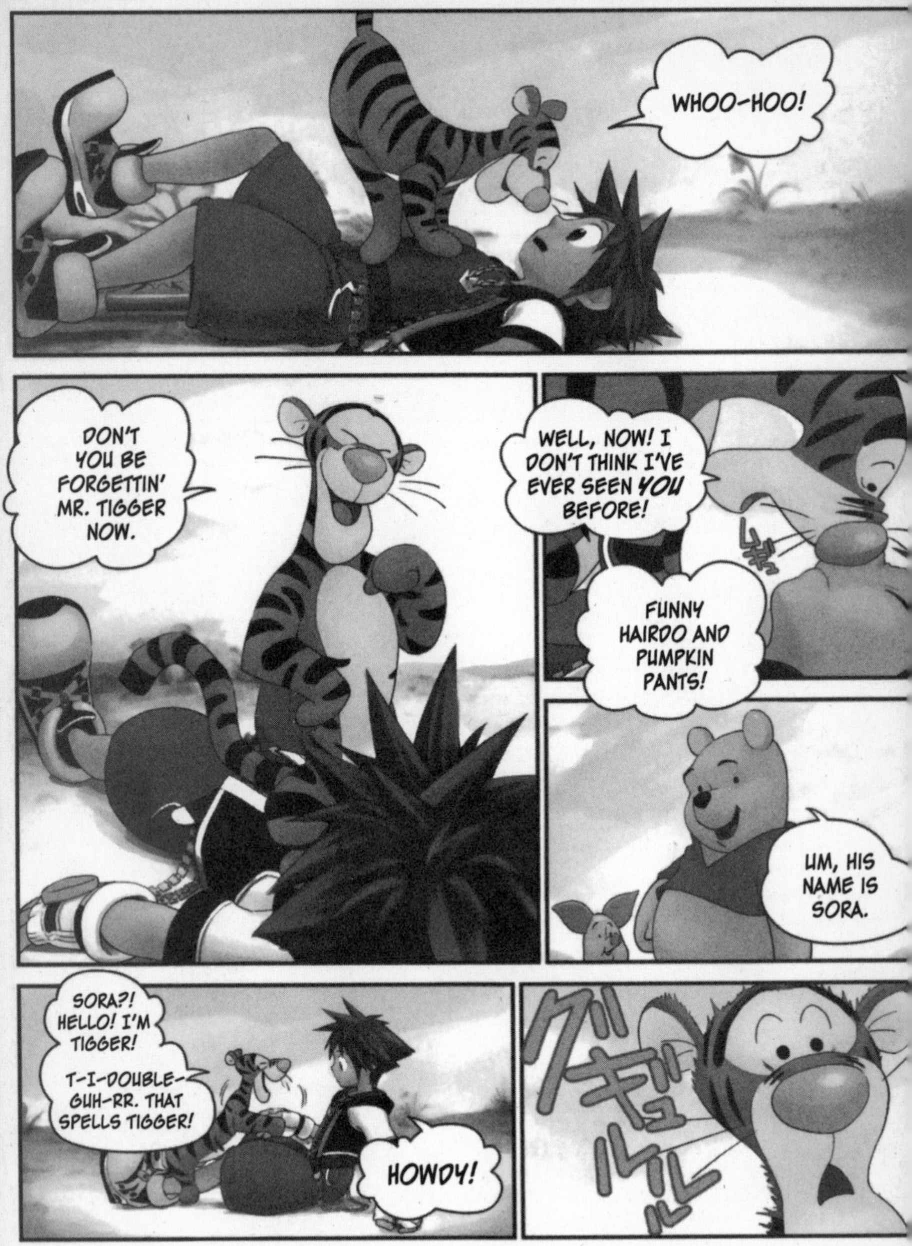
WHOO-HOO!
DON'T YOU BE FORGETTIN' MR. TIGGER NOW.
WELL, NOW! I DON'T THINK I'VE EVER SEEN *YOU* BEFORE!
FUNNY HAIRDO AND PUMPKIN PANTS!
UM, HIS NAME IS SORA.
SORA?! HELLO! I'M TIGGER!
T-I-DOUBLE-GUH-RR. THAT SPELLS TIGGER!
HOWDY!

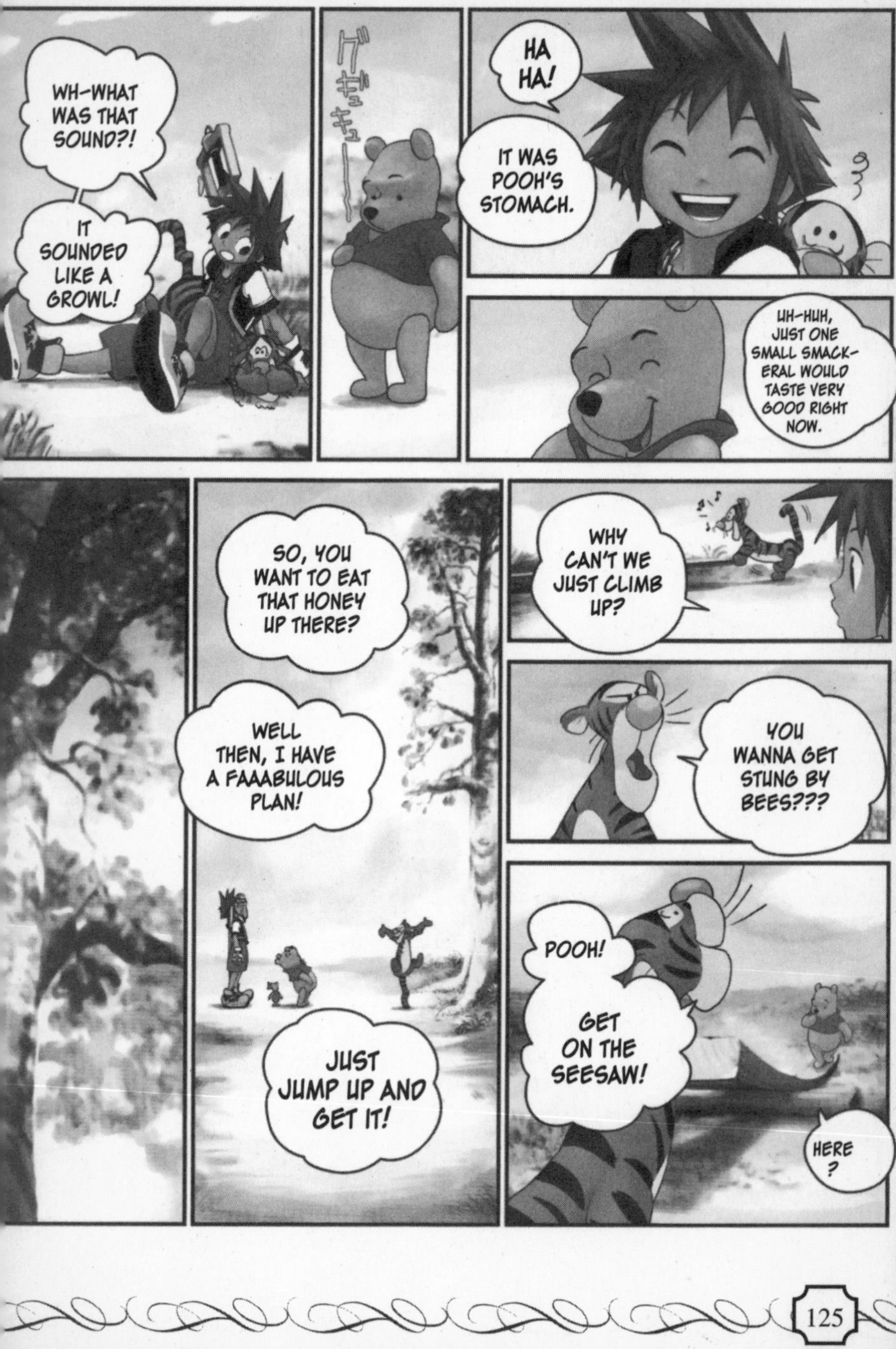
WH-WHAT WAS THAT SOUND?!
IT SOUNDED LIKE A GROWL!
グギュキュー
HA HA!
IT WAS POOH'S STOMACH.
UH-HUH, JUST ONE SMALL SMACK-ERAL WOULD TASTE VERY GOOD RIGHT NOW.
SO, YOU WANT TO EAT THAT HONEY UP THERE?
WELL THEN, I HAVE A FAAABULOUS PLAN!
JUST JUMP UP AND GET IT!
WHY CAN'T WE JUST CLIMB UP?
YOU WANNA GET STUNG BY BEES???
POOH!
GET ON THE SEESAW!
HERE?

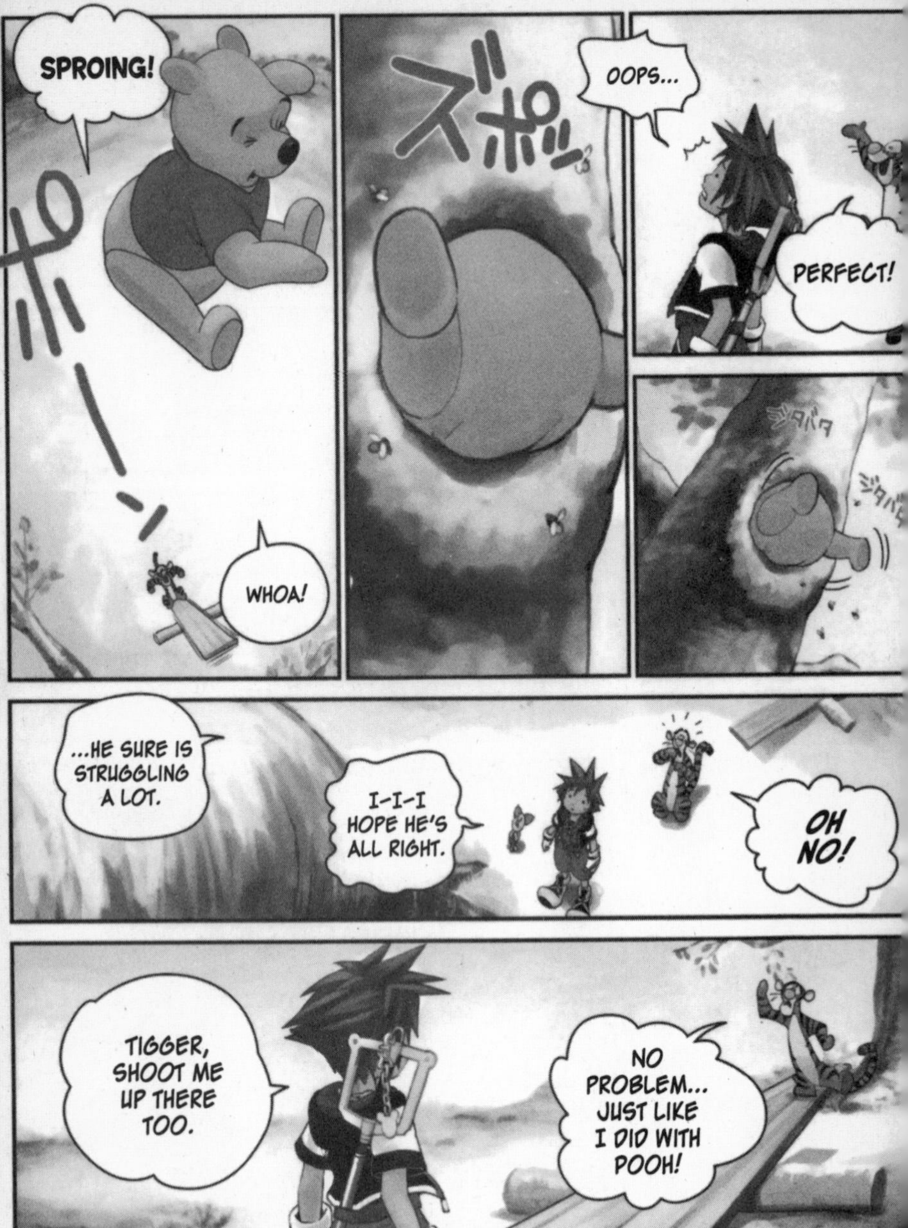
SPROING!
ポーン
WHOA!
ズポッ
OOPS...
PERFECT!
ジタバタ
ジタバタ
...HE SURE IS STRUGGLING A LOT.
I-I-I HOPE HE'S ALL RIGHT.
OH NO!
TIGGER, SHOOT ME UP THERE TOO.
NO PROBLEM... JUST LIKE I DID WITH POOH!

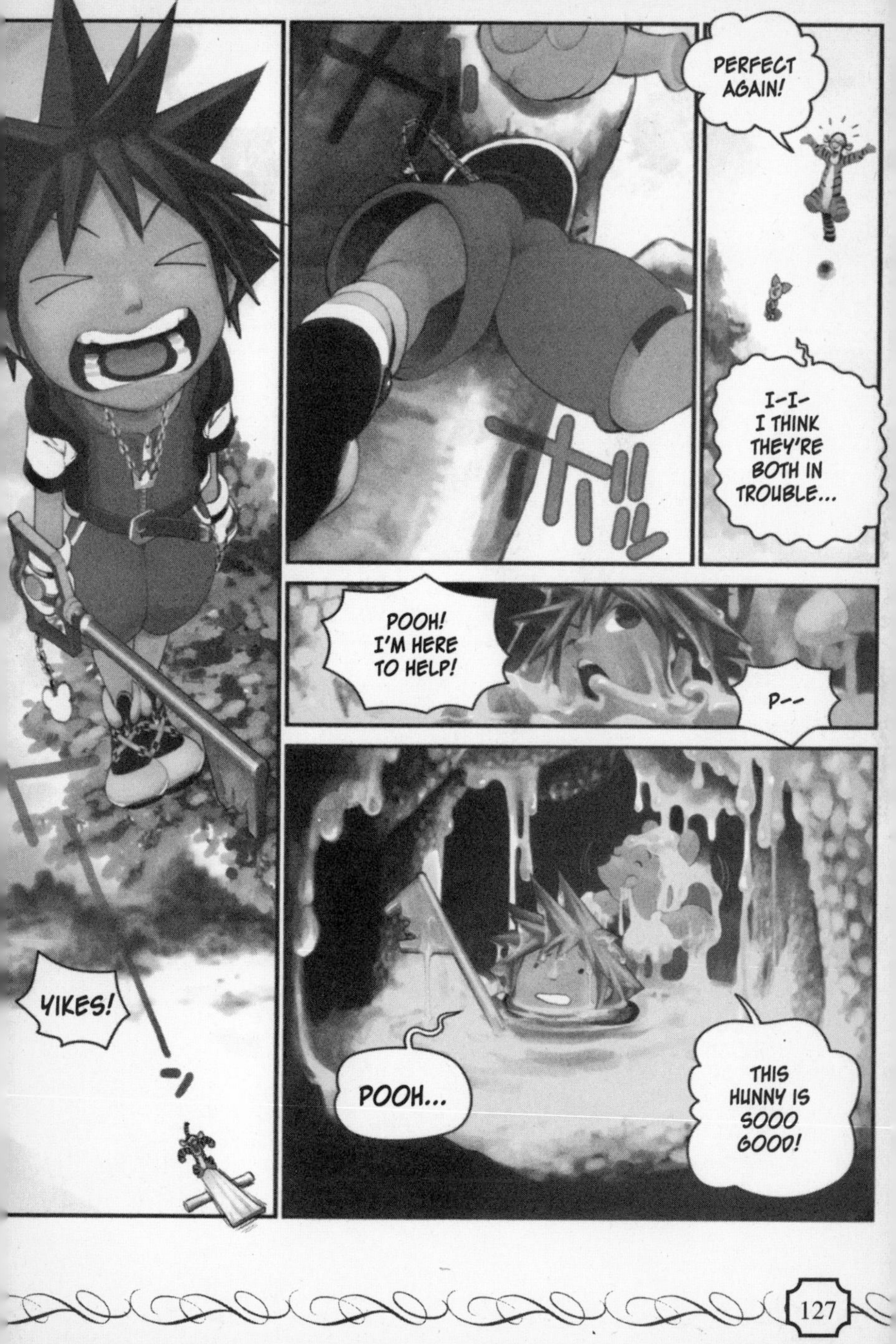
YIKES!
PERFECT AGAIN!
I-I- I THINK THEY'RE BOTH IN TROUBLE...
POOH! I'M HERE TO HELP!
P--
POOH...
THIS HUNNY IS SOOO GOOD!

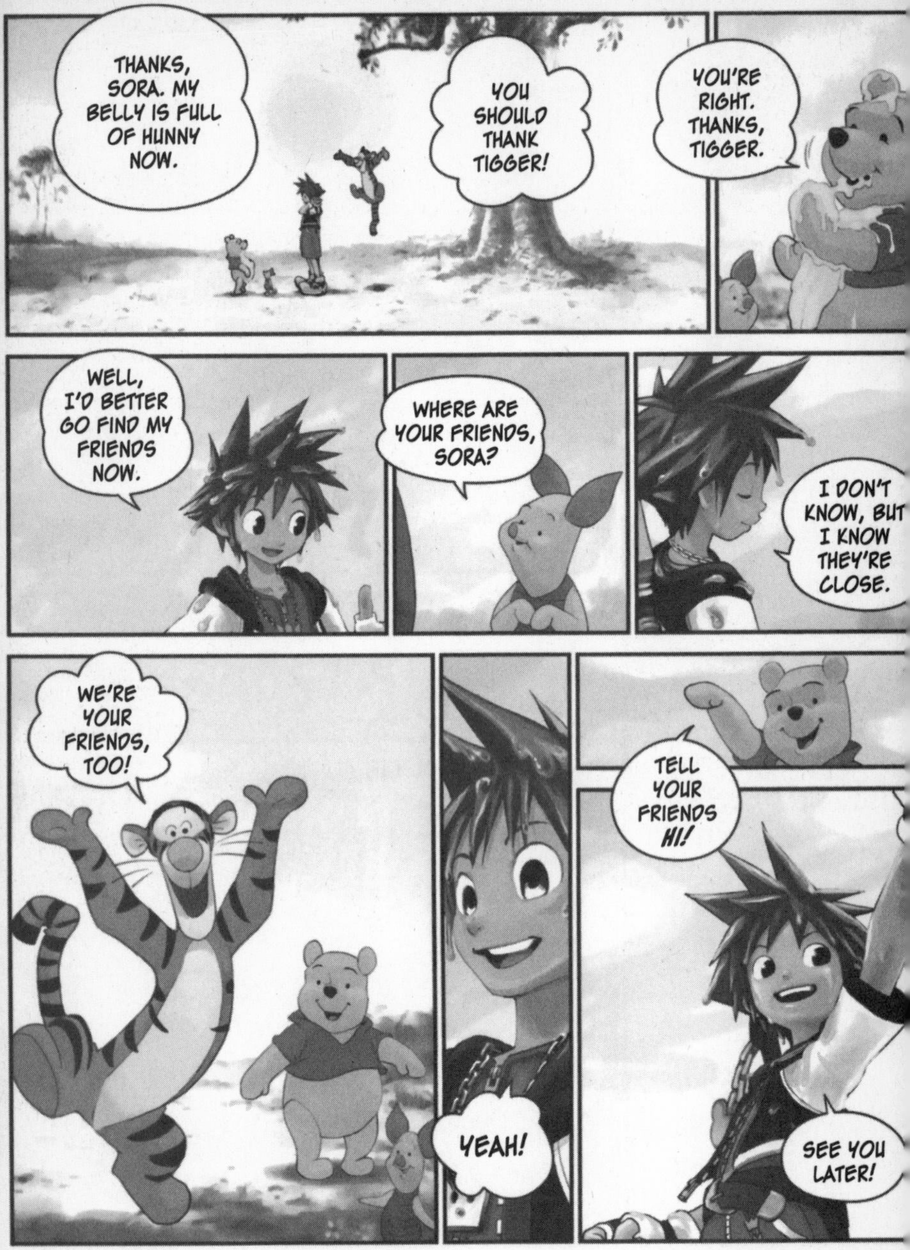
THANKS, SORA. MY BELLY IS FULL OF HUNNY NOW.
YOU SHOULD THANK TIGGER!
YOU'RE RIGHT. THANKS, TIGGER.
WELL, I'D BETTER GO FIND MY FRIENDS NOW.
WHERE ARE YOUR FRIENDS, SORA?
I DON'T KNOW, BUT I KNOW THEY'RE CLOSE.
WE'RE YOUR FRIENDS, TOO!
YEAH!
TELL YOUR FRIENDS HI!
SEE YOU LATER!

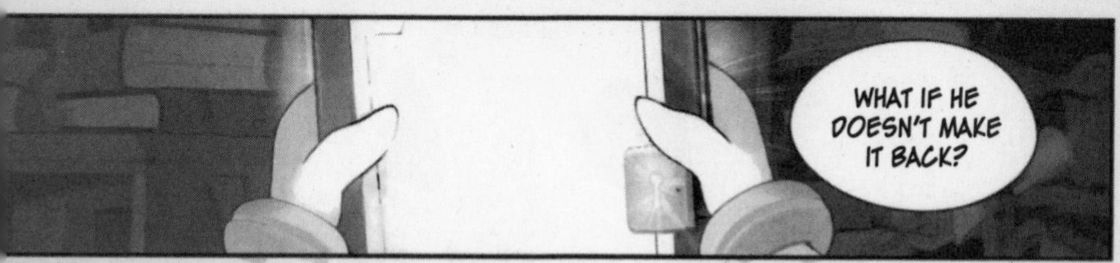
WHAT IF HE DOESN'T MAKE IT BACK?

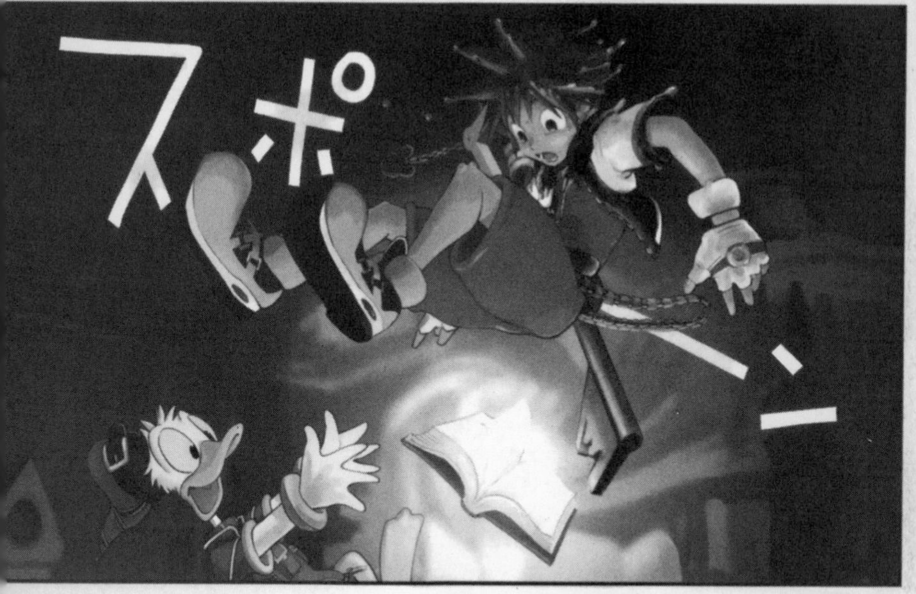
スポ

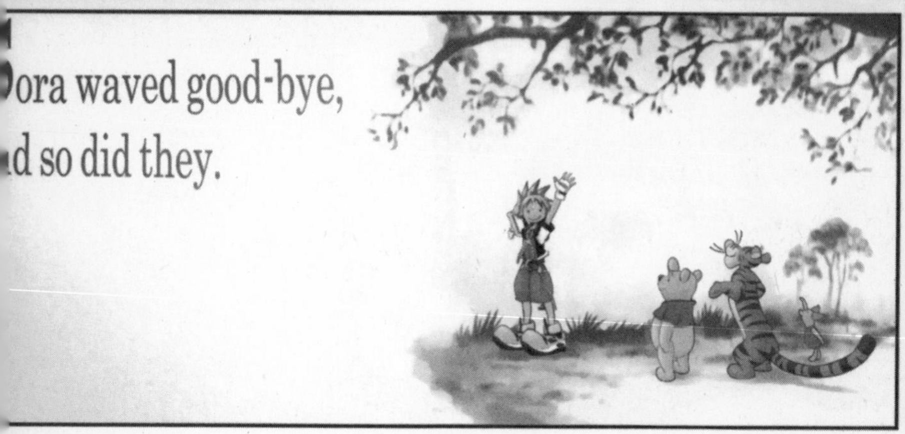
ora waved good-bye,
d so did they.

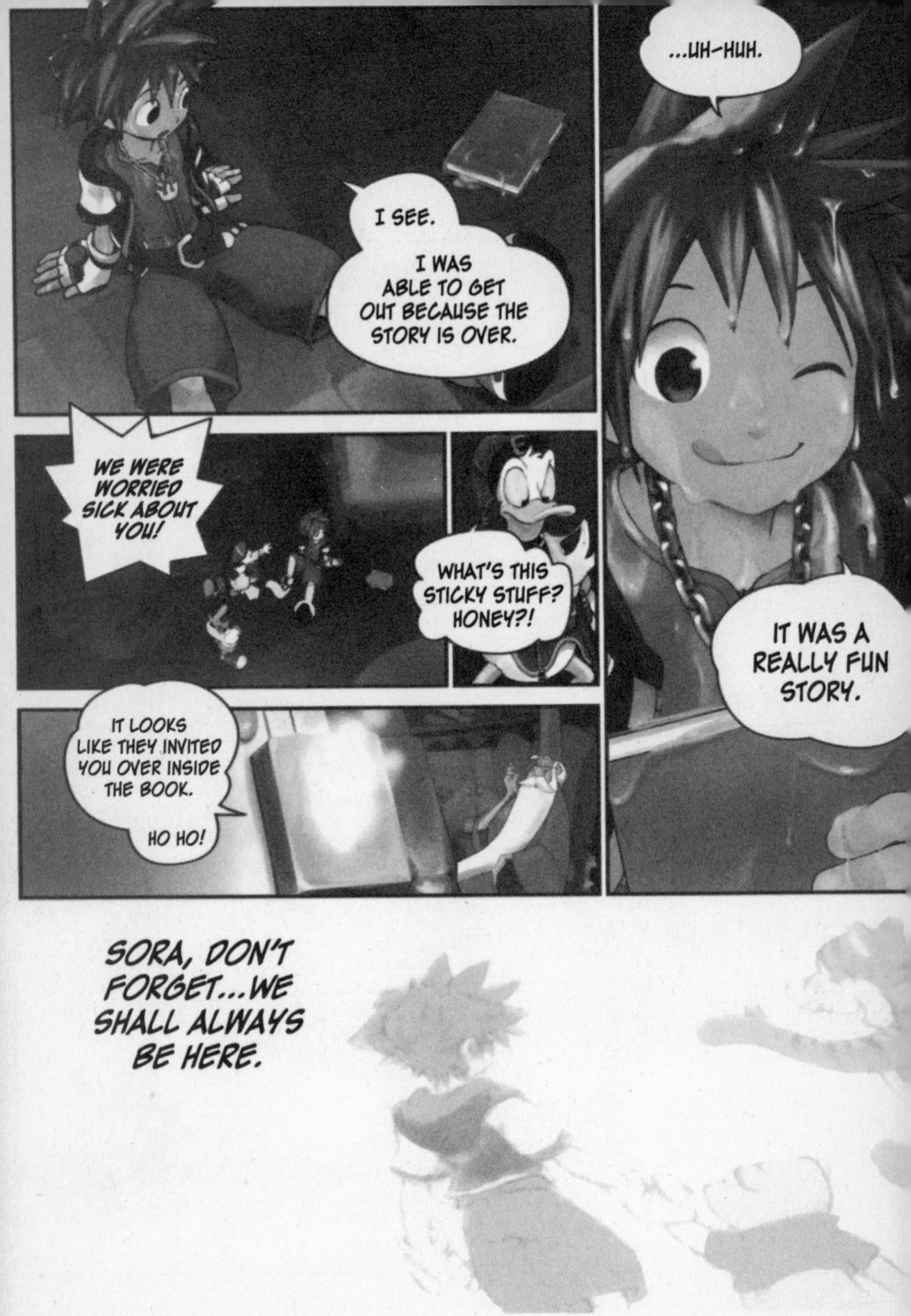
I SEE.
I WAS ABLE TO GET OUT BECAUSE THE STORY IS OVER.
WE WERE WORRIED SICK ABOUT YOU!
WHAT'S THIS STICKY STUFF? HONEY?!
IT LOOKS LIKE THEY INVITED YOU OVER INSIDE THE BOOK.
HO HO!
...UH-HUH.
IT WAS A REALLY FUN STORY.
SORA, DON'T FORGET...WE SHALL ALWAYS BE HERE.

IF YOU'D LIKE TO VISIT AGAIN, THAT IS.

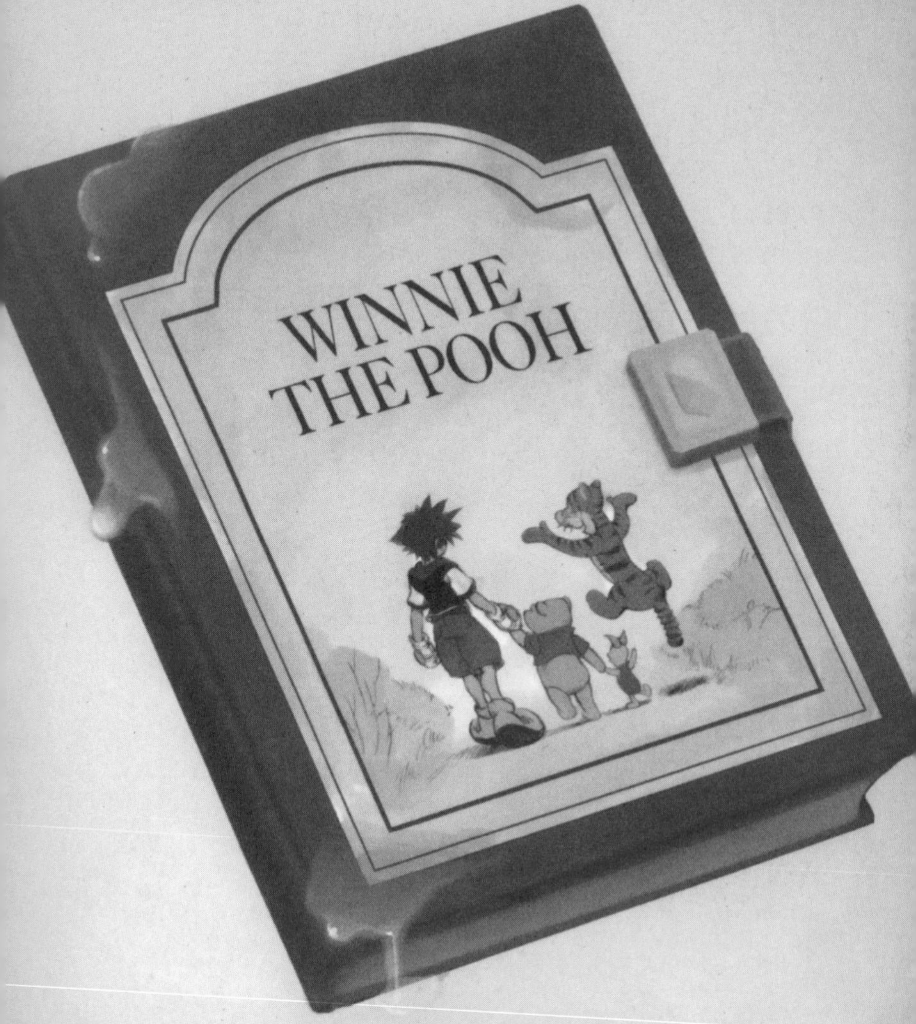
WINNIE
THE POOH

THE END

In Volume 1 of

Disney · SQUARE ENIX

KINGDOM HEARTS
CHAIN OF MEMORIES

Sora's
Adventure
Continues!!

- Aladdin
- All Grown Up
- The Amanda Show
- Avatar
- Bambi
- Barbie™ as the Princess and the Pauper
- Barbie™ Fairytopia
- Barbie™ of Swan Lake
- Chicken Little
- Cinderella
- Drake & Josh
- Duel Masters
- The Fairly OddParents
- Finding Nemo
- Future Greatest Stars of the NBA: LeBron James, Dwyane Wade and Carmelo Anthony
- G.I. Joe Spy Troops
- Greatest Stars of the NBA: Tim Duncan
- Greatest Stars of the NBA: Kevin Garnett
- Greatest Stars of the NBA: Allen Iverson
- Greatest Stars of the NBA: Jason Kidd
- Greatest Stars of the NBA: Shaquille O'Neal
- The Incredibles
- The Adventures of Jimmy Neutron: Boy Genius
- Kim Possible
- Lilo & Stitch: The Series
- Lizzie McGuire
- Madagascar
- Mucha Lucha!
- Pooh's Heffalump Movie
- Power Rangers
- The Princess Diaries 2
- Rave Master
- Romeo!
- Shrek 2
- SpongeBob SquarePants
- Spy Kids 2
- Spy Kids 3-D: Game Over
- That's So Raven
- Totally Spies
- Transformers

COLLECT THEM ALL!

Now available
wherever books are sold or at
www.TOKYOPOP.com/shop

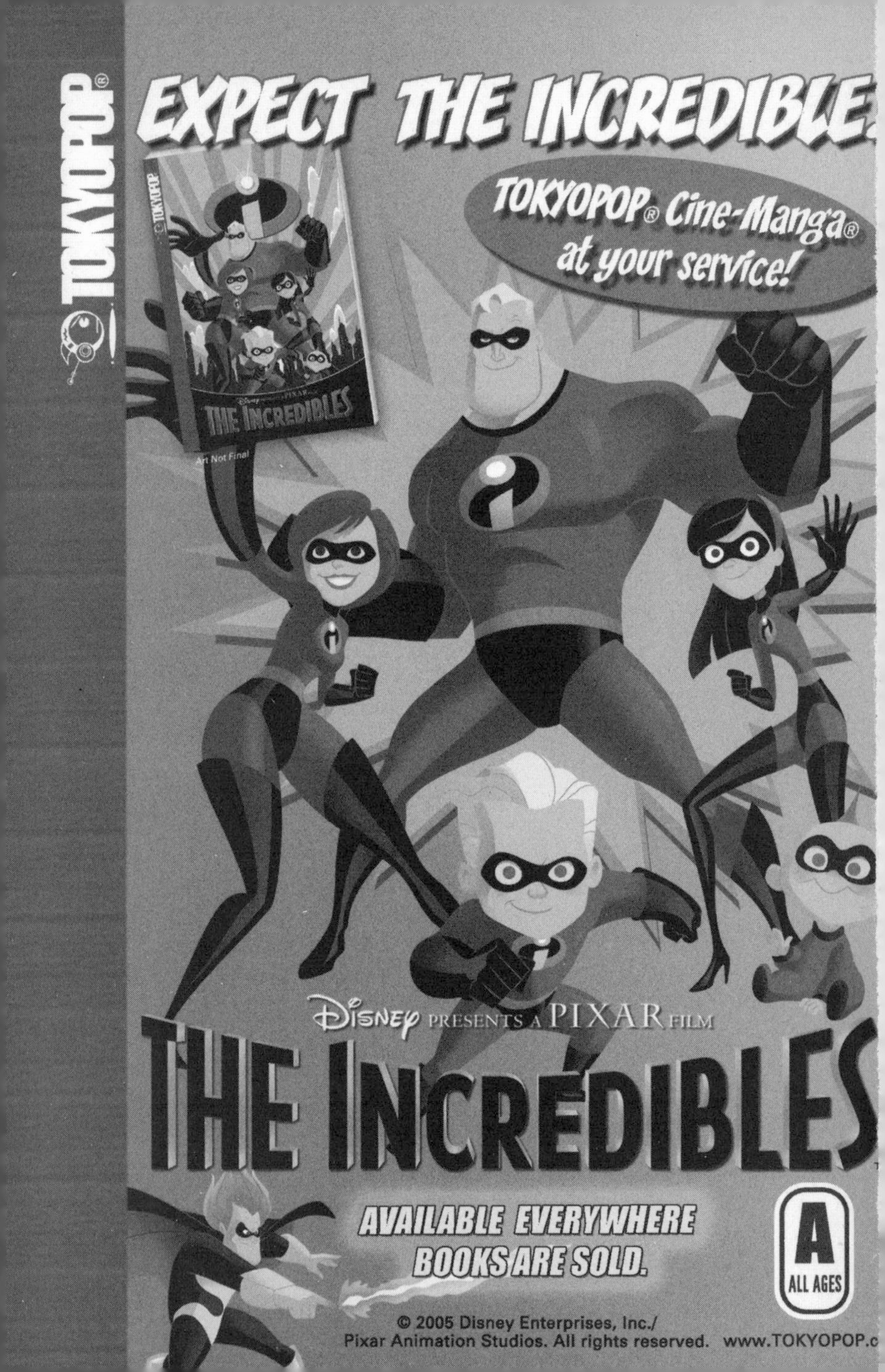
TOKYOPOP®
EXPECT THE INCREDIBLE.
TOKYOPOP® Cine-Manga®
at your service!
Art Not Final
DISNEY PRESENTS A PIXAR FILM
THE INCREDIBLES
AVAILABLE EVERYWHERE
BOOKS ARE SOLD.
A
ALL AGES
© 2005 Disney Enterprises, Inc./
Pixar Animation Studios. All rights reserved.
www.TOKYOPOP.c